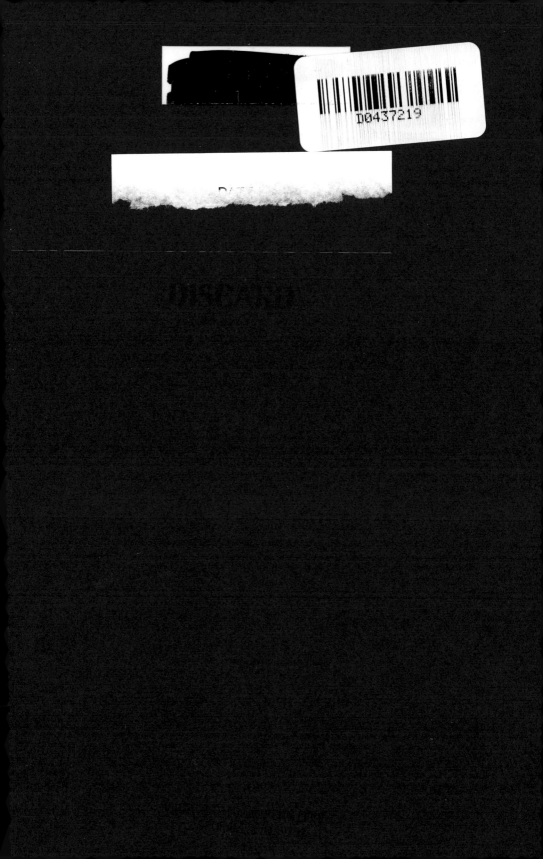

The Dialogics of Dissent

The
DIALOGICS
of DISSENT
in the English Novel

CATES BALDRIDGE

MIDDLEBURY COLLEGE PRESS
Published by University Press of New England
Hanover and London

Middlebury College Press

Published by University Press of New England, Hanover, NH 03755

Printed in the United States of America   5   4   3   2   1

CIP data appear at the end of the book

Portions of chapter 4 have appeared in *Studies in the Novel*, 25(2), Summer 1993, and *The Journal of Narrative Technique*, 23(1), Winter 1993.

An earlier version of chapter 7 appeared in *Studies in English Literature*, 30(4), Autumn 1990.

For my parents,
who never doubted

Contents

✳

Acknowledgments

❋

When one's mind has been changed about controversial issues by voices that one used to disdain, there will always be those willing to lend a sympathetic ear and converse in a spirit of inquiry and excitement about how and why and whither one's view of things has been transformed—and those others, who, feeling fearful and betrayed, will simply walk away from the conversation. Such, I imagine, are the rewards and risks of all dialogic enterprises. Luckily for me, the vast majority of my colleagues at Middlebury have proved to be of the former rather than the latter humor. Among them, Elizabeth Napier, Alison Byerly, and Paul Monod have read all or portions of the manuscript, and contributed many valuable suggestions. Farther afield, I would like to thank Gary Saul Morson, whose painstaking comments both showed me what yet remained to be done, and saved me from a number of embarrassing mistakes. Those errors that remain are, of course, entirely chargeable to myself. I also owe a debt to all the organizers of and participants in the International Bakhtin Conferences, for their efforts continually remind me how vigorous and diverse and inexhaustible is the field in which we labor, and bring a sense of community and solidarity to an often solitary process.

Preface

*

There was a time some decades ago when it was merely assumed that the novel was a site of subversion, when it was regarded as a genre uniquely equipped to expose the machinations of power, to speak for the downtrodden and the forgotten, and to suggest ways of arranging our private and social lives undreamed of by bourgeois orthodoxy. If, under such a conception, all literature deemed worthy a place in the canon was declared to be a criticism of life, the novel was seen to embody the rougher and sharper edges of this critique, for, New Critical valorizations of detachment notwithstanding, there appeared little that smacked of complacency in even its most elaborate aesthetic patterns, and its detailed discriminations of character and feeling could always be credited with being so many diagnoses of what a pitiless capitalism or a straitened imagination or an outmoded Christianity was doing to us. It was as though nearly every novel likely to be studied in an undergraduate classroom carried as its unwritten but palpable subtitle "The Way We Live Now," with Trollope's angered inflections wholly intact. Recently, of course, the situation has become wholly reversed, and today the genre is much more likely to be charged with collaboration than with giving any aid and comfort to the Resistance. Whether a text be Jamesian or Jeremiacal, the outcome is the same—eventually criticism forces it to betray its guilty allegiance to the liberal subject and the discourses that sustain him, a confession which paints the novel not as the scourge of middle-class hegemony but rather as its velvet police baton, relentlessly disciplining us in our easy chairs and seminar rooms. What appears to be subversion, we are inevitably informed, is merely the prearranged charade of Power, a feigning of distress designed to lure us into believing that we are somehow dismantling the Bastille, when in actuality we are walling ourselves up in textual Panopticons. Novelists, like Shelley's poets, have thus become, in an ironic and despairing sense, the unacknowledged legislators of the world—legislators in a thoroughly rubber-stamp Assembly, producing decrees that, whatever their rhetorical splendor, cannot help but function as so many *lettres de cachet*.

The Dialogics of Dissent takes issue with this prevalent critical consensus, for my central argument is that any balanced perspective on the politics of the novel must take account not only of the ways in which it seconds and promotes the hegemonic discourses of bourgeois culture but of those means by which it occasionally obstructs, exposes, decenters, and subverts them. To be sure, the past decade has seen the publication of a number of forceful readings of the genre that, drawing to one extent or another upon on the works of Michel Foucault, have usefully cleared away much sentimentality and unsupported optimism. These attempts to expose the manner in which the novel's formal structures and paradigmatic plots exert a carceral influence over the reader have consistently displayed erudition, ingenuity, and subtle discrimination. However, one can admit all of this and still maintain that such readings' implicit or explicit suggestions that novels are entirely incapable of acting as sites of dissent and resistance posit a relationship between a culture and its literary forms that is unacceptably simplistic, mechanical, and unmindful of social diversity. To counter this polarized view of the political work performed by the genre, I will call frequently upon the theories of Mikhail Bakhtin, a thinker whose placement of novelistic texts within bourgeois culture gives due weight to the fact that any society is composed not just of complementary but of competing vocabularies, and to the various ways in which novels are specially adapted to depict these contending social languages in dialogue, a process whose effects are frequently subversive of hegemonic structures. The result, I hope, will be a more well-rounded view of the novel as a literary form that, although largely the product of middle-class ascendency and thus inevitably complicit in its attempts at self-perpetuation, need not therefore be conceived of as the wholly submissive handmaiden of the powers that be. As I intend to show, novels are capable both of throwing up sticky formal obstacles to attempts at thoroughgoing hegemonic appropriation and of dialogically testing, critiquing, and even subverting their own dominant discourses through their representations of cultural vocabularies in collision.

A secondary purpose of this study is to suggest—largely through the example of its critical praxis—the extent to which Bakhtinian strategies of reading may be integrated with those of neo-Marxism. I am fully aware that this is an enterprise which must be approached with a good measure of caution and tact. Bakhtin himself was not a Marxist, and he made it clear that certain of his key concepts were incompatible with those of dialectical materialism: "Dialogue and dialectics. Take a dialogue and remove the voices (the partitioning of voices), remove the intonations (emotional and individualizing ones), carve out abstract concepts and judgments from living words and responses, cram everything into one abstract consciousness—and that's how you get dialectics."[1] Fortunately, as the concepts contained within the "neo" of neo-Marxism have multiplied over the preceding decades (sometimes to the point where they seem to transform the main term beyond recognition), the role of dialectics has concomitantly diminished. Indeed, as the twentieth century draws to its close, it becomes clear that nearly all of the notions associated more closely with Marxism's prophetic, rather than its analytic, mode have fallen into irrevocable disrepute. However, what remains once the dead tissue has been removed continues—and will continue—to be widely productive, especially in the field of literary criticism, to which recent attempts at reconciling neo-Marxism with deconstruction, new historicism, and the genealogies of Foucault amply testify.[2] The fact is that Marxist categories of thought so permeate the assumptions and methodologies of contemporary hermeneutics that, in a very real sense, "we are all Marxists now."[3] As I hope my readings of individual texts will demonstrate, there is much common ground between the kind of criticism practiced by Raymond Williams and Terry Eagleton and that undertaken by Bakhtin, provided one is willing to be flexible rather than dogmatic. After all, Bakhtin's conception of literature is, like Marxism's, relentlessly social in nature, and many of the former's theories of how cultural vocabularies become inscribed within texts and thence perform cultural labor comprise, so to speak, a superstructure inconceivable without the undergirding base provided by the latter. And, to turn the tables, Marxism needs Bakhtin in order to fulfill its analytic potential, for if it is true, as Fredric Jameson says, that a Marxist criticism which involves only a "negative hermeneutic"—that is, a methodology content merely with its "demystifying vocation" of demonstrating "the ways in which a cultural artifact fulfills a specific ideological mission"—is unacceptable,[4] then Bakhtin is the figure who can most profitably supplement such a program by illuminating the various ways in which novels are not just the reactive products of class society but often engines for change within them.

My third but not, therefore, least important aim has been to produce fresh and perhaps provocative interpretations of six eighteenth- and nineteenth-century novels. I have chosen the texts included here because in each case the application of Bakhtinian theories not only reveals subversive energies other methodologies might wish to ignore or deny, but results in readings that either challenge (or at least markedly refine) a particular critical orthodoxy or bring to light an important aspect of the work not hitherto discussed. What unites my half-dozen novels is that they are all documents that appear consciously designed by their authors to valorize and defend various aspects of bourgeois hegemony. This criterion of selection was mandated by my primary purpose, since if new historicist and neo-Foucauldian critics have demonstrated the power of their approach by discovering carceral structures in texts popularly associated with dissent, any Bakhtinian rejoinder must search out resistance and subversion in works of an unmistakably conservative cast. It is my belief, however, that the resulting chapters contain something more than just so many workings-through of Bakhtin's theories of novelistic resistance and that they may therefore stimulate reappraisals of the texts from other directions as well.

This book is organized into two parts whose functions are related but nevertheless distinct. In the first section I focus upon novels in which a desire to vigorously endorse a particular middle-class orthodoxy clashes with a particular formal requirement of the genre. Here the resulting narrative dissonance blunts the desired ideological effect and exposes a number of latent contradictions within bourgeois structures of thought and feeling. In the second section the focus turns to a pair of works in which the presence of, or concern with, what Bakhtin terms "dialogism" promotes a subversive counter-discourse to the texts' overt political doctrines. These novels, while betraying none of the vexed formal blockages and elisions of the former group, nevertheless wind up promulgating two diametrically opposed ideological positions at once, a fact that cannot help but decenter the conservative vocabularies they clearly intend to present as "natural," "commonsensical," and unanswerable. The chapters that begin each of the sections are not solely introductions to the readings of individual texts which follow, for they include general discussions of the various relationships between bourgeois culture and the novel and also endeavor to provide an explanation of those Bakhtinian concepts that can most usefully supplement or directly challenge neo-Marxist, neo-Foucauldian, and new historicist critical presuppositions. Let me say here that I have endeavored throughout (partially excepting my Conclusion) to aim this book at readers who are not necessarily specialists in Bakhtin;

rather, my implied audience are those persons who, while interested in questions of dissent and resistance within the novel, have as yet undertaken no systematic study of Bakhtin's theories relating to these subjects. At the same time, I trust that my expositions of such concepts as hidden polemic, heteroglossia, and dialogism have been undertaken with sufficient economy to keep those more familiar with such critical tools from losing interest. At any rate, I can assure the specialist reader that even the two "introductory" chapters spend as much time deploying pieces of Bakhtinian ordnance as they do explaining their workings.

Finally, as anyone who has found inspiration in the writings of Bakhtin must acknowledge, a book such as this is both a response to previous utterances and an anticipation of the responses it will itself provoke. The former, of course, are easier to acknowledge since they can be affixed here and now to a name and a title, whereas the latter necessarily involve speculation and will no doubt arrive in part from wholly unexpected quarters. Still, I can very well envision the form some of those replies will probably take, and I feel it may be useful to anticipate at least one of them at the outset. This study, because it argues for the presence of political obstruction, dissent, and subversion within the novel, is at odds with the prevailing mood within cultural poetics, a mood which, reversing that exemplified in the familiar fable, is not likely to bode well for the bringer of good news, who is more likely than not to be branded with the hated name (hated especially in academic circles) of naïf. Indeed, there seems to be a pervasive but unspoken competition ongoing within the profession of English to see who can deliver the direst tidings about the prospects for resistance within literary texts in order to thereby claim the mantle of supreme toughmindedness. If I decline to participate in this footrace and in fact attempt to run somewhat against the tide, it is not because I think the current fashion for pessimism has led others to willfully misread texts or compromise their true opinions. Rather, I only mean to suggest that it has encouraged them to look in only one direction down what, properly understood, is a two-way street. It is therefore not so much to refute but to expand this keen but one-sided view of the novel and its political implications that I have undertaken to add my voice to a conversation already productive of much valuable insight.

I

Monologic Disruptions

CHAPTER ONE

Novelistic Form and the Limits
to Cultural Collaboration

✳

In what ways are the formal properties of the novel complicitous in sustaining bourgeois hegemony? In recent years, the answer most frequently
given (or assumed) seems to be "in *every* way." Of course the myriad in-
terrelationships between the novel's "rise" and the contemporary ascents
of capitalism, individualism, urbanization, and the liberal state have been
critical commonplaces for thirty-five years,[1] but more and more the claim
is made that the genre is a superbly calibrated mechanism for promoting
middle-class categories and assumptions, the more so because it often does
its pacifying work while falsely appearing to give aid, comfort, sanction,
and ammunition to society's discontents. This, at any rate, is the argument
of such critics as D. A. Miller in *The Novel and the Police*, Nancy Armstrong in *Desire and Domestic Fiction*, Lennard J. Davis in *Resisting Novels*, and Jon Stratton in *The Virgin Text*.[2] In all fairness, this new orthodoxy
has nurtured a number of ingenious—even brilliant—readings of novels
once touted by a more sentimental, essentialist, and Romantic hermeneutic
as oppositional through and through, and certainly no one would wish us
back to the days when the mere presence of aesthetic form was taken as
guaranteeing the presence of oppositional energies. Still, might it not be
worth considering whether, amid the previous decade's attempt to rid ourselves of the last vestiges of politico-critical naïveté and behold the carceral
nature of our culture without any comforting squints or sidelong glances,
we have imagined the scene before us as bleaker than it really is, distancing
ourselves from the wishful thinking of the past with a burst of ablutionary
but perhaps equally falsifying pessimism? The purpose of this brief chapter will be to initiate the argument that those who see novels as seamlessly
collaborationist with dominant cultural discourses are overlooking the extent to which certain formal properties of the genre can complicate, deflect,
and sometimes even soundly thwart authorial attempts to promulgate

bourgeois ideologies. In what follows, the writings of Mikhail Bakhtin will be employed to construct an overview of these potential contradictions between novelistic structures and middle-class orthodoxies and to thereby lay the theoretical groundwork for the readings of specific eighteenth- and nineteenth-century novels, which will comprise the remainder of this book's initial section.

What characterizes the critics named above is an intention to completely overturn the long-standing notion endorsed by both general readers and academic specialists that novels can comprise a site on the "margins" of culture from which society's dissident energies may be discharged to good effect toward the dominant modes of thought and feeling underwritten by liberal-capitalist hegemony. For an understanding of the guiding assumptions of this recent variety of generic analysis, we can turn to Stratton's *The Virgin Text*, which he describes as "a rewriting of the history of the novel":[3]

Texts are always constructed, and constituted, within a framework of lived practices. These practices develop over time and have to be learnt by the members of the society as an aspect of their socialisation. From this point of view it is possible to understand the movement of literature under capitalism as a movement towards a particular formulation. I do not mean this in the classical and teleological bourgeois sense of the importance and value of the modern novel form, but rather that the modern novel form is acceptable to our society because it partakes of fundamental attributes of our society's ideology. Hence we are not talking about the inevitable elaboration of the "correct" form of the novel but the gradual articulation of a form, and content, of writing which is determined by, and reinforces, the presuppositions of the evolving society.[4]

There is much in this formulation that is unobjectionable. Stratton is undoubtedly right, for instance, when he notes that there is no "perfect" form of the novel that exists outside its cultural constitution—the genre, being a social artifact (or better, a social process), possesses no *essential* form but rather evolves according to the pressures exerted upon it by hegemonic discourses, discourses it in turn has helped to construct and sustain. There can exist no Platonic ideal of the novel, then, though we might allow for a Jamesian one, as long as we remain cognizant of the fact that James's strictures are themselves the contingent products (and producers) of middle-class hegemony.

One of the shortfalls of the analysis, however, is its insufficient historical breadth. From reading it, one might get the idea that the novel sprang full-grown from the head of the first spinning jenny or copyright act, instead of taking shape, at least in part, from the cobbled-together parts of other, already existent genres of both long and short duration, some of which were labeled "literary" and some of which were not. This oversight may strike some as venial, but it has important consequences, for when a recognition of the novel's precapitalistic progenitors is elided, it then becomes all too easy to speak about the form as if it were wholly the work of bourgeois capitalism and thus a tool not just well suited but *flawlessly designed* to sustain middle-class hegemony. The hidden metaphor in Stratton's account is one of willed human manufacture—liberal society "thinks up" the novel and then crafts it precisely to suit its own specific purposes, much as an engineer invents a laborsaving device—but when speaking about a cultural realm one must employ such tropes sparingly and with caution, for novels are not machines. To take an analogous case, if one were discussing biology and made the claim that evolution had provided every species now extant with an array of physiological attributes perfectly harmonized to meet the dangers and exploit the possibilities of its environment, one would stand accused of distorting the operations of natural selection—an indictment of "vulgar Darwinism" would no doubt be handed down. The truth, of course, is that human beings are burdened with appendixes and that other species suffer both from their own sets of vestigial organs and from special vulnerabilities to certain competitors that are the direct results of special advantages enjoyed over others. If, then, the field of cultural poetics is one it is still especially difficult to speak about without recourse to frequent metaphors from other realms of inquiry— none of which will ever be wholly satisfactory—it still makes more sense to see the novel as having evolved from a process somewhat akin to natural selection than to talk about it as if it were built to specification from a mechanical drawing. It is a curious thing indeed how certain critical methodologies, whose antihumanism is nothing if not strident, are nevertheless inclined to overly anthropomorphize when it suits their purpose.

A better description than Stratton's of the relationship between a genre and its surrounding culture—one that takes sufficient account of the conflicting wills and contradictory aims that a society brings to bear upon any literary practice—is offered by Gary Saul Morson and Caryl Emerson in their encyclopedic study, *Mikhail Bakhtin: Creation of a Prosaics:*

Genres form not by legislation but by accretion. The genuine results of a historical process, they resemble a patchwork rather than a preconceived design. One cannot understand them unless one recognizes that they are compromises, never designed from the outset for the purpose they currently serve, but adapted for that purpose from forms previously serving other purposes. Like most products of evolution,

they are imperfectly suited to their present use—and for that very reason are relatively adaptable to future uses, to which they will also be acceptably but not
optimally suited. Made from ingredients at hand, they become part of a culture's
mixed plate—its prosaic *satura*—of hastily confected offerings.[5]

Bakhtin's refusal to lose sight of the role of chance, accommodation, and
the conscious and unconscious weight of tradition in all instances of genre
building stands as a needed corrective to theories of the novel that, while
insisting that we always historicize, seem oddly oblivious to *literary* history. As Terry Eagleton points out, taking due account of the persistence
of the past when scrutinizing the formal structures of a genre does not
mean abandoning materialism for aestheticism: "just as [in] Marxist economic theory each economic formation tends to contain traces of older,
superseded modes of production, so traces of older literary forms survive
within new ones," a state of affairs that impels us to see genres as "partly
shaped by a 'relatively autonomous' literary history of forms."[6] Thus, although it is fashionable these days to see the structural diffuseness and
complexity of the nineteenth century's "loose baggy monsters" as so much
camouflage masking a very efficient hegemonic weapon,[7] it is important
to recall that the novel, like all genres, is the product not of one century
but of many, and that, like a physiological attribute, it is "at once designed,
undesigned, and ill-designed."[8]

Despite the pertinence of the novel's literary genealogy to investigations
of the genre's supposed collaborations with bourgeois hegemony, it will
not be the purpose of this book's first half to investigate how identifiable
vestiges of older forms render certain novels recalcitrant to the aims of
their society's dominant discourses. I began with the topic in order to better
introduce a set of resistances to middle-class orthodoxies, which, far from
being (unfairly) dismissible as the products of generic "remnants" or "ex-
ogamous fragments," spring directly or indirectly from a structural requirement—that of character development—which the novel seems to
share with few if any previous literary genres and which is traceable to
specifically bourgeois-capitalist cultural pressures. If it can be convincingly demonstrated that a formal imperative mandated by liberalism itself
is an instigator within novels of a mode of discourse potentially subversive
of liberal categories and parameters,[9] then it will at least be necessary to
concede that certain new historicist and neo-Foucauldian claims about the
relentlessly carceral influence of the texts we read, study, and teach will
have to be significantly qualified. Such a demonstration would, in fact,
suggest that to paint the genre as always and everywhere complicit with

hegemonic forces is to turn a blind eye to social complexity and to succumb to a variety of essentialism just as potentially misleading as its much-denigrated Romantic opposite.

For Bakhtin, character development, while not the only structural feature that sets the novel decisively apart from its predecessors, is nevertheless a definitional aspect of the form. The hero of the Classical epic, in contrast to figures like Tom Jones or David Copperfield, enters his work "a fully finished and completed being" who has "already become everything that he could become." Furthermore, in the Homeric text all of the hero's "possibilities are realized utterly in his external social position," for his "view of himself coincides completely with others' views of him," and thus he possesses no secret inner life to either nurture or escape.[10] When we turn to other ancient fictional genres, we also discover personalities incapable of evolving in anything like a "novelistic" manner, for, whereas in the Greek romances and tales of ordeal the protagonists may be sorely and frequently tested, their victory lies precisely in emerging morally unscathed from their many trials; and although stories such as *The Golden Ass* may take as their subject the hero's change of form or state, these alterations appear as magical metamorphoses or other examples of transfiguration that punctuate rather than permeate a character's life.[11] Classical biography and autobiography are likewise bereft of the kind of evolving personalities associated with the novel, a fact that might seem strange given the later genre's obvious similarities in matters of focus and subject with works such as Augustine's account of his own life. True, in the *Confessions* we begin to detect a private existence within the subject that does not completely coincide with his public persona, but here the trajectory of the protagonist's career hinges upon a single momentous event whose unsurpassable importance depletes all of the other occurrences in the text of their life-shaping power by rendering them either forerunners or recapitulations of itself, a pattern that also characterizes many of the Puritan autobiographies of the seventeenth century, whose more direct influence upon the novel is not in question. In another theater, Plutarch and his imitators, though concerned with more secular subjects, also fail to conceive of character as something that is constructed by the random events of day-to-day living; instead, biographies of the ancient world tend to visualize their subjects' lives in a strictly retrospective manner, taking the mature public self as the endpoint and evaluating all previous events not as contingent and locally influential but as so many early manifestations of what the subject was later to be. Under such a conception, says Bakhtin, "character itself does not grow, does not change, it is merely *filled in*,"[12] an observation that underscores the extent to which modern-day biography may owe its own perspective on personal development to the historical intervention of the novel. Passing on to the medieval and Renaissance periods, we can recognize that chivalric romances are in some respects more akin to novels than to the ancient forms—after all, the knights who populate them are individualized to a much greater degree and willfully go in search of adventures that hold out the promise of changing the course of their lives. Here again, though, figures like Lancelot and Tristan cannot really be said to anticipate modern fictional questers such as Pendennis or Stephen Dedalus, for their lives are haunted by prophecies of their destiny and revelations of their fate which are literal rather than symbolic,[13] clear signals that the illusion of a character potentially able to change in any number of ways, depending on the circumstances—an illusion so crucial to the novel's unique perspective on the relationship between personality and time—is simply not being striven for.[14] Finally, we can note that even those prose genres still thriving when novels (as conventionally defined) first arrived on the scene—apologues and religious allegories such as *Pilgrim's Progress*—exhibit much the same lack of what might be called "casual causality," for here, though the protagonists' attitudes and opinons do unmistakably alter in an incremental fashion over the course of the narrative, the characters are made to follow a more or less formulaic path whose mileposts are both clearly visible within the text and previously known (at least in outline) by the audience, and whose presence banishes the sense of contingency and "freedom" we associate with the heroines and heroes of works such as *Clarissa*, *Emma*, and *Great Expectations*. It is by now obvious that any notion of a "relatively autonomous literary history of forms" must make allowances for ruptures as well as continuities if it wishes to help explain the rise of novels from such progenitors as these.

What constitutes one of the novel's most decisive breaks with the past, then, is its representation of protagonists whose personalities alter and develop, usually in small and discrete steps, as a direct result of seemingly nonpredetermined experiences over the course of an extended narrative. Characters in novels, when first encountered, are usually figures whose biographies have not been inscribed in any other text and who therefore appear to possess a relatively "open" future, in which willed action and blind circumstance (in varying proportions) will combine to determine the direction of their subsequent careers.[15] Of course, this openness and freedom are always qualified, at least in the eighteenth- and nineteenth-century novel, by a countervailing tendency toward conservation and consistency. In bourgeois fictions change must always be "reconciled to the idea of a stable ego," an ego demarcated by "the unique pattern of past changes which constitute [its] individuality" and that therefore "allows for some possibilities of development and excludes others."[16] For our purposes, the most important point about this well-understood formal aspect of the novel is that it has been accused of underwriting hegemonic assumptions and categories of thought in a number of ways. It has often been said, for instance, that the manner in which characters evolve in novels makes the forces that shape personality in the real world of capitalism more transparent, rational, and benign than they really are, providing readers with a sanitized account of the manipulations and obfuscations that have alienated them from their communities, their labor, and themselves. An additional indictment is lodged by Lennard J. Davis, who accuses novels of predominantly depicting persons who move from states of mind that bourgeois-capitalist structures define as unproductive to those that they define as useful, thus staging a variation on the "before-and-after" pictures so common in advertising:

It might be worth considering the normative ways in which characters change. Usually the change is from unfeeling to feeling (Gradgrind, Casaubon, Dombey), from crime to moral realization (Moll Flanders, Fanny Hill, Magwitch), from naïveté to world weariness (Jude Fawley, Dorothea Brooke, Raskolnikov), from repression to mature sexuality (Lucy Snow, Jane Eyre, Emma Bovary). Thus the consummate composite character used to be an unfeeling, repressed, naïve outcast who becomes an integrated, feeling, moral, world-weary, sexually mature being. Obviously, I am fooling around with categories a bit, but in a way the pattern of change is to transform the character from one of them to one of us. Again, the move is normative, creating humans in the image of an idealized, middle-class image of themselves.[17]

Thus, to identify with fictional personages is to follow them from cultural "outgroup" to cultural "ingroup," shedding attitudes obstructive to hegemonic designs with every turn of page.

I wish to take issue with this contention of Davis's on two counts. First of all, it seems to me that his description of characters moving steadily and inevitably from heresy to conformity significantly underestimates the extent to which hegemonic discourses within a novel can be disrupted and decentered by the *dialogic* processes through which fictional psyches eschew one ideological ensemble and adopt another, even when those psyches are headed in the general direction of the cultural norm. This point will be touched upon briefly below, but its full articulation must await my second section, in which, again with the aid of Bakhtin, current ideas about the novel's supposed ability to represent divergent cultural discourses at length, without simultaneously undercutting the orthodox ones it wishes to valorize, will be directly challenged. For the time being, however, I would direct the reader's attention not to the questionable assumptions that inform Davis's list but to a set of texts it does not touch upon at all. Although some of the novel's protagonists are, as he rightly says, introduced to us as maladjusted beings who subsequently rid themselves of opinions and attitudes antithetical to middle-class normality, we also frequently encounter heroes and heroines whose consistent *championing* of hegemonic discourses is what defines them, from first page to last, as the text's center of sympathy and whose ordeal is precisely that of contending against other characters who willfully violate, or inadequately uphold, or do not properly understand bourgeois values. To anticipate a little, we can certainly name the Vicar of Wakefield, Fanny Price, Agnes Grey, and Oliver Twist as belonging to this alternative group, though a complete roster would of course be considerably longer. Not surprisingly, such characters inhabit novels that seem to be purposefully designed as strident endorsements of the status quo, supremely conservative documents that appear unwilling to risk depicting their protagonists in even a temporary state of ideological "error." At first glance the existence of such a class of texts does not seem to affect Davis's argument since, if their protagonists are already paragons of sorts, then character development must be present only in sparing amounts. In truth, however, while such heroes' or heroines' abilities to "safely" evolve may indeed be greatly curtailed, the *formal pressure to depict them as doing so* does not abate at all, resulting in a situation in which the structural requirements of the genre are at loggerheads with the text's desire to stridently endorse centripetal bourgeois discourses, and thus in which a good deal of inconsistency and even incongruity infects the unfolding of the plot. Now, of course, such novels can, in a breezy manner, be labeled as the results of so many bad artistic judgments, of so many errors of craft, but to say this is to admit in the same breath that a heightened intention to valorize middle-class orthodoxies appears destined to conflict with a formal desideratum of the novel, which, as Stratton says, is itself a contingent product of middle-class ascendency. Indeed, all of the texts I deal with in this first section are "problem novels"—books that seem to flaunt their author's stated literary tastes (*The Vicar of Wakefield*), to be troubling exceptions to the remainder of their author's canon (*Mansfield Park, Oliver Twist*), or to offer a striking contrast with the productions of the author's literary coterie (*Agnes Grey*). And while it has been generally understood that all of the above works more or less "fail" in some way, explanations of their deficiencies as the results of conflicts between ideological intentions and a structural imperative have rarely if ever been put forward. It may be, then, that a new awareness of such contradictions will henceforth prove helpful in deciphering the discordant or ambiguous or undecidable aspects of texts possessing a similarly conservative cast. Much more important, however, it is my hope that the chapters which immediately follow will clearly demonstrate that in certain ways novels are formally unsuited to the vigorous seconding of bourgeois dogmas and assumptions, and thus that currently fashionable blanket assertions about the novel's *necessary* collusion with hegemonic practices must be regarded as telling only half the story.

By touching upon some of Bakhtin's central theories concerning how social discourses are represented in the novel, we can gain a better idea of why investigations of the relationship between the progress of character development and a particular novel's political coloring need not inevitably lead to a verdict of thoroughgoing cultural conformity. To begin with, the genre is, by historical standards, still a young and developing one, and because it grew and matured together with the capitalist state in which we yet abide, it is especially well suited to record the social dynamics of bourgeois liberalism: "Only that which is itself developing can comprehend developments as a process. The novel has become the leading hero in the drama of literary development in our time precisely because it best of all reflects the tendencies of a new world still in the making; it is, after all, the only genre born of this new world and in total affinity with it."[18] As stated above, this does not mean that novels are the perfect repressive tools of middle-class hegemony; rather, it suggests that, when it comes to depicting life under liberalism, they possess a kind of evolutionary advantage, allowing them to represent our cultural processes *as processes* more readily and thoroughly than can other literary forms. David Goldknopf agrees, insisting that "in the novel, the heightened time-sense of the age was transformed, at the behest of the ego-centered consciousness, into a sharpened recognition of change or process, adding a depth-dimension to the flat vista of [eighteenth-century] empiricism. It was as though one meaning of experience, the conscious absorption of the present moment, gave way to another meaning, a change in the condition of the absorbing agent."[19] This ability to record incremental change over time is important because one of the elements that distinguishes capitalism from previous economic systems is the extent to which it has thrown together people whose disparate cultural vocabularies, once kept relatively separate by the absence of widespread urbanization and industrialization, now struggle with one another in a manner that leads to unprecedented social ferment, antagonism, interchange, and hybridization—to employ Bakhtin's term, the liberal state is characterized by its "heteroglossia." Clearly, such a phenomenon can be investigated thoroughly only by a genre with a good deal of diachronic range, which is just what the novel possesses in strength. Because it takes as its subject the jostling and jockeying of characters within a sociolinguistic landscape whose geography is dominated by issues of class, economic stratification, and unequal political privilege, and because it can follow this contention at length and in detail, the genre remains the most sensitive register we have of one of our culture's centrally constitutive activities. Lionel Trilling is cognizant of the classical novel's special proclivity for, and competence at, depicting the myriad conversations spawned by bourgeois class relations when he asserts that it

tells us about the look and feel of things, how things are done and what things are worth and what they cost and what the odds are. If the English novel in its special concern with class does not . . . explore the deeper layers of personality, then the French novel in exploring these layers must start and end in class, and the Russian novel, exploring the ultimate possibilities of spirit, does the same—every situation in Dostoevsky, no matter how spiritual, starts with a point of social pride and a certain number of rubles.[20]

Thus, whenever a character in a novel speaks, he or she reveals a perspective on reality shaped by concrete cultural factors such as class, occupation, gender, or generation, meaning that when fictional persons interact, what really come into proximity and often into conflict are the various self-interested and partial descriptions of the social system they articulate. As Bakhtin puts it, "a particular language in a novel is always a particular way of viewing the world," and therefore "the speaking person in the novel is always, to one degree or another, an *ideologue*, and his words are always *ideologemes.*"[21] This political contest, however, is not always orchestrated in the same way, and texts in which there is something akin to a level playing field offer a radically different view of hegemonic structures from those in which the author has rigged the game. In "monologic" novels there is one particular take on reality—usually that of the narrator or the protagonist—which the text unequivocally endorses. Here the author's own ideological positions are the only ones allowed to fully resonate, while opposing perspectives are doled out to secondary characters in such a way that they "no longer [appear] as signifying ideas, but rather as socially typical or individually characteristic manifestations of thought."[22] Labeled as the idiosyncratic products of some special social circumstance, biographical trauma, or psychological lacuna, they become not valid alternatives to the reigning authorial discourse but so many counters that, by their obvious deficiencies, merely underscore the infallible, unanswerable speech emanating from the novel's ideological center. A "polyphonic" novel, by contrast, is one in which "a character's word about himself and his world is just as fully weighted as the author's" and in which those figures whose social perspectives oppose that of the narrator are represented *"not only [as] objects of authorial discourse but also [as] subjects of their own directly signifying discourse"*(Bakhtin's italics).[23] This does not mean that the author remains neutral (an impossible undertaking); it means only that she endeavors to present the worldviews of even her villains as if from the inside, granting these dissenting ideological positions their full status as coequals with the one she chooses to inhabit. Finally, within a polyphonic novel it is possible for the characters' differing social vocabularies to interact "dialogically." When this occurs, the conversation between clashing social perspectives creates an exchange in which "each language reveals to the other what it did not know about itself, and in which new insights are produced that neither wholly contained before." Furthermore, the languages come to reflect a new self-conscious understanding that, far from unproblematically reflecting reality, they each merely give voice to one possible viewpoint among many, all of which are equally limited by cultural circumstances, and thus they lose their naive belief in their own "authoritative" (i.e., unquestionable) status.[24] After a character has been involved in a dialogic exchange, he sees the social field from a Copernican rather than a Ptolemaic perspective, and the contingent nature of all cultural discourses—hegemonic and subversive alike—begins to reveal itself.

As one would expect, such ideas have met with their share of skepticism from critics unwilling to credit literary texts with even a minimum of oppositional efficacy. Davis himself, for instance, doubts that the genuine ideological accents of the speech of any class can be rendered in novels in a manner adequate to support Bakhtin's claims about their effects because, as he rightly points out, there is a great deal of difference between the dialogues in even the most naturalistic novel and the actual conversations of human beings as captured on tape recordings. The talk that emerges from novelistic characters is severely regularized, denuded of many of the pauses, false starts, trailings off, stammerings, facial expressions, and involuntary bodily movements that we know accompany our real-world verbal communications and that often contribute more than the words themselves toward getting our actual—as opposed to our polite or conventional—message across.[25] This acknowledgment that much is left out, however, need not lead to the conclusion that the ideological colorings Bakhtin speaks of also necessarily go by the wayside. Many of the unrepresented conversational aspects which Davis notes are, after all, lapses in cerebration rather than elements of a socially learned repertoire, and for this reason would not often vitally contribute to a reader's understanding of a character's specific cultural perspective. Rather, such an ideological orientation would much more likely come to light as a result of the repeated use of certain key words, the misunderstanding of another person's speech, a class-bound interpretation of some common event, and so on. The truth is that Davis's chronological focus here is simply too narrow, for a novel contrasts the varying strands of heteroglossia over time, and dialogism cannot be effected within the space of a snapshot. If long duration is, as we have seen, the novel's métier, then any judgments of the genre's political effects must remain mindful of this fact.

A more important criticism put forward by Davis, however, takes the form of an assertion that dialogism cannot genuinely occur in *any* literary work. "Natural conversation," he says, "is social, interactive, and communal by nature, whereas dialogue in novels is not. It is monolithic, nonnegotiable and, in that sense, not egalitarian and democratic since it proceeds from the absolute authority and unity of the novelist." In addition, real conversations are unplanned and can be voluntarily entered or abandoned, but those in novels are designed in a "linear" fashion to illuminate character, reveal conflicts, or provide information; and of course the fictional speakers serve at the pleasure of the author, all of which robs them of precisely the qualities Bakhtin wishes to find within them: "the linear nature of the exposition . . . points to the reality that, rather than Bakhtin's notions of heteroglossia or dialogicity in novels, control descends from the author who may label linguistic signs as two voices but ultimately controls the essence of conversation—its form. Rather than many voices, on this formal level, the novel contains one voice—that of the author." In one sense, of course, this is undeniable, since most books are not written by committee, but here again, the fact that the dialogues in novels are more *efficient* than those in real life seems to be employed as the proof for a much larger claim—in this case, that strong sympathetic imaginings and keen sociological observations cannot flourish alongside an authorial intention to get on with the plot. The trouble here is really with Davis's use of words like "authority" and "control," because the way he invokes them tends to deny in an a priori fashion the possibility of an other-directed and inclusive rather than a self-reflective and narrowing agenda on the part of an author. Nearly all of us have ourselves participated in countless conversations where the heteroglossia of our culture was dialogized (Davis does not deny that they in fact occur outside of texts). To then claim that an author's attempts to represent these types of encounters must inevitably rob them of their social particularity and conflictual resonance to the point where their value as registers of ideological diversity is fatally compromised is to caricature the extent to which our state of cultural subjection (or psychological solipsism) hobbles the process of literary production. Many novels are monologic, but were the genre as a whole as monologic as Davis appears to believe, it is very doubtful that interpretive disagreements concerning specific works would be nearly so numerous as they have hitherto been.

It should be noted in passing that dialogism does not merely occur when two or more characters in novels have face-to-face conversations. David Lodge, responding to Davis, explains that such a narrow understanding of the concept

> is based on a misunderstanding, or misrepresentation of what Bakhtin means by the dialogic in fiction. The dialogic includes, but is not restricted to, the quoted verbal speech of characters. It also includes the relationship between the characters' discourses and the author's discourse (if represented in the text) and between all these discourses and other discourses outside the text, which are imitated or evoked or alluded to by means of doubly-oriented speech.[26]

This claim will be strongly borne out by the chapter on *Mansfield Park*, where the voice Austen so stridently attempts to refute is located largely, though not exclusively, offstage. Thus, even if Davis's description of novelistic conversations were more persuasive than it is, it still would not refute Bakhtin's assertions about the genre's dialogic potential.

Why this potential should be especially linked with character development and why it is sometimes capable of throwing up obstacles against authors determined to valorize bourgeois patterns of feeling can be understood if we look again both at the kind of "normative" novels Davis lists and at those counterexamples I will soon be focusing upon. In texts of the first variety, where the protagonist begins in a state of ideological "error" and must evolve into "one of us," this progress toward orthodoxy, however emphatically the reader's attention is drawn to it, cannot by itself ensure that the relativizing influence of dialogism will be wholly absent. This is so because a hero or heroine is, even in the twentieth-century novel, a character with whom the author and audience must, almost by definition, identify to some extent, and this act of identification cannot be deferred too long—that is to say, it must precede his or her arrival at the Beulah Land of cultural conformity that usually comprises the book's denouement, as a mental review of any of the novels in Davis's schedule will confirm. Indeed, Bakhtin would likely maintain that in some of the works there cited even the protagonist's initial ideological position, however disquieting to middle-class pieties, facilitates the process of identification only because it is allowed to fully "sound," to carry with it the coherence and conviction that allows us to experience it as if from the inside and thereby to feel that we are engaged with a human being instead of a straw man and reading a novel instead of an apologue. To employ one of Davis's own examples, although *Middlemarch* clearly wishes us to understand that Dorothea's early combination of asceticism and idealism is impractical and potentially subversive of social order, does this mean that, when she has "come around" in the final chapter, the narrator's middle-class discourse promoting the inevitability of incremental reform and the wisdom of diminished expectations emerges *completely unscathed* from its encounter with the heroine's youthful rhetoric of bold action, "excessive" altruism, and the pursuit of fame? In monologic novels "individuality kills the signifying power of the [dissenting characters'] ideas"[27]—that is, the views of those who ideologically oppose the narrator are completely discredited as being the result of some social or psychological deficiency: is this *all* that there is to be said of Dorothea's youthful voice in the first half of *Middlemarch* and of its persistent echoes in the second? One could now go on to raise even sharper questions about the havoc Moll Flanders's "conversion" wreaks upon the middle-class piety and respectability she finally embraces; the fact is that, by the time many a protagonist gets around to finding the straight and narrow, it often seems neither. The point is that if a text truly is dominated by a single, authoritative ideological deduction, then it is quite likely to transform "the represented world into *a voiceless object of that deduction*" [Bakhtin's italics],[28] in which case it is difficult to see how a satisfying *protagonist* could emerge at all within the type of novel we are now discussing. These issues will be dealt with at length in my second section, where Mr. Thornton's and Sydney Carton's dialogic pilgrimages from the margins to the center of bourgeois life will be shown to seriously undermine the very orthodoxies toward which the texts are obviously leading them.

Consider now the contrasting type of novel, in which the hero or heroine enters the book pretty much in accord with the text's overall ideological position, a set of works that is, if anything, more "normative" than those on Davis's list. Whereas, in the previous case, the juxtaposed presence of identification and character development made dialogism difficult to avoid completely, here the relative impeccability of the heroine's initial cultural perspective means that the novelistic imperative toward her moral evolution will, since dialogism may accompany it, pose a constant threat to the text's political stability. The result, at least in the novels scrutinized in the following chapters, is that arrested or problematic character development can be seized upon both as an example in itself of the potential conflicts between a vigorously conservative ideological agenda and a central formal requirement of the genre, and as a useful beacon for illuminating this conflict as it applies to other novelistic structures—irony, for instance, in *The Vicar* and narrative momentum in *Mansfield Park*. We shall also discover that, when push comes to shove, political considerations win out over formal ones; the texts "fail" to one degree or another because they do not quite fit our sense of what the novel should be. Again, the outcome of this struggle is not surprising, since the presence of such a dilemma is itself the mark of a peculiarly conformist political intention, an intention that now stands revealed as the major reason these texts seem so different from the rest of their authors' oeuvres. The most important point to keep in mind, however, is that whether a writer from Davis's list stumbles into it or one from mine scrambles to avoid it, the dialogic potential within the novel remains a lurking impediment to any attempts at unswerving collaboration with the discourses of bourgeois hegemony.

It might be objected that the above discussion, because it insists that character development is an "imperative" within the novel, is guilty of essentializing the genre, of arbitrarily positing the dramatization of evolving personalities as an element all "real" novels "ought" to include. If there is no Platonic ideal of perfect novelness, then why can't texts that portray static protagonists be unproblematically ranged alongside those that depict changing ones? And isn't all this talk of "failure" just an attempt to justify an expression of personal taste by erecting around it a dubious theoretical scaffolding? The answer is that character development, like any other formal requirement of the genre—that it be in prose, that it be of a certain length, that it contain both action and dialogue, and so on—is not something that most readers *just happen* to desire in novels but something that they have been led to prize by cultural discourses emanating wholly from within bourgeois hegemony. Recall Stratton's claim that the novel takes the form it does not because of some inherent transhistorical essence yearning to express itself, but rather because it "partakes of fundamental attributes of our society's ideology" and that, when we speak about the genesis of novelistic structures, we must envision "the gradual articulation of a form, and content, of writing which is determined by, and reinforces, the presuppositions of the evolving society." Thus, there is simply no difference between the formal aspects of any genre and the public expectation that they will in fact be present; for if the anticipated formal structures are absent from a work, the audience will simply classify it as belonging to a different genre, and there can be no appeal to "inherent" structures in the case of a wholly cultural production like a literary text. If "taste is morality," it is also ideology, and the taste for reading about persons whose personalities develop arose and became quasi-institutionalized contemporaneously with the preference for reading about "ordinary" people rather than Hercules or Lancelot—as Davis says, the accusation that a book's characters do not develop is a "recurring complaint in early novel criticism."[29] By the time E. M. Forster gets around to informing us that a protagonist should be "capable of surprising [us] in a convincing way,"[30] he is merely codifying a cultural proclivity of long standing, one that both shaped and was in turn shaped by the novel from its earliest days.

The point that must again be emphasized is that this yearning for character development, though both a product and producer of certain bourgeois capitalist ideologies, is not by any means perfectly suited to the purpose of abetting those discourses in a consistent or unambiguous way. We are, in fact, in the presence of a historical irony. The demand for character development most likely resulted from a general desire to see the burgeoning capitalist culture's new literary form reflect the rising sense of individual possibility that seemed to be everywhere emerging as traditional economic and social arrangements were superseded.[31] If middle-class readers were now, relatively speaking, freer to choose their places of residence, their occupations, their mates, their amusements, and their religion, then the corresponding idea that one's possible biographical scenarios had been multiplied—the feeling that "anything can happen, anything is possible"—undoubtedly helped to sow a preference for characters whose fates were not, like Tristan's or even Christian's, already formed in advance, especially in a genre that purported to distinguish itself from its predecessors through a heightened respect for everyday verisimilitude. And even if it can be convincingly shown that these supposed "new choices" were largely illusory or trivial, it will not change the fact that the demand for character development in the novel inevitably brought with it dialogizing energies potentially disruptive to dominant structures of feeling, since even if the range of economic, erotic, and peregrinational possibilities in literary texts far outstripped those available in life, the spectacle of social languages in conflict would have continued to undercut hegemonic claims for totalizing competence regardless. Furthermore, this holds true even if one admits that character development may have operated as a pacifying substitute for the self-transformations denied by economic and cultural realities,[32] for the accompanying dialogism offers not an additional vicarious satisfaction but a relativizing perspective on one's accepted way of life that may be anything but comforting. It is, in fact, the counterhegemonic side effect of a certain form of ideological pabulum.

Even this mild formulation may strike some as carrying with it the whiff of essentialism, since it might seem that the novel's dialogic potential, as this chapter defines it, is a universally effective oppositional energy, potentially able to decenter every conceivable kind of power structure, feudal, Communist, theocratic, or other. This point, however, is moot. It was bourgeois capitalism alone that produced the novel, and it is more than doubtful whether any other cultural configuration could ever have done likewise. Edward Said notes, for instance, that there was no novelistic tradition in Arabic countries until the form was borrowed from Europe in the twentieth century,[33] and we know that within Western societies resistance to the genre has usually sprung from traditionalist groups who also fear many concomitant aspects of the modern, liberal dispensation. Indeed, as W. J. Harvey has pointed out,

we may fairly say that the novel is the distinct art form of liberalism, by which I mean not a political view or even a mode of social and economic organization but rather a state of mind. This state of mind has as its controlling centre an acknowledgment of the plenitude, diversity and individuality of human beings in society, together with the belief that such characteristics are good as ends in themselves. It delights in the multiplicity of existence and allows for a plurality of beliefs and values . . . . Tolerance, scepticism, respect for the autonomy of others are its watchwords; fanaticism and the monolithic creed its abhorrence.[34]

The problem with this formulation, of course, is that it is overly laudatory. Still, it seems true that bourgeois liberalism's partially enacted virtues of tolerance and diversity are what allows the dialogic novel to expose those of its discourses that, under the benign mantle of evenhandedness, exclude, disempower, and brook no debate. Dialogism subverts the status quo by demonstrating that the blindnesses and self-interested viewpoints which motivate the speakers in liberalism's permitted debates also apply to those as yet unanswered cultural monologues that have hitherto seemed above the fray.

Once more, however, this first section deals not with the enactment of dialogism but rather with its avoidance. Here we will observe the ways in which a desire to infuse the text with a monologic ideological polarity— to draw a political *cordon sanitaire* around the protagonist—introduces contradiction and instability into the very heart of the narrative enterprise. In *The Vicar of Wakefield*, in *Mansfield Park*, in *Agnes Grey*, and in *Oliver Twist*, attempts to render the novel a univocal vehicle for cultural orthodoxy end up, because of the structural havoc they create, exposing all the more clearly the contingency, partiality, and answerability of the orthodox discourses they were intended to articulate and sustain. We thus emerge from these pointedly conservative texts not with our bourgeois prejudices confirmed, but with a better understanding that, however intimidating a reputation novels may now enjoy within liberalism's ideological arsenal, their dialogic potential frequently renders them swords of a cumbersome and two-edged variety, and that even the most subtle attempts to blunt the one inconvenient blade can result in the entire weapon appearing less than formidable, and its wielder somewhat comical.

CHAPTER TWO

Wakefield's Vicar,
Delinquent Paragon

*

A controversy over the nature and extent of the irony directed at *The Vicar of Wakefield*'s titular hero has nearly monopolized critical discussion of the text for at least the past quarter-century. Even in recent years, commentators have tended to center their arguments upon an allegiance either to the camp of those who insist that *The Vicar* scathingly indicts its narrator[1] or to those who assert that only a gentle irony is directed at Primrose and that he exits the text as more or less an ideal figure.[2] My argument, briefly put, will be that both schools in this dispute are half right and that this can be so because Goldsmith, at the very centerpoint of his novel, and for reasons that are thoroughly political, becomes frightened of where his own deployments of irony are taking him and attempts to rewrite his hitherto debunked protagonist as a character above reproach. Moreover, I will contend that the two most often discussed problems arising from the text—the seeming instability or intermittence of its ironic perspective and the marked divergence in tone and content between its first and second halves—are both the result of the author's endeavor to belatedly cancel or "take back" the inherent irony of his chosen genre in order to endorse certain middle-class orthodoxies.[3]

While the character of the Vicar therefore changes, it cannot be said to develop "novelistically," as that term has been defined in the previous chapter, for although the hero enters the novel displaying one set of characteristics and exits it sporting decidedly different ones, this moral transformation takes the form of a desperate leap rather than an incremental progression. It will not be my overall purpose in this chapter, however, merely to point out that character development is problematic in Goldsmith's tale, for this fact must be obvious to all; rather, it will be to demonstrate how that disconcerting leap of the protagonist's is mandated by, and can in turn be used to illuminate, contradictions between the formal structures of the novel (in this case, the novel of sentimental comedy) and an authorial desire to reproduce hegemonic discourses.

To properly explicate this issue, I will be obliged to look at *The Vicar* from what some may consider an unusual perspective. What both sets of critical partisans described above have in common is their focus upon how well or ill the hero orders his *religious* life, and while the issue is sometimes whether or not he lives up to the pious standard he himself espouses and at other times whether he does or does not follow a path from error toward some doctrinal truth approved by Goldsmith, the spiritual element is almost always uppermost. What I intend to do here is to shift the entire discussion of the Vicar's supposed faults and virtues into a more secular vein.[4] Without wishing to discount the religious issues that are undeniably present in Goldsmith's fiction, I want to put them temporarily aside and focus instead on a more worldly aspect of the narrator: rather than inquiring how good a clerical shepherd he is, I will investigate how good or ill an exemplar of emerging middle-class values he becomes. My belief is that when we see *The Vicar of Wakefield* as a book that reveals the difficulties, perils, and contradictions endemic to the middling orders' strategies of conceiving the world—and then, in its second half, as one that tries extremely hard to cover them up—we will discover an important aspect of the text largely ignored by the conventional critical debate. From this new perspective the novel's hero will emerge as a Pyrrhic champion of bourgeois values, a hero who, in a sense, prevails against those whose class-specific notions and practices he finds anathema, but one whose hard-won "victory" is called into serious question by the text's eleventh-hour attempt to erase the irony it has already offered up to us—an attempt that cannot help but fail.

But did Goldsmith really have a significant investment in recognizably "middle-class" or "bourgeois" ways of thinking? A number of recent studies have argued that what Defoe, in 1719, referred to as people inhabiting "the middle station"—people he distinguished as being free from "vicious living, luxury and extravagances on [the] one hand, [and from] hard labour, want of necessaries, and mean or insufficient diet on the other"[5]— were by midcentury far advanced in the process of "creating . . . a bourgeois culture that was destined to become the dominant national culture."[6] Thus, by "the middle of George III's reign" we can speak of "a powerful and extensive middle class"[7] whose habits of mind appear largely congruent with those of their nineteenth-century descendants. Now, one can admit this and yet still object that the author was, after all, a Tory and therefore unlikely to champion a set of values often associated, in 1766, with Whiggism. This is an important issue to raise because it will help define just what it means to talk about "bourgeois" values in *The Vicar.* One must admit right off, for instance, that Goldsmith had no love for the captains of industry (or more properly, lords of commerce) proliferating during his lifetime. It has been amply demonstrated, for instance, that Dr. Primrose's famous political diatribe in chapter 19 is essentially the same argument put forth by Goldsmith in *The Traveller* and elsewhere, and that both works are ardent in their "anti-commercialism . . . anti-imperialism . . . [and] anti-capitalism."[8]

To concede, however, that Goldsmith was in some ways a nostalgic Tory yearning for a precapitalist social contract is not to place him outside that structure of ideas and emotions which can properly be labeled "bourgeois," for there is much more to the term than a Whiggish attraction for laissez-faire economics and overseas empire. In truth, many of the sustaining energies of middle-class life flow from discourses concerned not with the marketplace but with the private sphere, discourses that promote a veneration for the family hearth and the domestic virtues it supposedly both fosters and protects. Peter Earle has demonstrated that, as early as the first decades of the eighteenth century, we find among the "middle station" the development of "a sensibility that sees the beginnings of 'Victorian' attitudes to the 'home' and to the place of middle-class women within it," a process that has "never been reversed" and that leads "inexorably to the even more middle-class middle class of the nineteenth century and today."[9] Such a championing of the nuclear family and its homespun tranquility is a major concern of Goldsmith's in both *The Deserted Village* and *The Traveller*, as these lines from the latter attest:

> Eternal blessings crown my earliest Friend,
> And round his dwelling guardian saints attend;
> Blest be that spot, where chearful guests retire
> To pause from toil, and trim their evening fire;
> Blest that abode, where want and pain repair,
> And every stranger finds a ready chair;
> Blest be those feasts with simple plenty crown'd,
> Where all the ruddy family around
> Laugh at the jests or pranks that never fail,
> Or sigh with pity at some mournful tale,
> Or press the bashful stranger to his food,
> And learn the luxury of doing good. (4:249)[10]

As for reconciling such attitudes with the author's Toryism, Paul Langford points out that emerging middle-class conceptions of domesticity "likely . . . promoted certain political tendencies in a party sense," and points to a contemporary of Goldsmith's who asserts that family life "makes Tories of us all [, for] see if any Whig wishes to see the beautiful Utopian expansion of power within his own walls."[11] There is no necessary contradiction, then, between Tory politics and the emerging cult of the familial fireside. We shall find, however, that, try as it might to idolize bourgeois notions of domestic felicity, *The Vicar of Wakefield*, when considered in its totality, emerges more as a testament to its author's overt and covert fears about their ability to prevail than as his proclamation of their inevitable triumph, and that this dichotomy between intention and result is directly traceable to a conflict within the text between the discourses of the middling orders and novelistic form.

The extent to which *The Vicar* depicts the family hearth as the keystone of middle-class safety and prosperity can be seen in the novel's initial pages, where we find that Dr. Primrose conceives of his marriage not only as a personal blessing but as a pillar of state. He is, for instance, of the opinion that "the honest man who marrie[s] and [brings] up a large family, *[does] more service* than he who continue[s] single, and only talk[s] of population" (37, italics mine).[12] This notion of a civic duty to reproduce— and thereby to re-produce the domestic occasion—allows him to see his children both as "the supports of [his] declining age" and as "a very valuable present made to [his] country," which he "consequently look[s] upon as [his] debtor" (38). As if to ensure a large and healthy brood, the Vicar has selected a wife not with eros, but with motherhood in mind, for we are told that he chose her "as she did her wedding gown, not for a fine glossy surface, but such qualities as would wear well" (37). Not content, however, to support the commonweal singlehandedly, he makes it his special mission to marry all of Wakefield, "exhorting . . . the bachelors to matrimony" (40), with the result that the town's lack of unmarried men soon makes it a subject of public comment.

What the Vicar hopes to gain by all this—what he seems to posit as the ultimate benefit of a thoroughly bourgeois hearth surrounded by a community of similar establishments—is that middle-class ideal, a rigorous stability. He asserts with satisfaction that, having ordered things so well, his family has "no revolutions to fear, nor fatigues to undergo; all [their] adventures [are] by the fire-side, and all [their] migrations from the blue bed to the brown" (37). As if to reassure us that he has rendered his family's existence essentially plotless, he provides a schedule of his household's unexceptional activities:

The little republic to which I gave laws, was regulated in the following manner: by sun-rise we all assembled in our common apartment; the fire being previously kindled by the servant. After we had saluted each other with proper ceremony, for I always thought fit to keep up some mechanical forms of good breeding, without which freedom ever destroys friendship, we all bent in gratitude to that Being who gave us another day. This duty being performed, my son and I went to pursue our usual industry abroad, while my wife and daughters employed themselves in providing breakfast, which was always ready at a certain time. I allowed half an hour for this meal, and an hour for dinner; which time was taken up in innocent mirth between my wife and daughters, and in philosophical arguments between my son and me. (50)

The phrase "little republic" has struck several critics as particularly telling, especially those ill-disposed toward Primrose. Richard J. Jaarsma, for instance, sees it as an indication that the Vicar's relationship with his family "is not that of a father, but of a dictator."[13] What I wish to draw attention to, however, is what the metaphor has to say about Primrose's desire to wall his family off from the outside world, for to liken one's family to a nation-state is to imply that it has—or has need of—borders, defenses, controls on immigration, and the like. This is the argument touched upon by Thomas R. Preston, who sees the Vicar as being chastised by Goldsmith for, in Miltonic phrase, practicing merely a "fugitive and cloistered virtue." As Preston puts it, Primrose "attempts to turn his family into a little paradise, where the closed family circle becomes a haven from the world, making a separate peace."[14] Now it is a commonplace that this is precisely what the bourgeois home is *expected* to do—to act as a haven from and an antidote to a morally suspect public sphere; and where I would differ from Preston is in the notion that Goldsmith sees domestic moral shelter as spiritually stifling or somehow unnecessary. Certainly the author's contemporaries within the middle station were familiar with his "commonwealth" metaphor and used it approvingly. For example, a sermon of 1766 insists that "private and familiar intercourse forms a kind of separate republic, which has laws of its own, distinct from those of the state, tho' influenced by them," and Langford maintains that it "remained a common conception of the period" to see "the family, . . . the 'natural society of wife and children,' [as] the fundamental form of political organization."[15] Far from denigrating such cloistering separateness, it seems to me that *The Vicar of Wakefield*, taken as a whole, strongly *attempts* to endorse the kind of spiritual "protection" the bourgeois hearth is supposed to provide. Furthermore, the protagonist's use of the "little republic" metaphor is quite appropriate given his political situation, for there really does exist an enemy without the battlements with which to contend: the squirearchical vices of opulence, sensuality, intemperance, and impiety embodied in the younger Thornhill.

There is, however, a serious breach in the familial defenses, for during the text's first half Goldsmith appears to inhabit the formal structures of the novelistic subgenre of sentimental comedy without qualm, which means that his protagonist is ironized by being presented as less than the exemplar of middling virtues he believes himself to be. Primrose's failings revolve around a familiar contradiction between middle-class rhetoric and middle-class reality: although the bourgeois mind preserves its integrity and stakes out its moral raison d'être by positing an impious, licentious, and sexually predatory squirearchy and aristocracy posed menacingly above it,[16] the acquisitive dynamic endemic to middle-class life and the related hunger for status and "respectability" means that bourgeois aspirations are at war with bourgeois apologetics—that there is built into the middle-class mind a desire to become what it defines itself against. Earle traces this paradox at least as far back as Defoe, insisting that "one part of him admired the ease of upwards social mobility in England and welcomed that climax of the career of a successful man in the middle station which enabled him to convert his capital into a rentier income and buy himself a life of genteel leisure. It was after all his own ambition. But the other part of Defoe spent much of his writing career lambasting the life-style of existing gentlemen."[17] As we shall see, this contradictory tendency is both exposed and elided in *The Vicar:* from the beginning of the book through chapter 16, Primrose is gently satirized as a self-proclaimed champion of his class who nevertheless reaches after that which he publicly associates with moral corruption; he is laughingly exposed as a zealous soldier in the army of bourgeois virtues who all the while yearns to join the ranks of the enemy. But at the text's halfway mark, Goldsmith suddenly becomes uncomfortable with what he has wrought and attempts to reverse the polarity of his tale, thereby fashioning the work's second half into something decidedly at odds with its first.

In *The Vicar of Wakefield*'s initial sixteen chapters the Primroses, like the Hebrews of the Old Testament, fall repeatedly, though their punishment is merely the mild irony doled out by sentimental comedy.[18] Here the protagonist, full of pronouncements about "disproportioned acquaintances" and "disproportioned friendships [which] ever terminate in disgust" (54–55), nevertheless seems curiously unable—especially for a "dictator"—to keep his family from aspiring to link themselves with the local squirearchy by way of matrimony or from otherwise scheming to rise above their station. Bear in mind too that this is the man who will later, in his political diatribe to the disguised butler, refer to all members of the upper classes as "tyrants" ravenous for ever-expanding power and hastening the virtual enslavement of their fellow countrymen. Despite the Vicar's alarming rhetoric, when it comes to praxis, he fails repeatedly to keep his family satisfied with their middling run of life, and what is especially interesting (and funny) about these failures is the silence and evasion in which he attempts to wrap them.

To begin with, when Squire Thornhill first sets eyes on the family daughters during the course of a hunt, the Vicar's commands to his family to retire are apparently ignored: "I was instantly for returning in with my family; but either curiosity or surprize, or some more hidden motive, held my wife and daughters to their seats" (53). Strangely, this act of blatant insubordination moves the republic's strongman to no rejoinder—the squire gets his introduction. Once Thornhill is gone, the Vicar begins to tell his family that he has some "apprehensions . . . from [Thornhill's] character," but the timely arrival of the squire's gift of venison stops his mouth, and afterward he "continue[s] silent, satisfied with just having pointed out danger, and leaving it to their own discretion to avoid it" (55). The next day, when the family has undertaken to entertain Thornhill, Primrose seems equally unwilling to state his concerns clearly, and relates the incident by way of phrases that obfuscate the question of how or even whether he objected out loud to the household's outlay: "it may be easily supposed what provisions were exhausted to make an appearance. It may also be conjectured that my wife and daughters expanded their gayest plumage upon this occasion" (59). On those days when the Vicar *is* roused to pronounce his nay, there quickly follow admissions that such measures have proved feckless. Chapter 9, for instance, ends with Primrose being "obliged to give a peremptory refusal" to the idea of his daughters accompanying the squire and his two "ladies" home after an excursion, and chapter 10 begins with the news that he "now began to find that all [his] long and painful lectures upon temperance, simplicity, and contentment, were utterly disregarded" (72). To round out this catalog of Primrose's derelictions, we can take note of his curiously vague description of how he is overcome in argument by his wife, this time over the question of whether the family colt is to be sold to buy a horse of a more respectable caliber:

"This at first I opposed stoutly; but it was as stoutly defended. However, as I weakened, my antagonist gained strength, till at last it was resolved to part with him" (81). The Vicar, usually so verbose about the minutiae of his many debates, here invokes the passive voice to render obscure the details of his latest abandonment of principle.

When we consider the elisions cited above alongside those more straightforward instances of the Vicar's desire for a landed connection—his worry, for instance, that Sophia will fall for a "man of broken fortune" such as Burchell (57) or his willingness to use Farmer Williams as a pawn to attract the squire toward Olivia[19]—the contradiction upon which Goldsmith builds his ironic case against Primrose becomes clear. I have emphasized the Vicar's comic silences because a good deal of critical attention has been directed to the question of why Primrose waxes so frenetic and verbose in the book's second half, becoming "an authority on monarchy, commerce, drama, penology, and the criminal code."[20] To put the case succinctly, I believe that what comes after the midpoint of *The Vicar* is an attempt to compensate for and refute the undermining of middle-class discourses carried out by the sentimental comedy of the first sixteen chapters. It is my contention that *The Vicar* shifts gears (and practically genres) halfway along because Goldsmith suddenly becomes appalled at the cumulative effects of his own irony, at his own text's laughing insistence that the bourgeois hearth is fatally *permeable*, open to all the depredations of squirearchical vices because each and every one of its denizens, including that middle-class "hero" Primrose, has been revealed as a traitor within the gates. What the second half of the text sets out to portray—quite *without* irony—is the middle-class domestic circle as an utterly *hermetic* structure, safely walled off against any upper-class intrusion, no matter how violent or prolonged, provided the paterfamilias acts as he should.[21] And so, as we shall see, the abrupt change in tone and content that so many readers have puzzled over will emerge as the text's desperate attempt to take back what it has already conceded, and in the process to convert itself from a sentimental novel into something more akin to a philosophical exemplum.

Evidence that Goldsmith requires the bourgeois hearth to emerge from the book much more resistant to undermining and compromise than it appears to be after chapter 16 can be gleaned from the Vicar's subsequent political harangue to the disguised butler. (Recall that the ideas expressed there are the author's as well.) As outlined by Primrose, the middling orders of society are in grave danger of being marginalized, for the "laws [of

Great Britain] contribute to the accumulation of wealth[,] . . . the learned
are held unqualified to serve their country as counsellors merely from a
defect of opulence, and wealth is thus made the object of a wise man's
ambition." The resulting plutocrats are busy at work corrupting the lower
classes, for "the possessor of accumulated wealth, when furnished with the
necessaries and pleasures of life, has no other method to employ the superfluity of his fortune but in purchasing power." They thus go about
"making dependents, by purchasing the liberty of the needy or the venal,
of men who are willing to bear the mortification of contiguous tyranny for
bread" (115). Each wealthy "orb" now possesses "a vortex of its own"
composed of "slaves, the rabble of mankind, whose souls and whose education are adapted to servitude, and who know nothing of liberty except
the name." Opposed to this unholy alliance of Opulence and Poverty, however, are a class who alone are qualified carry the torch of sweetness, light,
and civilization forward through the darkness:[22]

> But there must still be a large number of the people without the sphere of the
> opulent man's influence, namely, that order of men which subsists between the
> very rich and the very rabble; those men who are possest [*sic*] of too large fortunes
> to submit to the neighboring man in power, and yet are too poor to set up for
> tyranny themselves. In this middle order of mankind are generally to be found all
> the arts, wisdom, and virtues of society. This order alone is known to be the true
> preserver of freedom, and may be called the People. (116)

This is hardly an idiosyncratic view on Goldsmith's part. Rather, it is a
hallmark of that blending of middling virtues and Tory politics which
Langford terms "country ideology," an ideology whose "long-established
maxim" is that "the middle ranks, the smaller freeholders and tradesmen,
[are] well disposed to the cause of liberty, and innately more resistant to
authority than their superiors and inferiors alike. Noblemen could be considered tools of princes. The lower classes were inherently dependent on
power and patronage. Civic as well as moral virtue belonged with the
golden mean."[23] The *Vicar of Wakefield*, then, is not so much picking a
fight as joining one in progress.

Clearly, such a vision of chronic social warfare necessitates a middle
class which is immune from the kind of blandishments that the "rabble"
is seduced by, but if even the Vicar is chronically unable to withstand the
glittering fruit that Thornhill dangles before him, the battle is as good as
lost. The martial language I employ here is congruent with Goldsmith's
own, for he has this newly resurgent Primrose assert that the middling
orders, having no ally save the King, "may be compared to a town of which

the opulent are forming the siege" (116). What then will do but a kind of military discipline, a singleness of purpose of which the Vicar of the first half has shown a signal lack? The hero's political diatribe, coming only one chapter into the novel's second section, can thus be seen as *The Vicar of Wakefield*'s call to arms against itself, marking off a frightened recognition of what has already been given away and of how extreme any strategy of reclamation will need to be. And so, if the concluding portion of Goldsmith's novel turns decisively away from the ironic strains of sentimental comedy, it is because that supposedly "harmless" satiric mode is now perceived as having been pursued in a manner which has thoroughly undermined the bourgeois context that sustains it.

The work of refashioning the text's portrait of the middle-class family—of showing that what has gradually been revealed as a sieve is in fact a fortress—begins with Olivia's elopement in chapter 17. The specific episode during which the Vicar receives the first of his many doleful reports of disaster has often been pointed to as illustrating his spiritual pride, both in relation to the workings of divine Providence and to the doctrine of Original Sin, for it is here that Primrose asserts to his wife that though they "are now growing old . . . the evening of [their] life is likely to be happy" and rejoices that they "are descended from ancestors that knew no stain." I have no quarrel with such interpretations, but rather wish only to suggest (1) that the scene can also be read as a revelation of the Vicar's hubris concerning the supposed impermeability and bourgeois orthodoxy of his family circle, and (2) that this is the first such revelation which *Primrose himself*, not just the reader, is allowed to comprehend. This passage, in which the protagonist gives thanks for his family's "tranquility, health, and competence" and in which he claims to be "happier now than the greatest monarch upon earth" because such a potentate can boast "no such fire-side, nor such pleasant faces about it" (106–7), paints the Vicar as guilty not only of thinking himself the favorite of heaven, but as the entirely competent sculptor of an unassailable middle-class home. Learning at this very instant that his daughter has actually eloped with the enemy, the Vicar cannot help but discover the long-running joke we have hitherto enjoyed behind his back—clearly, that particular vein of irony and laughter must now be abandoned. Instead, from this point on, the hero's Job-like sufferings[24] will begin to constitute a "proof" of the middle-class hearth's ability to endure any challenge from the outside world by means of its internal fortitude and cohesion.

Once his genuine misfortunes commence, the Vicar almost instantly marshals newfound energy toward shoring up his domestic circle, in both a physical and spiritual sense, even as it comes under renewed and redoubled attack. We can see this when, after his odyssey to regain the absconded Olivia is completed in the face of long odds and sickness (and recall that it is during this trek that he delivers his middle-class call-to-arms to the butler), he returns home to find his family in mortal danger. Previously, in chapter 3, a child of his also had been in peril of her life, but whereas at that time the Vicar was too overcome to assist her, here he is apparently so stirred by the threatened loss to both himself and the state that he rushes into the burning structure and manages to carry out his "treasures" (141). This deed, which begins to reestablish the mantle of paterfamilias about the Vicar's shoulders, is soon followed by another act of domestic restoration. When Deborah threatens to make Olivia's return to the family fold into a kind of perpetual separation by refusing to forgive her, Primrose, reversing his earlier posture toward his helpmeet, refuses to stand by "a silent spectator" to her disruptive behavior. Indeed, he now addresses his wife with "a degree of severity in [his] voice and manner . . . which," he claims, "was ever followed with instant submission." Not only is his tone different, but his rhetoric begins to paint a picture of his family as a city under siege, whose denizens must put an end to "dissention among each other" in order to "shut out the censuring world" (143), a motif that will become more pronounced as the novel proceeds.

The physical dimensions of his establishment having been reduced by fire, the Vicar redoubles his efforts—now by means of moral persuasion—to saturate its ethical atmosphere with middling virtues. There are several interpolated stories in *The Vicar*, but it is only at this point in the family's fortunes that we get one directly from Primrose's lips. Significantly, "Matilda's Story" is about the power of domestic ties to prevail over even the cruelties and dislocations of war. During the course of it nations are shaken, *besieged cities fall*, atrocities are committed, but the family unit emerges reunited from the ashes to at last enjoy "all the happiness that love, friendship, and duty could confer on each" (145). Indeed, as the Vicar delivers ever more frequent eulogies upon the bourgeois ideal, he points to the ramshackle condition of the family's new dwelling as confirmation that "the hearth" is a habit of mind, not an edifice. He invites George, for instance, to "observe this bed of straw, and unsheltering roof[,] those mouldering walls, and humid floor," and yet to understand that "even here" the son sees before him "a man that would not for a thousand worlds exchange situations" (146). His bully pulpit in full swing, Primrose draws ever more of his figures from the domestic scene, commenting that "the good are joyful and serene, like travellers that are going towards home; the wicked but by intervals happy, like travellers that are going into exile" (147). The ears of his family now ringing with such panegyrics upon the joys of the fireside, the Vicar feels able to assert that, despite the family's reversals and Olivia's declining health, a state of bourgeois normalcy has been restored beneath his roof: "Thus, once more, the tale went round and the song was demanded, and chearfulness condescended to hover round our little habitation" (147).

It is at this point that Goldsmith ratchets up the pressure upon his besieged "little republic" by bringing Squire Thornhill to bear directly against it. Just before Olivia's seducer makes his unexpected appearance, the family has been consoling itself with a rendition of the novel's most celebrated verses, "When lovely woman stoops to folly." For our purposes, what is noteworthy about them is the unambiguous allegiance they pay to bourgeois sexual morality, expressing as they do the customary punishment exacted by middle-class literature upon those characters who transgress as Olivia has:[25] "Her only art her guilt to cover/ . . . is to die" (148). This selection is sung by Olivia herself, at the request of her mother, who, feeling "a pleasing distress, and [weeping], . . . loved her daughter as before" (147). It appears then, that the Vicar's stepped-up campaign of middle-station moralizing has paid off, and just in time too because the major onslaught against his hearth and home is just beginning. When it comes, the squirearchy's proposal is nothing if not direct: "We can marry [Olivia] to another in a short time, and what is more, she may keep her lover beside; for I protest I shall ever continue to have a true regard for her." Primrose, predictably, responds with anger and disgust, banishing Thornhill from his sight while making it clear that he feels their relative moral positions are almost allegorically the reverse of their places in the social hierarchy: "Go, and possess what fortune has given thee, beauty, riches, health, and pleasure. Go, and leave me to want, infamy, disease, and sorrow. Yet humbled as I am, shall my heart still vindicate its dignity" (149). The Squire exits with a few thinly veiled hints about his power over the Vicar's family, which much alarm Deborah and the children; but the protagonist remains resolute, likening himself to "one of those instruments used in the art of war, which, however thrown, still presents a point to receive the enemy" (150). This metaphor can stand as a concise synopsis of what the text seems to be trying to make of the bourgeois family as it approaches its climax, for if Primrose can in fact be shown to be morally armored in this way, it would seem to go far toward counteracting the appearance of dangerous permeability the family earlier displayed, though it would also directly contradict the first section's ironic portrait of the protagonist.

The next day, of course, the Vicar is taken away to the jail, his wife and children in tow. It strikes me that the overall purpose of the prison scenes, from a secular perspective, is to demonstrate convincingly that the bourgeois family is capable of taking anything upper-class power and persuasion can dish out without fragmenting or compromising its organizing principles. One of the things Goldsmith seems to be doing throughout the novel is arguing that the strengths of the domestic circle are not dependent upon the physical surroundings with which they are usually associated in literature, memory, and imagination. As the chapters have proceeded, the family has been forced to inhabit ever-narrower and less genteel homes, and now the ultimate test is at hand: they are to be incarcerated in a dwelling where the presence of the two class enemies the Vicar cited in his speech to the butler are everywhere felt, for the jail is run by lower-class lackeys who take their orders from the manor house. In such a place, where, as the Vicar warned, "the laws govern the poor, and the rich govern the law" (116–17), the family's survival will depend upon how well they have *internalized* the precepts of middling domesticity. That the Vicar has seemingly succeeded in this regard is shown early on, when his first night's sleep amid the straw and filth is passed with "the utmost tranquility till morning" (155). His two smallest children also readily adapt, little Bill "lov[ing] every place best that [his] papa is in" (156). One would, of course, like to believe, for Goldsmith's sake, that such strained passages are meant to be taken tongue-in-cheek. The context of strident bourgeois recuperation, however, leaves us little room for optimism, for *The Vicar of Wakefield* now more closely resembles a kind of cheerily inverted *Rasselas* than the ironic novel it at first appeared.

As far as the older members of the family go, the Vicar wastes no time in reproducing the ordered daily routine that, however faultily, kept his "little republic" running in the outside world. Sophia is "particularly directed to watch her declining sister's health," Deborah is to attend to her husband's wounds, while Moses will support the family by "the labor of [his] hands" (156). Even in the depths of prison, idleness is to be banished, rational amusements pursued, and all of the middle-station pieties observed. Not that all this works a miracle in the characters of Deborah and the children, for their subsequent collusion in deceiving their father about

Olivia's "death" underscores anew their willingness to betray middle-class principles for expediency's sake—to foolishly deal with the squirearchy on its own terms. This seems, however, to be largely a result of Goldsmith's views about the female sex's supposed weakness of will and sparseness of ethical faculties. More important is the fact that, through Primrose's unceasing efforts, Goldsmith manages to turn *The Vicar* into a fable of familial survival within the prison house whose contrast to *Little Dorrit* could not be clearer. Here there very definitely *is* an inoculation against the "prison taint," and one that is readily available in the bromides of domestic conduct books.[26] Where Dickens's Marshalsea is only a dark parody of a home, Goldsmith has the Vicar turn his jail into a reasonable facsimile of the ideal the protagonist once enjoyed. When, for instance, Jenkinson opines that Primrose's offspring are "too handsome and too good for such a place as this," the Vicar replies that his children "are pretty tolerable in morals, and if they be good, it matters little for the rest," for their familial loyalty "can make a dungeon seem a palace" (159).

It is Primrose's efforts to reform his fellow prisoners that most clearly foregrounds what the entire second half of the text has been grimly intimating—that the middling domestic order is a state of mind possessed of so many inarguable virtues and inherent defenses that one can construct it even amid the most inhospitable surroundings. Thus, the hero begins his project of moral improvement confident that it "might amend some, but could itself receive no *contamination* from any" (157, italics mine). (Recall that in the novel's first half the Vicar's susceptibility to "contamination" was both chronic and funny.) Carrying his middle-class message to the depraved masses through a carriage both impermeable and implacable—he credits his own "perseverance and address"—Primrose turns the moral tide of the prison "in less than six days" (161). Success assured, he now goes on to do for the jail what he once did for the town of Wakefield, inscribing his domestic virtues upon the face of the community, until the borders of his "little republic" encompass all who reside within the writ of his moral persuasions: "I did not stop here [at having them make and sell tobacco stoppers], but instituted fines for the punishment of immorality, and rewards for peculiar industry. Thus in less than a fortnight I had formed them into something social and humane, and had the pleasure of regarding myself as a legislator, who had brought men from their native ferocity into friendship and obedience" (162).

If we now recall again the Vicar's likening of himself to "one of those instruments used in the art of war, which, however thrown, still presents a point to receive the enemy," we can appreciate the full resonance of the phrase's language. When the prophylactic and proselytizing strengths that Goldsmith hopes are inherent in Primrose's bourgeois outlook become manifest under trial, the protagonist can "receive" enemies in the sense both of defending against them and persuading them to join him. The episodes involving the prisoners have revealed a morality that the text would have us believe is not only hermetically sealed off from contamination but also persuasively expansive. This having been said, though, it is still the protective, contraceptive nature of the Vicar's ideology that Goldsmith is, in the main, out to emphasize—its resistance to the temptations and threats thrown out by plutocratic power that triumphed so often and so amusingly in the novel's first half. As the chapter heading above the story's climax reminds us, *"Let us be inflexible, and fortune will at last change in our favour"* (177).

When critics mainly concerned with *The Vicar*'s religious aspects approach its final pages, it is not "inflexibility" that they find there, but proof that the Vicar has remembered few if any of the spiritual lessons he supposedly learned (at much emotional cost) in prison.[27] A look at the book's concluding paragraph makes clear the basis of such criticisms: "I had nothing now on this side of the grave to wish for, all my cares were over, my pleasure was unspeakable" (199). Viewed from our secular perspective, however, the passage is a testament to how urgently the author wants to represent the domestic circle as having emerged *essentially unchanged* from its cruel buffetings at the hands of Thornhill and fate. This is another passage in which one would desperately like to discover irony at work, but if my argument about the text's attempt to recover in its final chapters the middle-class confidence dispersed by its own earlier irony is at all convincing, then any such hopes must be wistfully abandoned—the scene is intended to be taken straight.

It might seem that one could now charge that the supposedly secular aims of the text are compromised by the disposition of the Vicar's daughters at the novel's end—after all, they do marry into the upper classes, thereby seeming to crown their father's initial backsliding, not his subsequent reformation, with "success." What in fact happens, however, is that the plot falls out such that both the younger and elder Thornhills wind up appearing much more like members of the middle station than the squirearchy. Young Thornhill, of course, is simply stripped of his wealth (it goes to Olivia) and made to work for his living as a "companion at a relation's house," where he is "very well liked and seldom [sits] at the

side-table, except when there is no room at the other" (198). Where the
nephew is forced into a more middling mode of living, the uncle has gradually adopted it over the course of a varied life, as exemplified by his
masquerading as the moneyless gentleman Burchell. His bourgeois characteristics involve much more than clothing and deportment, however, for
his mind is thoroughly imbued with a veneration for the domestic hearth
only slightly less zealous than Primrose's. When at last unmasking, for
instance, he affirms what his frequent visits to the parsonage have already
prepared us to hear, that he has "at [the Vicar's] little dwelling enjoyed
respect uncontaminated [note the word!] by flattery, and [has] received
that happiness that courts could not give, from the amusing simplicity
around his fire-side" (181). What is more, he has been long about the task
of procuring a wife who will be bound to him not on the basis of a political
alliance or the uniting of established fortunes but upon the middle-class
basis of rational affection[28]—a quest that, until he met Sophia, was pursued "in vain, even amongst the pert and the ugly" (195). Thus, when the
Vicar descends upon the wedding morn to find his family "as merry as
affluence and innocence could make them" (197), we need to read the
word "innocence" in terms of class allegiance. Fate and his own steadfast
middle-station orthodoxy have seemingly delivered to Primrose the best
of both worlds: the money that satisfies the yearning for upward mobility
has been gained through an alliance with husbands who have been denuded of their threatening squirearchical traits. The protagonist can be so
smugly self-satisfied in the novel's final paragraph because he has just presided over the unlikely merger of abundant Mammon with correct Morality.

   To affirm all this is *not*, however, to assert that *The Vicar* has succeeded
in recasting the bourgeois ideal into the safely hermetic mold it tries so
desperately to represent, for the sheer contrivance of the final pages is
evident to every reader. Even those critics who claim, with some justice,
that Primrose becomes "closer to us"[29] or "grows in stature"[30] or trades
a cloistered for an active virtue wind up having to apologize for the novel's
ending; and those who attempt to do more are driven to rather lamely
remind us either that the text's author was not a nineteenth-century realist
or that after all it is the Vicar, not Goldsmith, who is telling the tale.[31] The
reversal-laden climax is a tour-de-force in its own way, of course, but as
a piece of novelistic fiction it is ridiculous. What such clanking awkwardness reveals, though, is not so much artistic incompetence as a sacrifice of
novelistic form to political imperatives. As Macaulay famously pointed out,

the first half possesses "all the vivacity of comedy," while the second half lacks "that consistency which ought to be found even in the wildest fiction about witches, giants and fairies."[32] To repeat this judgment from within the perspective we have adopted here is to say that irony cannot be successfully "taken back"—once a character has been exposed to its illuminating glare he cannot be reclothed in immaculacy. Or to adopt Maurice Shroder's terminology, the usual tendency of the novel as a genre is to be "deflationary," for "the novelist is [most often] the *eiron*, while his protagonist . . . is an *alazon* who learns, through disillusionment, that he is not a hero after all."[33] Thus, Jaarsma both puts things too strongly and misjudges Goldsmith's feelings about the middle station when he asserts that "the character of Primrose stands as one of the most savage indictments of bourgeois values in eighteenth-century literature"[34]; it is much more accurate to say that the novel mounts one of the century's most incompetent (or inconsistent or belated) *defenses* of those values.

We can now turn back for a moment to the critical controversies concerning the novel's ironic stance, for in light of what has been argued here, the position of both the contending camps can be shown to be partially correct, though incomplete. To those who insist that Primrose is meant to be an ideal figure, guilty only of the most venial faults, one must reply that, however "gentle" the satire is in the first half of the novel, the protagonist's behavior there puts a great deal that the author held valuable into perilous danger. We, unable to share Goldsmith's deep-seated allegiance to bourgeois domesticity, may insist upon calling his midpoint about-face a terrible overreaction, or indeed a betrayal of one of his genre's most promising formal properties. Still, we must attempt to understand, if we cannot approve of, the author's panicked retreat from his own irony. To those readers, on the other hand, who maintain that Primrose is savaged throughout the text, I would suggest that they are mistakenly assuming (or hoping) that the tone of the novel's opening chapters is carried through to the end, projecting irony onto scenes that we are meant to receive at face value.

Our peculiarly secular focus upon *The Vicar* can perhaps suggest an answer to another puzzle within Goldsmith criticism. Why, it has been asked, did a man who apparently possessed such a healthy contempt for the kind of sugary endings common in sentimental novels wind up fashioning one himself? Is it possible that an author capable of writing, "How deceitful are those imaginary pictures of felicity! and, we may add, how mischievous too!" (I, 17), could in good conscience pen *The Vicar of Wake-*

field's conclusion as well? Answers have generally fallen into two categories. On the one hand, it is conjectured that Goldsmith might have been satirizing the genre as a whole, consciously creating a sickly-sweet finale that, by its absurd exaggeration, would bring the fashion of sentimentalism into disrepute. On the other hand, he might have been at some level profoundly attracted to such fables and thus simply might not have been able to help himself—after all, he wrote the hypersentimental "History of Miss Stanton" too.[35] As Ricardo Quintana puts it, though Goldsmith had "as quick a sense as anyone of the fatuous character of much popular fiction," he "could not bring himself to disown romance," for "his heart still clung to it."[36] This may be so, but we should supplement such speculations by reiterating that the very extremity of the novel's ending seems to support the notion that it is a troubled reaction to the ironic undermining accomplished near its own beginning. If Goldsmith's finale is seamlessly providential even though he professed a distaste for similar performances elsewhere, then we can with greater confidence conceive of it as the author's anxious overcompensation for his previous "class treachery." Primrose, taken apart with such seeming ease at the novel's outset, must be pointedly and completely restored to bourgeois orthodoxy, even at the cost of that verisimilitude and consistency "which ought to be found even in the wildest fiction about witches, giants and fairies."

Another reason that even the most sugary tropes of Sentimentalism might prove irresistibly attractive to Goldsmith can be discerned by way of Bakhtin, who offers an insight into the historical context of Sentimentalism:

> The aspect of opposition to the old literary language and the correspondingly high poetic genres it sustained is of crucial importance in the Sentimental novel. While setting itself in opposition to the lowly and gross heteroglossia found in life—which is subject to being ordered and made respectable by Sentimentalism—Sentimentalism also opposes the quasi-elevated and false heteroglossia found in literary language, which is subject to exposure and invalidation by Sentimentalism and its discourse.[37]

In other words, Sentimentalism is the prose genre most amenable to a bourgeois middle class at a time *before* that class became dominant or even assumed it's "classical" nineteenth-century form—*before* its values infused the reigning, quasi-official ("authoritative," Bakhtin would term it) literary language of the day. This thesis is seconded by Langford:

> . . . sentiment, in the broad sense in which it finally predominated, had a special appeal to middle-class England at a time of economic growth and rising standards of living. Gentility was the most prized possession of all in a society obsessed with the pursuit of property and wealth. It could be purchased, but only if the code of genteel conduct was sufficiently flexible to fit the diverse social and educational

circumstances of the purchasers. The emphasis on feeling provided this flexibility and removed the sense of repressive social exclusiveness which marked a more aristocratic view of the world.[38]

To a mind defensive and frightened about the survival of its own social stratum, a mind willing to divide all classes outside "the middle order of mankind" into "tyrants" and "slaves . . . moving in the vortex of the great," Sentimentalism's opposition to both the discourse of the aristocracy and the mob may appear so powerful a virtue as to render its equally obvious faults less noisome. Bakhtin is always reminding us that the novel has special properties that thrust it more urgently into political struggles than is true of other genres. *The Vicar of Wakefield* is Goldsmith's only novel (even employing Bakhtin's expansive use of the term), and thus the ideological attractions of Sentimental fiction may go far toward explaining why Goldsmith said one thing as a critic and yet acted quite the opposite as a novelist.

Perhaps the best way to conclude this chapter is to return to the novel's title page and examine the epigram. "Sperate miseri, cavete faelices": "Take heart, you who are miserable; take heed, you who are happy." Martin Battestin, his eyes fixed quite firmly (and properly) on the religious aspects of Goldsmith's text, asserts that its message, as well as that of *The Vicar* as a whole, is that "affliction, teaching a man humility and self-knowledge, 'comes by God's permission and providence.' "[39] By means of our more secular optic, however, we can discern not so much a message being imparted as a fear being expressed. Indeed, the epigraph is a kind of synopsis of the tale's political plot structure as a whole. When Primrose is happiest, he is in the greatest danger of surrendering ideological ground to his upper-class foes; when he is most hard-pressed by them, he is most adamant in his defense of middle-class dicta. So what the phrase's first half records is the text's desperate hope—that when class warfare threatens, the "middle order of mankind" will remember its principles and find anew the strength to resist plutocratic temptations. The second half, however, conveys what the text tries to forget and to make us forget—that when seemingly safest, the bourgeois ideal may well rupture as a result of its own internal contradictions, its own hankering after the wealth and power it has supposedly identified with sensuality, cruelty, and impiety. What transforms the epigraph's pleasing caesura into the novel's gaping one is that the irony which illuminated that contradiction in the book's early pages cannot be so easily forgotten.

CHAPTER THREE

The Anti-Romantic Polemics of
Mansfield Park

*

There operates within all of Jane Austen's novels a tension between the author as narratist and the author as moralist, which springs from Austen's attempt to promote and protect the bourgeois values of stability, equanimity, and repose. At times—and especially in *Mansfield Park*—this tension intensifies to the point where it takes on the lineaments of paradox. As D. A. Miller explains, that which "motivates the narratibility of [Austen's stories] coincides with what the novelist strongly disapproves of," while the desired state of closure—consisting of perfect clarity, calm, and order—is frustrated by narrative itself because "only insufficiencies, defaults, deferrals, can be 'told.' "[1] Thus, an Austen novel "must be on the wrong track when it moves on track at all. For the novelist's ideal—what she calls [in *Sense and Sensibility*] 'the reality of reason and truth'—is a great good place where movement . . . is impossible."[2] What this chapter will attempt to explain is why and how, in *Mansfield Park* as nowhere else in her canon, Austen champions the middle-class desideratum of tranquility so relentlessly as to bring herself into conflict with the structural necessities of her chosen medium.[3] Rather than seeking to explain Austen's "problem novel" as the result of a so-called evangelical phase in the author's life,[4] I will instead suggest that the text's oddness is shaped by the many polemics within it aimed at certain Romantic texts, a few of which place the book at odds with the enabling constraints of the novel. Answers are called for: Austen's texts usually uphold bourgeois hegemony while still managing to emerge as intensely satisfying examples of narrative art; if *Mansfield Park* is her one book that consistently frustrates our novelistic expectations, it is reasonable to ask whether an *exacerbated* desire to champion middle-class pieties—or to counter some antithetical discourse—may be at least partially to blame. All readers sense polemics at work within the story of Fanny Price; what I hope to do is to clarify what their targets are and to suggest thereby how ideological fervor may be responsible for producing a heroine who "triumphs by doing nothing"[5] and whose priggish attitudes have alienated generations of readers.

There has lately been a good deal of confusing debate about whether or not Jane Austen is herself a Romantic.[6] It seems to me that much of the muddle adhering to this question arises from four interrelated mistakes or shortcomings: an insistence that Austen be either wholly for or wholly against "the Romantic movement" (as defined by twentieth-century critics), a failure properly to distinguish between different modes or strands of Romanticism, a desire to minimize the obvious affinities between Gothic fiction and certain varieties of Romantic poetry, and a lack of historical imagination in reconstructing how the emerging Romantic texts must have looked to a committed moral realist like Austen.

We can begin to correct these errors by acknowledging that Wordsworth seems to have contributed to Fanny Price's perceptive faculties in a quite benign manner.[7] Her description of a starry night at Mansfield—"Here's harmony! . . . Here's repose!" (139)[8]—her paean to "memory" (222), and her transparencies of Tintern Abbey and "a moonlight lake in Cumberland" (174) all suggest that Austen perceives of that poet as a valuable educator of the senses, who has fostered in Fanny an ability to reflect and empathize which often dwarfs that of her acquaintances, especially that of the Crawfords. Such a reception of Wordsworth should not really surprise us, since, as George Levine has shown, the realism that Austen wrought upon her two inches of ivory is not so different from what the poet was trying to achieve: if *Lyrical Ballads* attempts to speak in the "language really used by men," realism also "presumes that the 'ordinary' . . . has a value hitherto ascribed almost exclusively to the experience of the select few" and promises "to give back with greater authenticity by Wordsworthian strategies the very romantic powers taken away [by its] rejection of [romance] conventions." Austen, like the author of "Simon Lee," seeks to "choose incidents and situations from common life, and . . . to throw over them a certain coloring of the imagination." In doing so, she manages to achieve Wordsworthian ends "without Wordsworthian fuss."[9]

It is in fact the term "*common* life" that I believe holds the key to Austen's harsher treatment of some of Wordsworth's visionary company, for there is, of course, a mode of Romantic discourse, present in both poetry and prose, that eschews everyday settings, mundane occurrences, and unexceptional characters in favor of extremes of environment, action, and motivation.[10] Whereas Wordsworth asserts that "the human mind is capable of being excited without the application of gross and violent stimulants,"[11] both Byron and the Gothic novelists seem to operate from far different premises, filling their literary productions with exotic settings, dizzying narrative momentum, episodes of violence, and anguished emotional states. And while it is often tempting to dismiss the improbable action in many Gothic novels as so much sensationalism devoid of intellectual content, such texts do espouse, however deficiently, the central Romantic tenet (if we again except Wordsworth) that truth can be discovered through extreme states of consciousness. This is a position with profound implications: whereas Pope and Fielding declare that the true and the beautiful are graspable only from the balanced and reasonable center of public life, Byron and the Gothic novelists see illumination as a product of the passionate margin or isolated promontory, the result being that Augustans and Romantics observe many a social institution through different ends of a telescope. As Robert Kiely points out, "most early romantic novelists were not political or social radicals, yet they had chosen the one genre in which to give free play to private vision and extreme emotion was to come into inevitable conflict with the idea of a well-regulated society."[12]

That Austen—as a late Augustan novelist who wishes her productions to be not merely amusements but blueprints for cultural harmony as well—should perceive the literary representation of such extremes of plot and characterization as a genuine threat to her values is beyond question. The way of life defended (though never glorified) throughout her fictions rests upon the bourgeois foundations of tranquility, moderation, and prudence. To suggest that illumination is to be sought in tumult and virtue in excess is to attack directly Austen's insistence on the necessity of continuity and predictability as the ground of all beneficent actions, whether aimed at preservation or rational change. To quote Levine again, "Austen . . . resist[s] romantic extravagances of feeling, and [does] not sentimentalize her miniatures with Carlylean infinitudes[, for] such feelings would [be] both destructive and seductively falsifying in a world dependent on clarity of moral vision."[13] Furthermore, the depiction of flamboyant and attractive protagonists in Gothic castles or outside the walls of harems immediately and inevitably stamps as false or trivial the virtues available to be practiced beside the middle-class hearth. Ruskin, for instance, insists that tales of romance lead people into moral danger by rendering "the ordinary course of life uninteresting, and increas[ing] the morbid thirst for useless acquaintance with scenes in which we shall never be called upon to act."[14] As Conrad's Marlow learns to his cost, the proximity of exotic exultation and existential insight renders all bourgeois knowledge "an irritating pretence" and makes those who subscribe to it appear "so full of stupid importance."[15]

Thus, for an early nineteenth-century novelist of Austen's esthetic and political proclivities, a great moral chasm opens in the contemporary literary landscape between texts that portray reality as chronically "absolutistic" and those that depict it as the thoroughly "mediated" affair she believes it actually to be.[16] By an "absolutistic" text I mean one that—to paraphrase the helpful categories of Joseph Wiesenfarth—valorizes individual freedom over social restraint, involves its characters in mysterious or magical riddles rather than situations susceptible to the workings of reason, foregrounds large existential questions rather than everyday concerns, and portrays love as a transcendent force beyond the writ of social restraints. A "mediated" text, on the other hand, tends to value the community's interest in stability over the individual's in liberty, to position its characters in situations they can negotiate by means of reasoned choices, to foreground questions of manners and politics, and to portray love as one emotion among others and subject to the usual array of communal pressures.[17] Under this (admittedly generalizing) schema, Gothic novels and Byronic narratives such as *Childe Harold's Pilgrimage* and *The Giaour* (both available to Austen as she wrote *Mansfield Park*)[18] would merit the label "absolutistic," whereas any work by Austen herself would best typify what is meant by a "mediated" text. Such a distinction was surely obvious to Austen, since, as we shall see momentarily, she drew attention to it often enough, and since both Gothic novels and Byron's poetic productions appeared to be winning a war for the hearts and minds of the reading public during her working life. An anonymous review of 1818, for instance, laments that "we have been spoiled for the tranquil enjoyment of common interests, and nothing will now satisfy us in fiction . . . but grand movements and striking characters," going on to note that Jane Austen "never operates among deep interests, uncommon characters, or vehement passions."[19]

Absolutistic texts are dangerous (from the middle-class perspective) because they make people dissatisfied with the small rewards that "real" life (that is, the bourgeois social contract) can deliver and because they persuade their readers that strong emotions are *intrinsically* admirable, regardless of the antisocial desires that may underlie them or the pernicious social evils they may generate. Just how widespread Austen believes the baleful effect of such texts to be can be discerned at numerous points in her fictions. Recall, for instance, that *Udolpho*'s tales of locked chests and wasting prisoners have rendered Catherine Moreland unfit to properly face reality in "the central part of England" (202), and that the "impassioned descriptions of hopeless agony [and] . . . a mind destroyed by wretchedness" (121)[20] in *The Giaour* and the *Bride of Abydos* have turned *Persuasion*'s Captain Benwick into a posturing melancholic. (It is significant that Anne Elliott counters the Captain's Romantic fever by prescribing an antidote of realism—or rather, reality—consisting of the "works of our best moralists, . . . collections of the finest letters, [and] . . . memoirs of characters of worth and suffering" (121–22).) In *Sanditon*, the enemy is once more prose, but both the fault and the effect remain the same, as we can see from Sir Edward Denham's half-deranged description of his reading habits:

The Novels which I approve are such as display Human Nature with Grandeur—such as shew her in the Sublimities of intense Feeling—such as exhibit the progress of strong Passion from the first Germ of incipient Susceptibility to the utmost Energies of Reason half-dethroned,—where we see the strong spark of Woman's Captivations elicit such Fire in the Soul of Man as leads him—(though at the risk of some Aberration from the strict line of Primitive Obligations)—to hazard all, dare all, atcheive [*sic*] all, to obtain her. —Such are the Works which I peruse with delight, & I hope I may say, with amelioration. They hold forth the most splendid Portraitures of high Conceptions, Unbounded Views, illimitable Ardour, indomptible [*sic*] Decision—and even when the Event is mainly anti-prosperous to the high-toned Machinations of the prime Character, the potent, pervading Hero of the Story, it leaves us full of Generous Emotions for him;—our hearts are paralized—.[21]

As one Victorian commentator explains, Jane Austen "seems to have had an ethical dread of poetic rapture."[22]

In stressing Austen's likely quarrels with the absolutism of Gothic and Byronic texts, I do not mean to give short shrift to those points of opposition frequently mentioned by other critics, though I do think their conclusions can be refined. A case in point is Tony Tanner's discussion of Romanticism's attitude toward the individual's adoption and substitution of personae. There he reminds us that within some Romantic discourses there is a strong suggestion that "the self can only come to full realization of itself through experiments in different roles and by trying on different masks," and that "one of the prevailing Romantic convictions is that we are very much more than the conscious mind tells us, [and] that a man is a crowd of almost infinite possibilities." Inevitably, such "role-playing must make against stability and fixity: if the self is fluid, there is no limit to what it might do, no knowing how it might behave."[23] Although I agree that Austen does in fact grasp the danger Tanner points to, I would submit that she depicts it as largely a matter of readers in a mediated bourgeois world adopting the inappropriately absolutistic personae that Gothic and Byronic texts imply are within their grasp. Thus, when *Udolpho* lets Catherine Moreland play the part of a menaced heroine and Byron's poetry allows Captain Benwick to feign the irremediable melancholy of Childe Harold, these texts are portrayed by Austen not only as undermining the determinate social identities that she sees as vital to the maintenance of social equilibrium, but also as granting readers license to fantasize their lives as places where the large questions of life and death, salvation and damnation, unspeakable evil and angelic goodness are everyday affairs, a latitude that weakens their hold on mundane middle-class existence as (she would insist) it must be lived. Such alternative roles pose a further threat to bourgeois stability in that they are in large part defined by emotions rather than duties or class position, thereby legitimating the notion that an individual's feelings can be powerful or exceptional enough to exempt her—temporarily or perhaps even permanently—from the constraints and responsibilities of middle-class society that Austen again posits as "natural" or "simply the way things are."

Along these same lines, we must not ignore the manner in which tensions between mystery and disclosure, certainty and obscurity, and assertion and irony are handled by Byron and the Gothic novelists, nor fail to mark how antithetical their practices in this regard are to, on the one hand, Austen's Augustan beliefs in the possibility of sufficient knowledge, eventual illumination, and a limit to the undermining potential of irony—and, on the other, to her provisional acceptance of Wordsworth's claims for a beneficent spiritual gnosis accessible in nature. Nina Auerbach (in the midst of an otherwise wrong-headed attempt to paint Austen a thorough Romantic) asserts that in most Gothic fictions "all roads, even the most apparently open and winding, lead ultimately to some sort of prison." Furthermore, "in all of them, the journey to prison is presided over by a darkly ironic narrator. In all, the devil is in control, and like Melmoth, he is a laughing sardonic devil whose jocularity is corrosive. . . . Romantic fiction, then, is the laughing denial of Romantic hopes for illumination."[24] Clearly, for someone whose two greatest novels turn upon their heroines' long-delayed but entirely sufficient moments of *anagnorisis*—"Till this moment, I never knew myself"—such visions of perpetual night and irony without end constitute dangerous reading. Once again, though, such an objection must be seen as one aspect of the larger quarrel between fictions that depict the world as thoroughly mediated and those which insist that it can chronically participate in the absolute. These darker varieties of Romantic irony are not compatible with middle-class existence, recognizing as they do no sanctions more sovereign than their own claim to a totalizing, antinomian vision. Once readers are ravished into believing that the solutionless dilemma of Childe Harold is their own, the "irritating pretenses" of mediated constraints will count for little.

It might be objected at this point that if one wants to see Austen Gothic-bashing, one need go no farther than *Northanger Abbey*, and that *Mansfield Park*, despite its remarkable structural similarities to the earlier novel (which remained unpublished when *Mansfield Park* appeared), contains none of *Northanger Abbey*'s straightforward parodies of Gothic settings and situations. If there are no "mysterious" cedar chests in *Mansfield Park*, what evidence can there be that it too is an anti-Radcliffian document? We can commence the answer by citing Bakhtin's distinction between parody and what he terms "hidden polemic." In the former, the author takes up residence in an antagonistic discourse and "introduces into that discourse a semantic intention that is directly opposed to the original one." Two voices can thus be said to clash, but it is hardly a fair fight, for "in parody the other person's discourse is a completely passive tool in the hands of the author wielding it. He takes, so to speak, someone else's meek and defenseless discourse and installs his own interpretation in it, forcing it to serve his own new purposes."[25] In hidden polemic, however, something quite different occurs. There

the author's discourse is directed toward its own referential object, as is any other discourse, but at the same time every statement about the object is constructed in such a way that, apart from its referential meaning, a polemical blow is struck at the other's discourse on the same theme, at the other's statement about the same object. A word, directed toward its referential object, clashes with another's word within the very object itself. The other's discourse is not itself reproduced, it is merely implied, but the entire structure of speech would be completely different if there were not this reaction to another person's implied words.[26]

Hidden polemic is in fact employed in *Northanger Abbey*, for there occur episodes in which stock Gothic situations, rather than being blatantly parodied, are instead *alluded to*. Such passages, though turning up only sporadically, resonate—as Bakhtin asserts they must—much more widely and with a more serious timbre than Catherine's straightforwardly parodic scrapes with chests, parchments, and the bedchambers of deceased wives. They do this by positing "mundane" versions of Gothic scenes, character types, and moral atmospheres—versions that, because they are simultaneously shown to be, in Wordsworth's phrase, "simple produc[ts] of the common day," make up through our new sense of their pervasive relevance what they inevitably lose in Gothic amplitude. Thus, the absolutistic discourse of Monk Lewis and his compatriots is drained of its authority by means unavailable to the mere parodist; for if horror can be convincingly *transposed* from the lonely keep to the drawing room (and this can be done to effect only while both settings are kept *intact* before the reader's eyes by means of hidden polemic), then the mediated discourse of Austen's realism can claim the virtues of both genres simultaneously.

Examples of hidden polemic in *Northanger Abbey* include Mr. Thorpe's "kidnapping" of Catherine in his gig, as well as the heroine's physical tussle with her brother, Thorpe, and Isabella in the street as she tries to visit Miss Tilney, both of which "double-voiced" scenes speak through one side of their mouths about the action being portrayed and whisper disparagingly through the other about Gothic accounts of abduction and imprisonment. But perhaps the best opportunity to see how, in hidden polemic, the mode of writing under attack "acts upon, influences, and in one way or another determines the author's discourse, while itself remaining outside it,"[27] occurs when Elinor is forced to bring her friend the "intolerable" news of her expulsion from General Tilney's castle. The tidings, we discover, are delivered as a kind of mediated death sentence: "To-morrow morning is fixed for your leaving us, and not even the hour is left to your choice; the very carriage is ordered, and will be here at seven o'clock, and no servant will be offered you" (222–23). Once the heroine has digested the insult, her "swelling heart need[s] relief," especially since her protector, "Henry[, is] at a distance." When she attempts to divine the cause for her expulsion, she finds it, like many strange and sudden Gothic events, wrapped in a shroud of mystery: "It was as incomprehensible as it was mortifying and grievous. From what it could arise, and where it would end, were considerations of equal perplexity and alarm" (224). When she is at last apprised of the general's motivation by Henry Tilney, she arrives at an assessment of the former, which, in its phrasing, precisely balances the two discourses that have been at odds in Austen's prose. That is, she "heard enough to feel, that in suspecting General Tilney of either murdering or shutting up his wife, she had *scarcely* sinned against his character, or magnified his cruelty" (243, italics mine). "Scarcely": that is, she has been exaggerating, and yet she has not; she has been deluded, but not as thoroughly as she first thought. As Auerbach happily puts it, she has learned that the general "simultaneously is and is not a Montoni."[28] By such means are absolutistic texts repudiated in the same moment that their strengths are appropriated; by such methods does Austen "domesticat[e] the Gothic."[29]

In turning to *Mansfield Park*, we find that the most obvious instance of hidden polemic involves Gothic enclosures. The Portsmouth episode—an "uncharacteristically physical"[30] one for Austen—has been interpreted as "a cliché of the anti-Jacobin novel," its function being to depict "what a world run by revolutionaries would be like."[31] If, however, as I have been arguing, the novel's principal external antagonists are much the same as those of *Northanger Abbey*, then a different kind of reading suggests itself. After all, if one wishes to talk of clichés, there is no aspect of the Gothic more immediately familiar than the characteristic castle in which either nefarious men or malevolent spirits carry on their business. *Northanger Abbey* was named after a place in order to evoke the titles of the Gothic fictions it meant to undercut—Otranto, Udolpho, Wolfenbach, and the like. *Mansfield Park* also denotes an edifice, but here it stands for all that is opposed to the Gothic; and it is the Price's house that represents an abode filled with the kind of everyday (and therefore serious) "terror" and "horror" Austen wishes to discover residing in the realm of mediated life. Once arrived, Fanny experiences the claustrophobia besetting many a Gothic heroine: she is "almost stunned," and the "smallness of the house, . . . the thinness of the walls [brings] every thing so close to her" that "she hardly [knows] how to bear it." The dingy parlor, lighted only by the "solitary candle" under which her father reads the paper, drives her to a state of "bewildered, broken, sorrowful contemplation" (375). The Prices' home, she soon learns, is a place where things go bump in the night, for, as in the darkened corridors of Udolpho, doors are frequently heard to slam, unintelligible cries are uttered, and the tread of footsteps destroys all peace. Her disillusionment with the household growing apace, Fanny is made to sum up its physical and moral atmosphere in a sentence that could easily refer to any genuinely Gothic keep but whose diction demands that we relocate the evil it bespeaks in a more mundane realm and transpose it to a mediated key: "It was the abode of noise, disorder, and impropriety" (381). She comes to feel, no less than Radcliffe's Emily, a prisoner in Pandemonium:

The living in incessant noise was to a frame and temper, delicate and nervous like Fanny's, an evil which no super-added elegance or harmony could have entirely atoned for. It was the greatest misery of all. At Mansfield, no sounds of contention, no raised voice, no abrupt bursts, no tread of violence was ever heard; all proceeded in a regular course of cheerful orderliness; . . . [while what vexations did arise there] were as a drop of water to the ocean, compared with the ceaseless tumult of her present abode. Here, every body was noisy, every voice was loud. . . . Whatever was wanted was halloo'd for, and the servants halloo'd their excuses from the kitchen. The doors were in constant banging, the stairs were never at rest, nothing was done without a clatter, nobody sat still, and nobody could command attention when they spoke. (384)

Here, then, is an especially literal instance of Austen "domesticating" the Gothic, for this haunted house opens onto a city street, and the unquiet spirits that fill it suffer not from the presence of demonic forces but rather from the absence of bourgeois decorums and restraints.

We can discover a second instance of hidden polemic at work in the way in which thrill-mongering and restless ennui are distributed among the Crawfords, that pair who stand as Austen's depiction of what a supposedly glamorous Romantic irony really looks like in mediated precincts. The crucial text in this connection is quite probably *Childe Harold's Pilgrimage*, cantos 1 and 2, which appeared in March 1812. That the poem— like its author, an instant popular phenomenon—contains the kind of Gothic extremes that Austen has elsewhere objected to is beyond question, for its exotic settings and gloomy prospects are peppered with such items as a comradely reference to "Vathek! [William Beckford], England's wealthiest son" (1:275), a vividly exhaustive account of a bullfight (1:720–800), and an erotically charged description of a once meek but lately brutalized Spanish woman who now "o'er the yet warm dead / Stalks with Minerva's step where Mars might quake to tread" (1:565– 66). But such sensationalism is not here the main target of Austen's polemic; rather, *Mansfield Park* sets out to debunk an equally "dangerous" aspect of the poem: the unmistakable and (to the middle-class mind) scandalous voice of its hero, a blend of irreverence, dark irony, and world weariness that the reading public immediately (if unfairly) identified as conveying Byron's own sentiments. The ever-peregrinating Harold, "with pleasure drugg'd" and motivated by some unnamed sorrow "to go / And visit scorching climes beyond the sea," finds the mediated world so dulling that, in the midst of his "joyless reverie," he "almost [longs] for woe, / And e'en for change of scene would seek the shades below" (1:50–54).

If we now turn to the novel, we find the Crawfords likewise infected with a chronic hunger for novelty that disdains the familiar structures of bourgeois existence. Henry, for instance, possesses "a great dislike" for "any thing like a permanence of abode" (74) and is described as a man of "unsettled habits" (142), and Mary is a creature who forever "must move" because "resting fatigues [her]" (123), as does "doing what [she does] not like" (99). Moreover, the latter views her moral failings with an unmistakably Byronic self-consciousness that confesses faults and yet simultaneously closes off any prospect for improvement, declaring that "selfishness must always be forgiven you know, because there is no hope of a cure" (98), and thereby appropriating for the Midlands Harold's similar but darker lament:

> It is that weariness which springs
>   From all I meet, or hear, or see:
> To me no pleasure Beauty brings;
>   Thine eyes have scarce a charm for me.
>
> It is that settled, ceaseless gloom
>   The fabled Hebrew Wanderer bore;
> That will not look beyond the tomb,
>   But cannot hope for rest before.
>
> What Exile from himself can flee?
>   To zones though more and more remote,
> Still, still pursues, where'er I be,
>   The blight of Life—the Demon Thought. (1:849–60)

There is more than one parallel to be drawn from this passage, for Mary too gets little pleasure from beauty, finding the tour of Southerton "fatiguing," "the greatest bore in the world," and an empty ritual of "admiring what one does not care for" (123). Nor can she share any of Fanny's Wordsworthian raptures over the powers of memory and nature, detecting "no wonder in [the] shrubbery equal to seeing [her]self in it" (223). Austen would apparently have us believe that Fanny's ability to take pleasure in the world around her is in some way a function of her having actually encountered so little of it, a defense of stillness in which we can detect an allusion to the repeated Byronic refrain that drinking life to the lees leaves everything tasting flat.

Of course the Crawfords are flippant and airily cheerful though all of this, whereas Harold is much grimmer; but again, this is hidden polemic, not parody, and what Austen has in mind is not to appropriate Byron's exact words, but to treat the same structure of attitudes in such a way that Byron's glamorization of them will come to seem foolish and dangerous, a process that, as Bakhtin explains, involves keeping the poet both in and out of her sights simultaneously:

In the hidden polemic . . . discourse is directed toward an ordinary referential object, naming it, portraying, expressing, and only indirectly striking a blow at the other's discourse, clashing with it, as it were, within the object itself. As a result, the other person's discourse begins to influence authorial discourse from within. For this reason, hidden polemical discourse is double-voiced, although the inter-relationship of the two voices here is a special one. The other's thought does not personally make its way inside the discourse, but is only reflected in it, determining its tone and its meaning. One word acutely senses alongside it someone else's word speaking about the same object, and this awareness determines its structure.[32]

My surmise that *Childe Harold's* discourse lies behind the depiction of the Crawfords is rendered less speculative if one brings to mind the political implications of so many readers identifying the speaker of the poem with Byron himself. By 1813, when the bulk of *Mansfield Park* was being written, everyone knew who Byron was, which is to say that they knew about his class background. In fact, the publication of *Childe Harold* had come close upon the heels of his first speeches in Parliament. Austen, of course, has strong ideas about what is at stake, as far as social stability is concerned, in the behavior and public perception of the upper classes; she knows, as Tony Tanner puts it, that "property" must be wedded to "propriety," since "the one without the other could," in a society so dependent upon deference, "prove helpless to prevent a possible revolution." And thus in her fictions a securing of "the proper relationship between property and propriety" is "not the wish-fulfillment of a genteel spinster but a matter of vital social—and political—importance."[33] It is "propriety," of course, that the well-to-do residents of Mansfield violate when they stage the theatricals, and we can hear Edmund reminding the others of the word's relationship to property when he objects to seeing a play performed by "a set of gentlemen and ladies, who have all the disadvantages of education and decorum to struggle through" (150). Recall too that the instigator of the dubious project is the frivolous Mr. Yates, "the younger son of a lord" (147), and that he has just participated in a similarly disruptive venture at another country house. Thus, rather than positing Evangelicalism as the cause for Austen's disapproval of her amateur thespians, we can more profitably seek the reason in politics: the acting out of *Lovers' Vows*, like the writing out of *Childe Harold*, is simply an abdication of class responsibilities.

We must now pass on to those manifestations of engagement with absolutistic Romantic narratives that, although they comprise the most significant portions of *Mansfield Park*'s attack upon Gothic and Byronic texts, can no longer be labeled as hidden polemic. These remaining strategies

are two in number, one of which might be described as a cruder version
of what we have just observed, the other constituting a complete about-
face in which the kind of imitative disparagement that characterizes
hidden polemic is abandoned for an attempt to render *Mansfield Park* a
diametric counterimage to the Gothic. Where the former continues the attempt to siphon off absolutistic energies into the mediated world, the latter
rigorously eschews all narrative momentum in an attempt to exalt stillness
and stasis. Ironically, it is the very *successes* of hidden polemic that go
farthest toward illuminating the motivations behind both the inadequate
imitation and the problematic countermove. These two strategies also
share an unfortunate tendency to render Fanny an unpalatable heroine.

Bakhtin insists that hidden polemic is a very tricky business, a tightrope
act in which "the other person's discourse remains outside the limits of
the author's speech, [while nevertheless] the author's speech takes it into
account and refers to it."[34] What name are we to give to a strategy, however, that entails directly appropriating *individual key terms* of another's
discourse and inserting them into one's own? Not parody, surely; that
strategy requires more room, demanding that a narrator fully "inhabit"
another's language and make it speak to her own purposes, not a task that
can be accomplished with the importation of isolated words every now and
again. And not hidden polemic either, since there the alien discourse can
never be spoken directly. If no Bakhtinian label is convenient, though, the
specifics of just what occurs can be easily summarized: terms such as "terror," "horror," and "evil"—those hallmarks of the disparaged Gothic—
occur with incongruous frequency in the pages of *Mansfield Park*, and do
so in a way that has serious consequences for Fanny's characterization. If
this represents another attempt to transpose the energies of the absolutistic
texts into the mediated world, its effects are nevertheless at odds with those
produced by hidden polemic.

We can begin to enumerate what must be only a partial catalog of such
instances by noting Fanny's state of "continual terror" at the thought of
Mary's visits on Henry's behalf, a terror that drives her into hiding in order
"to avoid any sudden attack" (352) from that quarter. Mary finds her out
anyway, of course, and when she again prepares to urge her brother's suit,
Fanny feels "the evil ready to burst upon her" (353). In seemingly better
times, just previous to the ball in her honor, the heroine is "worn down at
last to think every thing [belonging to it] an evil" (273), while her friend's
offer of a necklace for the evening provokes from her "a look of horror
at the proposal" (265); soon after, "such [is] her horror" (281) at Sir

Thomas's suggestion that she open the ceremony that she summons courage enough to ask him to choose another upon whom to bestow that honor.
At Portsmouth, she feels that a letter from Edmund announcing his engagement "should be a subject of terror" (368), and the postman's knock
thus "bring[s] its daily terrors" too (391). When Henry later arrives in
that city, the "terrors" she feels push her to the point of "fainting away,"
and she must struggle "to keep herself alive" (392), while her father's
dinner invitation to her admirer causes a "thrill of horror" before he de-
clines, leaving her in a rare state of "actual felicity from escaping so horrible an evil" (398–99).[35] This strain of absolutistic diction reaches its
troubling crescendo when Fanny finally learns of Henry and Maria's
elopement:

> The horror of a mind like Fanny's, as it received the conviction of such guilt, and
> began to take in some part of the misery that must ensue, can hardly be described.
> At first, it was a sort of stupefaction; but every moment was quickening her per-
> ception of the horrible evil. . . .
> Fanny seemed to herself never to have been shocked before. There was no pos-
> sibility of rest. The evening passed, without a pause of misery, the night was totally
> sleepless. She passed only from feelings of sickness to shudderings of horror; and
> from hot fits of fever to cold. . . . [I]t was too horrible a confusion of guilt, too gross
> a complication of evil, for human nature, not in a state of utter barbarism, to be
> capable of! . . . [A]nd it appeared to her, that as far as this world alone was con-
> cerned, the greatest blessing to every one of kindred with Mrs. Rushworth would
> be instant annihilation. (429–30)

The most interesting attempt to separate the narrator from Fanny's
rhetoric in such passages has been undertaken by Michiel Heyns, who,
understandably bothered by the fact that the heroine uses the phrase "horrible evil" to describe both the elopement and the prospect of Henry "taking his mutton" at her father's house, declares that "a writer as sensitive
to language as Jane Austen does not inadvertently repeat as excessive a
phrase . . . on two such dissimilar occasions." His conclusion is that Fanny's assessment of events "suggests an untrained moral sensibility which
can surely not serve as the standard of judgement in the novel," and that
Austen is in fact distancing herself (and us) from her heroine by making
us understand that she has "no precise moral vocabulary in which to couch
and thus order her responses." In short, Fanny is intentionally portrayed
as immature, and thus "what distinguishes this novel from all Jane Austen's others . . . is that the irony at the expense of the heroine is never
resolved by enlightenment."[36] This is as good a defense of *Mansfield Park*
as one can devise, I think—one wants to believe it—but unfortunately,

Heyns's conclusion simply contradicts one of the strongest impressions that generations of readers have borne away from the novel: that Fanny Price is always right. Lionel Trilling's judgment of the mid-1950s—that in this novel Austen's "characteristic irony seems not to be at work" and that in fact the book "undertakes to discredit irony and to affirm literalness"[37]—has been reluctantly but consistently seconded in succeeding years, down through Tanner in the mid-1980s: "She is never, ever, wrong. Jane Austen, usually so ironic about her heroines, in this instance vindicates Fanny Price without qualification. We are used to seeing heroes and heroines confused, fallible, error-prone. But Fanny always thinks, feels, speaks and behaves exactly as she ought. Every other character in the book, without exception, falls into error—some fall irredeemably. But not Fanny. She does not put a foot wrong."[38] Even Heyns is forced to admit that the intention he ascribes to Austen makes a jumble of the text's conclusion, confessing that "what we cannot forgive Jane Austen is that ultimately she withdraws from the implications of this immaturity and asks us to accept it as a standard whereby to judge the events of the novel."[39]

A better method of accounting for the inappropriate diction that Heyns points to is to consider it in light of the anti-Gothic strategies previously discussed. When looked at in this way, one can understand how the text's proclivity for absolutistic terms might spring from an intention identical to that which motivated the hidden polemics we have already seen the novel employ. To loot the Radcliffian lexicon and to attempt to make the booty adorn Mansfield's mediated walls involves the by now familiar pattern whereby *Mansfield Park* contests the alien discourse and struggles to divert its emotional power into its own more mundane channels. The difference, of course, is that there is nothing "hidden" about *this* kind of polemic; the words in Fanny's mouth stick out like—well, a sore tongue. What is also different is the effect produced. Whereas the previous strategies suggestively disparage the haunted enclosures and histrionic poses of Gothic and Byronic texts without rendering the heroine overly judgmental, this cruder attempt manages to paint Fanny as the prig to which so many readers object. The absolutistic diction, wrenched from its proper context of extremity and placed at the disposal of the mediated heroine, merely makes Fanny's judgments seem extreme. Her shocked reactions and bitter censures are out of proportion to the situations that call them forth, and hence Fanny is diminished in our eyes.

But why does an author of Austen's caliber adopt so *clumsy* a strategy, especially when, as we have seen, subtler and more effective ones lie close to hand? Why would she feel compelled to so blatantly tamper with the novel's emotional thermostat, insisting that *we* feel "terror" every time Fanny recoils from a trivial or commonplace situation? The answer, I would suggest, must be sought in the overarching presence of the second, opposite-tending strategy mentioned above—the one that leads to D. A. Miller's "great good place where . . . movement is impossible." That is to say, this strange proliferation of "evils" is a kind of counterweight necessitated by the text's broad attempt to consistently associate almost all forms of narrative energy with moral depravity and social disruption—it is a compensation for the heroine's will-to-plotlessness. That *Mansfield Park*'s distrust of activity and liveliness has its genesis in bourgeois ideology, and that it contains an implicit anti-Gothic thrust, is not difficult to discern. The Crawfords must fall because they represent "the unbridled emotion of Romanticism as against the discipline and control of Augustan life,"[40] and their case is merely an exaggerated example of a theme visible in all Austen's novels.

Levine touches on our author's dilemma when he points out that whereas nearly all nineteenth-century realists were self-conscious about their subject matter and uneasy that the stories they meant to tell would prove banal, trivial, and uninteresting, Austen nevertheless feels strongly her self-imposed responsibility to test "Romantic energies against the pragmatic and ordering values of a finely civilized community."[41] *Mansfield Park*'s central complaint against absolutistic texts is not different in *kind* from *Northanger Abbey*'s: they are too full of startling incident to be anything but a caricature of life, and while their unflagging narrative energy may entertain light minds, they distort reality in order to deliver their incessant thrills and thereby wind up undermining the middle-class social order. Where the earlier and later novels differ is in the methods used to articulate this complaint, for whereas Catherine Moreland's story makes do with parody and hidden polemic, Fanny's seems bent upon purging itself of everything that might betray the slightest yearning for some experience more colorful or distracting than those that habitually inhabit the thoroughly mediated norm of bourgeois existence. *Mansfield Park*, unlike *Northanger Abbey* or any of Austen's other novels, seems to define nearly *all* energy and exertion as the devil's work and to valorize a stillness that finally appears more sterile than "finely civilized."

We can commence a discussion of this vitally important aspect of the text by singling out a startling motif: the novel's nearly maniacal use of the disparaging word "bustle" to describe just about any variety of motion and action. Several critics have drawn attention to the frequency with which this term is employed,[42] but what has gone unnoticed is how well its definition seems to synopsize Austen's complaints against her Gothic and Byronic adversaries. "To bustle" means "to bestir oneself or display activity with a certain amount of noise or agitation, to be fussily active," and usually implies an "excessive or obtrusive show of energy." Its secondary meanings include "to struggle, scuffle, [and] contend; to elbow one's way through a crowd." And finally, keeping Austen's concern for the Gothic's victim-readers in mind, we should note its transitive sense of "to cause to move precipitously and in disorder," to "hurry (a person or thing) in a fussy or over-energetic manner," and "to make (hot, etc.) by bustling." In short, to bustle means to expend much energy to no end or to a bad one, and the activities to which *Mansfield Park* attaches the term are legion. Aunt Norris, defrauded of announcing Sir Thomas's return, regains the household's attention by "trying to be in a bustle without having any thing to bustle about" and thereby "labouring to be important where nothing was wanted but tranquility and silence" (196), this last nevertheless being just what Sir Thomas quickly reestablishes at the disordered Mansfield by making known his preference for "a quiet family-party [over] the bustle and confusion of acting" (205). Meanwhile, Henry Crawford's assessment of the play is directly opposed to that of the novel's patriarch, his wistful reminiscence betraying an addiction to the very thing the text decries:

"It is as a dream, a pleasant dream!" he exclaimed, breaking forth again after few minutes musing. "I shall always look back on our theatricals with exquisite pleasure. There was such an interest, such an animation, such a spirit diffused! Every body felt it. We were all alive. There was employment, hope, solicitude, bustle, for every hour of the day. Always some little objection, some little doubt, some little anxiety to be got over. I was never happier." (236)

To all of which Fanny responds, "Oh! what a corrupted mind!" This accusation is later endorsed by the text when Henry's attraction to activity is shown to be bound up with his promiscuous libido: the elopement undertaken, he tires of Maria once "the bustle of the intrigue [is] over" (452). Sister Mary fares no better, displaying her own corruption by a preference for soldiering over ordination, the former having in her opinion "every thing in its favour; heroism, danger, bustle, fashion" (136). Maria, in a passage foreshadowing her fall, desires to "escape from [Sir Thomas] and Mansfield as soon as possible, and [to] find consolation in fortune and consequence, bustle and the world" (216). When Fanny herself is sent away from the somnolent estate, she encounters—and deplores—just what Maria craves, discovering her father's house to be a den of "noise rising upon noise, and bustle upon bustle," and her mother a woman whose "days [are] spent in a kind of slow bustle; always busy without getting on" (382). So relentlessly does the text utilize the word that, rather than assisting to finely discriminate between productive and pernicious actions, it places the entirety of exertion under a cloud, for it becomes difficult to point with confidence to an activity within the novel that could not conceivably be tarred with the label. (William's doings at sea?—we hear about them only in summary.) In the wake of its libeling passage through the text, the only safe alternative appears to be passivity—waiting, observing, sitting tight. The contrast with *Childe Harold* could not be more striking.

Moreover, Fanny's passive nature is deliberately celebrated by the text, as if defying us to find fault with such a trait. When the narrator informs us that the evenings after Sir Thomas's return are "all sameness and gloom, compared with the past" and Edgar voices the same opinion, Fanny is ready with an apologia for dullness, declaring that "the repose of his family-circle is all he wants" (211), reminding her cousin that "there was never much laughing in his presence" and pointing out that "no young people's [evenings] are [lively] . . . when those they look up to are at home." This is not by any means a complaint on her part, for she quickly admits that she is "graver than other people" and that "the evenings do not appear long" to her. For this admission, Edgar—and the text—pronounce her "more wise and discreet" (212) than the rest of the family. Indeed, the instances of almost agoraphobic passivity that the novel apparently asks us to swallow without flinching, giggling, or otherwise turning against Fanny are numerous. Provisionally accepting a dinner invitation strikes her as "a flight of audacious independence," the thought of actually winning at cards motivates her to throw the game, and gaining a library card leaves her "amazed at being any thing in *propria persona*, amazed . . . to be a renter, a chuser [*sic*] of books" (390–91)!

While the claim of some critics that, given her situation, Fanny's decision to say no to Henry's proposal is "to act and act violently"[43] can be dismissed as wishful overstatement, a more persuasive argument employed by her defenders insists that she is a "heroine of principle" who, merely through her denials, defends the individual's right to self-determination against a repressive patriarchal society.[44] One can agree that she does this and yet still find the *way* she does it problematic, for her defense of principle is carried on in a manner reminiscent of nothing so much as Melville's Bartleby. Fanny too "would prefer not to"; and although the principle she defends is not so obscure as the Scrivener's, her repeatedly misunderstood refusals do little to dispel our sense of her vexing passivity. Calling Fanny a bulwark of principle appears to be merely a rhetorically muscular recasting of Trilling's idea that she is a "Christian heroine" like Fielding's Amelia, a type of protagonist Trilling himself does not expect us to admire.[45]

A different kind of apology for Fanny's role might point out that in many a novel the heroes and heroines are more passive than the villains. True enough, but one can admit this and still posit a lower threshold of vitality below which the term "protagonist" cannot be comfortably applied (its root, after all, being the Greek verb "to contend"). And although a bourgeois heroine's scope of acceptable activity is necessarily circumscribed, here Austen's desire to contrast her own text with its bustling opponents drains Fanny of the minimum energy required to register upon many readers' sympathies. Where one critic complains that "Fanny is almost entirely lacking in the wit, vitality, and human propensity to error which engage our sympathies for Jane Austen's other heroines,[46] Marilyn Butler goes to the heart of the matter by insisting that "to some extent Fanny's is a negation of what is commonly meant by character."[47]

Where all this necessary vitality goes, of course, is into the breasts of the Crawfords, where it is immediately tainted by their moral shortcomings. Most readers would agree, for instance, that Mary "brings a tremendous impetus to the story," that "no matter what the situation, she serves as a stimulus to the narrative," and that she is "the perfect creature for a plot, the principle of liveliness and action incarnate in a young woman."[48] However, it is precisely this aspect of Mary—the fact of her being a dynamo of narrative momentum—that is represented as alternately both the root and symptom of her ethical failing. In this regard the novel can be said to begin with deceptive charity; for Edmund, in the first throes of infatuation, allows that "a lively mind . . . seizing whatever may contribute to its own amusement or that of others" is "perfectly allowable . . . when untinctured by ill humor or roughness" (95). But before long the text ensures that the only lively minds we see *are* tinctured in such a way, for Mary's jokes about prayer and ordination soon reveal a humor that is in fact "ill," just as her eventual inability to differentiate "folly" from "a complication of evil" betrays a discrimination too rough to be consonant with virtue. (How different from *Pride and Prejudice*, where the livelier minds are the ones most sensitive to ethical distinctions!) The case is the same with her brother, whose very knack for advancing the plot stands as proof of his inner vacuity. Just as Lovelace is Richardson's despised but indispensable "novelist within the novel,"[49] so too is Henry the fashioner of plots whom the text wishes to denigrate precisely for his ability to generate it:

> ". . . I do not like to eat the bread of idleness. No, my plan is to make Fanny Price in love with me."
> "Fanny Price! Nonsense! no, no. You ought to be satisfied with her two cousins."
> "But I cannot be satisfied without Fanny Price, without making a small hole in Fanny Price's heart." (239)

When Mary declares that this intention springs from his "idleness and folly," he counters by claiming that the true motivation is in fact a curiosity insatiably productive of narrative incident:

> ". . . I do not quite know what to make of Miss Fanny. I do not understand her. I could not tell what she would be at yesterday. What is her character? —Is she solemn? —Is she queer? —Is she prudish? . . . I must try to get the better of this." (240)

The narrator's distaste for the vital elements of plot produced by such a proclivity brings the initial paradox described by D. A. Miller into sharp relief: "Let *other* pens dwell on guilt and misery. *I quit such odious subjects as soon as I can,* impatient to restore every body, not greatly in fault themselves, to *tolerable comfort,* and to have done with all the rest" (466, italics mine). Indeed, at times like these, the narrator seems to embody something very akin to Freud's *Thanatos.*[50]

One can see Austen struggling with this self-wrought contradiction as the novel draws to its close, though she never succeeds in writing her way out of it. When Edmund comes to collect Fanny at Portsmouth after the catastrophe, we are saluted by a passage that, in its breathless straining to make us believe the whole polarity of the novel has been reversed, merely underscores what has hitherto been the problem with Fanny's depiction:

> There is nothing like employment, active, indispensable employment, for relieving sorrow. Employment, even melancholy, may dispel melancholy, and her occupations were hopeful. She had so much to do, that not even the horrible story of Mrs. Rushworth (now fixed to the last point of certainty), could affect her as it had done before. She had not time to be miserable. Within twenty-four hours she was hoping to be gone; her father and mother must be spoken to, Susan prepared, everything got ready. Business followed business; the day was hardly long enough. (431)

If we can sense a nervous dishonesty in the above, a similar lack of candor inhabits our farewell view of Sir Thomas. In surveying "Fanny's excellence" along with Susan's "usefulness," he reflects upon "the advantages of early hardship and discipline, and the consciousness of being born to struggle and endure" (456). The too-easy equation of Susan with Fanny is paralleled by that of "struggle" with "endure." We have had the opportunity of seeing Susan at Portsmouth, but all we know of Fanny is her life at Mansfield, and it is there, we are to understand, that her character is formed, for she is very much Mansfield's creature by the time she visits her parents. Thus, while Austen's syntax would have us believe that Fanny has both "struggled" and "endured," it is clearly only the latter term that can rightfully apply to her. This difference is not trivial: to struggle means to aggressively exert oneself against a foe or obstacle; to endure denominates something much more passive, the tolerant bearing of a burden or the patient suffering of a hardship. As before, when one catches Austen being careless with her diction, an explanation is demanded; in this case, I think, we can account for such fudging as her last-minute attempt to graft a measure of *virtú* onto Fanny's character, an energy her structural position in the novel demands, but that she has not been allowed to display.

Concern over the heroine's obvious passivity does seem to have given rise to one comparatively successful attempt at camouflage, this being Lady Bertram's characterization. Trilling admits never being able "to resist the notion that in her attitude to Lady Bertram Jane Austen is teasing herself, that she is turning her irony upon her own fantasy of ideal [i.e., static, untroubled] existence as it presented itself to her at this time."[51] My own interpretation is less generous, for Fanny's vegetative aunt strikes me as nothing so much as a kind of decoy designed to distract our attention from the heroine's own paucity of will. Lacking not only energy but also intelligence and discernment, she is the stalking-horse who makes Fanny appear positively robust by comparison; and the text, by keeping our eye running back and forth between the two, manages to obfuscate the fact that background characters can be unproblematically passive but protagonists cannot. What makes this strategic deployment of Lady Bertram more palatable than the efforts mentioned above is, of course, its consistent and tactful appearance throughout the text as well as its organic connection with the novel's other thematic concerns. Lady Bertram is no stopgap measure but rather one of Austen's comic inspirations.

At first glance, all that I have argued so far might seem to offer a challenge to some of Bakhtin's most important pronouncements about the novel as a genre, especially his notions about what makes some novels more "novelistic" than others. After all, here is the one work of Austen's which appears to engage a discourse alien to that of the narrator's in a variety of ways,[52] and yet the result is a tone that readers have so often found grimly off-putting and a heroine who inspires little sympathy and sometimes outright revulsion. Shouldn't *Mansfield Park*'s grappling with oppositional voices theoretically (that is, according to Bakhtin) make it the "strongest" of her fictions, since such a give-and-take of competing languages is what the genre's formal structures are peculiarly adapted to exploit and amplify? In truth, Bakhtin's formulations seem to suffer only if we forget the very real differences between the hidden polemics in *Mansfield Park* and the other strategies employed to discredit Gothic and Byronic texts, differences Bakhtin clarifies when he asserts that

heteroglossia-in-itself becomes, in the novel and thanks to the novel, heteroglossia-for-itself: languages are dialogically implicated *in* each other and begin to exist *for* each other (similar to exchanges in a dialogue). It is precisely thanks to the novel that languages are able to illuminate each other mutually; literary language becomes a dialogue of languages that both know about and understand each other.[53]

Thus, in a truly dialogic text, the narrator's language must display a "participatory orientation" toward other modes of discourse, the challenge being to "find itself in intimate contact with someone else's discourse, and yet at the same time [to] not fuse with it, not swallow it up, not dissolve in itself the other's power to mean."[54] Consider now what must happen in Austen's novel in order for hidden polemic to work: at some level, her plot, characterization, and tone *must become like that* found in the texts she is attempting to denigrate. For hidden polemic to operate, noisy dens of impropriety must be visited, dangerous theatricals must be performed, world-weary ladies and gentlemen must be allowed to work their (mediated) mischief. In such manner is Austen's text changed by—in some sense changed into—the kind of discourse it would have us reject, and the result is an interpenetration of styles and plot lines that leaves neither Gothicism nor moral realism untouched, a mutual illumination that can genuinely merit the label "dialogic." As much as we may applaud such strategies, however, it is precisely their dialogism that seems to have prevented Austen from employing them more frequently, for in *Mansfield Park* she appears much less committed to constructively arguing with the Gothic than to emphasizing the great gulf fixed between its absolutistic castle and her mediated park, and thus in the other strategies we have discussed no such dialogic exchange results. On the one hand, the importation of blatantly Gothic diction into the Fanny's world is just the kind of "fusing," "dissolving," and "swallowing up" of social vocabularies that Bakhtin warned would be unprofitable. On the other, in those passages in which Fanny is made to denigrate energy and eschew narrative momentum, we can see *Mansfield Park* attempting to fight the absolutistic texts by making itself as *unlike* its adversaries as possible, by recoiling from everything the enemy exalts in and twisting itself into a shape of maximal opposition. This is engagement of a sort, but one based upon flight rather than confrontation, upon distance rather than dialogue.

Austen once noted in a letter, "I have read the Corsair, mended my petticoat, & have nothing else to do."[55] This pointed juxtaposition of the doomed and swashbuckling Conrad with the mundane but necessary exertions of bourgeois life can stand as a synopsis of Austen's struggle against the absolutistic sensibility. She had early on taken up arms against it in *Northanger Abbey*, but there her castigations had been lighthearted and intermittent. What renders *Mansfield Park* her "problem" novel is that here the attack is sustained by a grim resolve and carried through with a comprehensive rigor. Indeed, at times the later text appears to take on the features of an outright manifesto, seeking to prove by its own unlikely existence that a novel can be fashioned whose defense of bourgeois stillness against Romantic exuberance is impregnable, and whose principled separation from the alluring dangers of narrative momentum is hermetic. As so many readers have attested, Austen accomplished enough of this ideological purpose to produce her most troubling work, the static career of whose immaculate heroine stands at cross purposes with the formal requirements of the genre she inhabits.

CHAPTER FOUR

Bildungsromans That Aren't:
Agnes Grey and Oliver Twist

*

It will be the argument of this chapter that a peculiarly vigorous invest-ment in certain discourses of middle-class pedagogy has important con-sequences for the process of Bildung in Anne Brontë's *Agnes Grey* and Charles Dickens's *Oliver Twist*. Within this pair of texts, a strident preoc-cupation with bourgeois anxieties concerning the formation and perpe-tuation of "good character" in the rising generation winds up doing character development no good at all. That is, while both Brontë and Dick-ens purport to show us inexperienced, youthful protagonists making their way into the complicated ethical world of adults, neither author produces the bildungsroman such a scenario would, at least provisionally, entitle us to expect. Instead, both Agnes Grey and Oliver Twist are rendered as beings who *must not* grow and mature, a state of affairs directly traceable to their authors' desire to trumpet the all-sufficient and inviolable nature of the virtues inculcated within the bourgeois domestic establishment.

At base, the conflict between ideological commitment and novelistic form we shall be tracing arises from the tendency of Victorian middle-class culture to nominate, with unprecedented stridency, the home as the primary location wherein each rising generation is groomed for the offices of adulthood and citizenship. The church, the school, the community all have their parts to play, but these institutions contribute influences that are conceived of as distinctly supplemental to the moral instruction im-parted, and the moral example provided, within the domestic circle. This ranking of the familial hearth so far above its more public allies in the business of pedagogy (in the widest sense of that word) is inextricable from the dichotomous conception of society's moral geography prevalent among middle-class Victorians. According to this dualistic view, the atmosphere of the world at large is radically corrosive of all needful virtues, for outside the sheltering walls of home lies a realm given over to the barely regulated rapine of getting and spending and the animal pursuit of sensual pleasures. Conversely, and indeed consequently, the home must be maintained as a place apart, a hermetically sealed realm into which no infected drafts may be suffered to intrude, for only there can children be raised up "sufficient to stand" against the solicitations of modern life, and the breadwinner solaced and refreshed from his daily battle with hard-hearted necessity.

This cultural conception, however, is fraught with anxiety, as is illustrated by a passage from Ruskin:

This is the true nature of home—it is a place of Peace; the shelter, not only from all injury, but from all terror, doubt, and division. In so far as it is not this, it is not home: so far as the anxieties of the outer life penetrate into it, and the inconsistently-minded, unknown, unloved, or hostile society of the outer world is allowed by either husband or wife to cross the threshold, it ceases to be a home; it is then only a part of that outer world which you have roofed over and lighted fire in.[1]

Images of refuge and siege permeate this discussion, and the charge is framed so perilously as to generate acute attendant worries: "But do not you see that to fulfil this, she must—as far as one can use such terms of a human creature—be incapable of error? So far as she rules, all must be right, or nothing is. She must be enduringly, incorruptibly good; instinctively, infallibly wise."[2]

This distinctively bourgeois orientation of mind toward the family and the moral education it provides can therefore be said to consist of a faith accompanied by a fear. The former takes the shape of a belief that the middle-class hearth is uniquely capable of shaping children into morally adequate adults, for any family circle tainted by the vices endemic to its class—vices such as those arising from working class "indecency" or aristocratic marriages of convenience, say—must, given the assumed connection between home and child, introduce (or reproduce) the "error" and "danger" that cannot help but blight each young shoot. But stalking such expressions of pedagogical hubris is the fear of inevitable defeat, a palpable anxiety that even one deviation from utter propriety and perfect judgment will invite disaster, and that the virtues fostered in even the most exemplary bourgeois home may not prove at all durable once the threshold of the "vestal temple" (Ruskin's phrase)[3] is left behind.

I

To begin our examination of *Agnes Grey*, consider the problems that a rigid, unconditional belief in the middle-class hearth's nearly exclusive responsibility for molding—and in its unmatched ability to mold—a child into a virtuous adult poses for character development, especially in the context of a bildungsroman. If a bourgeois heroine (possessing all of the proper ethical credentials required of such a figure) is to make her way into the world in order to complete her education and either discover or hone her inherent but as yet hidden abilities, she cannot in truth have much to learn, for any shortfalls in her stock of ethical knowledge—that is, in her ability to confront situations in a morally impeccable way—cast suspicions upon her familial upbringing and thus in turn upon her own credentials as a middle-class exemplar; for if the branch is rotten, so must be the fruit, and vice versa. Nor, when we recall the attendant anxieties concerning those virtues' durability outside the home, will it help matters very much to postulate that such a heroine could conceivably travel from a state of "inexperienced" moral goodness to one in which she has attained a merely "pragmatic" or "instrumental" knowledge of how to deal with the evils that so thickly inhabit the exterior world: such an "education" must either immediately smack of accommodation and moral infection or prompt a reflex of withdrawal and avoidance, the first of which endangers her adequacy as a protagonist, the latter of which outlaws all but the most episodically repetitive of plots. No, if the bourgeois ideology of the soul-sculpting hearth is insisted upon in an obsessive or programmatic way, then the bourgeois heroine must go forth from her parents' house essentially completed, thereby short-circuiting any chance for genuine character development and rendering the idea of a bildungsroman all but impossible.

Agnes Grey is particularly fertile ground for exploring this contradiction, not only because of Anne Brontë's ideological affiliations but because her young heroine hopes to achieve adulthood through employment as a governess, a fact that allows us to see the author's ideas of personal development applied not only to the central character, but to the even younger people she is supposedly helping to raise. Indeed, by the end it will be clear that the author chooses her heroine's occupation not only from a desire to "write what she knows" (Brontë herself was a governess) but to impart more strongly the political message she wants *us* to know: that a childhood spent around a properly middle-class hearth is the only guarantor of a virtuous adult. And though it is quite obvious that Brontë fully intends to write a classic novel of education, her unwavering allegiance to the Ruskinian conception of the family circle's responsibilities, competencies, and vulnerabilities simply prevents her from following through.

I will not spend time here demonstrating what every reader of *Agnes Grey* soon discovers: that the protagonist's home and upbringing are depicted as immaculately bourgeois. Instead, I will focus only upon those early scenes in which the text seems especially intent upon assuring us that we are about to peruse a conventional bildungsroman. Such passages engender clear expectations that Agnes (1) possesses latent talents which only rough experience can draw forth, (2) has important lessons to learn that can be imparted only outside her family circle, and (3) will be potentially endangered—or at least challenged—by the moral tone of life beyond the rectory walls. Although none of these expectations will in fact be fulfilled, we must look briefly at these misleading (though not consciously duplicitous) claims on Brontë's part, claims whose effect is to paint the novel's protagonist as a figure of damp clay rather than revealing her as the piece of fired porcelain she already is.

As to the first, we need only recognize that while Agnes's desire to aid her family monetarily does spur her to seek employment as a governess, this is not her only or even her most important motivation, for she simultaneously harbors more self-regarding hopes: "How delightful it would be to be a governess! To go out into the world; to enter upon a new life; to act for myself; to exercise my unknown powers" (12).[4] She wishes to help, but she also wishes to blossom; one eye may be turned back toward the household she is helping to support, but the bulk of her attention is focused upon her own entry into the realm of adulthood and the opportunity with which her first office will provide her for self-discovery and spiritual expansion. Having been provided with no evidence to the contrary, we as readers can do nothing but provisionally accept the heroine's assertion that there are aspects of her character yet to be revealed by her daily familial rounds. As she says to her mother, "You do not know half the wisdom and prudence I possess, because I have never been tried" (11).

The second of the text's early misrepresentations involves a supposedly worrisome tendency in the Greys' rearing of their daughter (I will reiterate momentarily why it must be "tendency" and not "error"). As Agnes explains, her parents' way of doing things has left her approaching encounter with the world at large ripe for narrative opportunities of the "hard knocks" variety:

Of six children, my sister Mary and myself were the only two that survived the perils of infancy and early childhood. I, being the younger by five or six years, was always regarded as the *child*, and the pet of the family—father, mother, and sister, all combined to spoil me—not by foolish indulgence to render me fractious and ungovernable, but by ceaseless kindness to make me too helpless and dependent, too unfit for buffeting with the cares and turmoils of life. (4, Brontë's italics)

This passage is interesting because it reveals the text's dilemma so well. To produce the heroine of a bildungsroman, Agnes's upbringing must leave something to be desired; and yet to produce a rigorously bourgeois heroine (which Brontë insists upon), it cannot really go wrong at all. Thus, we get the vague distinction between "foolish indulgence" and "ceaseless kindness," and the nervous, hedgy attempt to make one of the cardinal virtues of the middle-class hearth—its enveloping nature—into a quasi-fault. In the pages that follow, this pattern continues, with every "complaint" against her sheltered life being couched within a larger utterance that lauds the family's bourgeois accomplishments. We are told, for instance, that Agnes and her sister are brought up "in the strictest seclusion," but this, we immediately learn, is because their mother, "being at once highly accomplished, well informed, and fond of employment, took the whole charge of [their] education on herself, with the exception of Latin—which [their] father undertook to teach" (4). Truly, the protagonist's mother seems, as Ruskin would have it, "incapable of error" and "instinctively, infallibly wise." And as we shall see, this coddling does Agnes no harm whatsoever, for though she cannot change the families in which she is employed (the text insisting that *no one* can), she refutes Milton by demonstrating that even her thoroughly cloistered virtue is utterly impregnable.

This last notion brings us to the third false promise of the novel's initial pages: that ethical dangers worthy of our concern will threaten the heroine once she has ceased to dwell within the protective moral embrace of the family. These perils are suggestively played up on the day of her departure, when the forces of nature are called upon to furnish the heroine's journey with dubious auspices: "It's a coldish mornin' for you, Miss Agnes," observes her driver, "and a darksome un too." As the gig pulls away, Brontë employs the pathetic fallacy in order to suggest a wavering of faith and a fear of pitfalls unforeseen:

As we were toiling up, I looked back again: there was the village spire, and the old grey parsonage beyond it, basking in a slanting beam of sunshine—it was but a sickly ray, but the village and surrounding hills were all in sombre shade, and I hailed the wandering beam as a propitious omen to my home. With clasped hands, I fervently implored a blessing on its inhabitants, and hastily turned away; for I saw the sunshine was departing; and I carefully avoided another glance, lest I should see it in gloomy shadow like the rest of the landscape. (15)

As she approaches the home of her first employers, Agnes clearly reiterates the promise and peril that the text has assured us are coming, declaring that "for the first time in [her] life, [she] must stand alone—there was no retreating now—[she] must enter that house, and introduce [her]self among its strange inhabitants—but how was it to be done?" She doubts her abilities and once again casts blame for her deficiencies of spirit upon her sheltered rearing: "True, I was near nineteen, but, thanks to my retired life, and the protecting care of my mother and sister, I well knew that many a girl of fifteen, or under, was gifted with a more womanly address, and a greater ease and self-possession" (16).

What *should* happen next if the initial gestures toward deficiency and potential in Agnes are to be carried through is illuminated by Bakhtin, who draws a distinction between those types of plots associated with Greek romances or "novels of ordeal" and those underlying most nineteenth-century fictional prose narratives, in which some form of Bildung almost always figures. The former (classical or baroque) kinds of stories are "organized precisely as trials of the hero and heroine," but, crucially, these trials leave "no traces [either] in the world [or] in human beings. No changes of any consequence occur, internal[ly] or external[ly], as a result of the events recounted in the novel." This is because, rather than maturing or molding the hero, "the hammer of events shatters nothing and forges nothing—it merely tries the durability of an already finished product."[5] In other words, "the basic idea governing such plots is [the] testing" of a hero and heroine, who possess "a fixed identity, which nothing can change"; thus "the novel as a whole, and each adventure in it, [merely] *affirms* who the hero and heroine are."[6] In the eighteenth century, however, there begin to arise texts in which trials "not only *reveal* the hero and heroine, but *make* them" as well.[7] In these narratives, the hero displays "a lack of wholeness characteristic of living human beings," and any test he encounters will therefore be "not only a touchstone, but a school." Here "life and events, bathed in the light of becoming, reveal themselves as the hero's *experience*, as the . . . environment that first forms and formulates the hero's character and world view."[8] It is not too much to say that we expect all novels (in the conventional, not the special Bakhtinian sense of that term) to be novels of education because, as Maurice Shroder points out, "the *Bildungsroman* is not merely a special category; the theme of the novel [as a genre] is essentially that of formation, of education."[9] And even if there are important exceptions to this blanket statement, we do in fact expect to find character development at the heart of those texts which have long been designated specifically as bildungsromans—that is, works which deal with a central character's difficult journey from childhood into adulthood. Certainly the initial pages of *Agnes Grey* have been designed to herald the presence of a text of this last variety, in which the heroine's sheltered upbringing, her untried talents, and the looming dangers of the world will provide the opportunity for her to encounter tests that will build as they bruise and strengthen where they sting. As we shall discover, however, Brontë's beliefs and anxieties concerning the family hearth and the durability of its moral bequest to youth renders Agnes a character possessing "the inborn and statically inert nobility"[10] associated with Greek Romance rather than the pliable receptivity to becoming required by a genuine novel of education. In addition, the author's desire to champion the superiority of a bourgeois upbringing over all class rivals ensures that her charges, no matter how young, are depicted as *already irrevocably ruined.* Despite all of Brontë's assertions to the contrary, what we come to witness is a faultless protagonist flinging herself against an unyielding wall of moral stupidity, for in *Agnes Grey*, ideological commitment has preemptively closed off all the avenues of dialogic exchange.

The household of the Bloomfields, the first in which Agnes finds employment, is vaguely middle-class but has been corrupted by exaggerated pretensions to gentility. Mrs. Bloomfield has raised her children in what might be termed an aristocratic rather than a bourgeois spirit, valuing them, in one critic's words, as "tangential extensions of her own self-esteem and social aura," the "hard work of a mother's love interest[ing] her not at all."[11] What is striking are the extremes of delinquency which this—to the modern reader's eyes—moderately dysfunctional household has produced. Little Tom Bloomfield, it turns out, is about as far from the bourgeois ideal of the silent and angelic child as can be imagined—as a matter of fact, he is a veritable sadist. When Agnes hopes aloud that he will not use his spurs and whip so readily on a real pony as he does on his rocking horse, he replies, "Oh yes, I will. . . . I'll cut into him like smoke! Eeh! my word! but he shall sweat for it" (20)! Tom's violence against wooden animals, however, pales in comparison to the tortures he inflicts upon living ones. When Agnes notices some traps on the lawn and asks her charge what he does with the birds he catches, his reply is matter-of-factly chilling: "Different things. Sometimes I give them to the cat; sometimes I cut them in pieces with my penknife; but the next, I mean to roast alive" (22–23). The heroine, in the face of parental indifference toward

and avuncular encouragement of such pastimes, tries to persuade Tom into
more gentle courses, only to find "his face twisted into all manner of con-
tortions in the ecstacy [*sic*] of . . . delight" (48) at the discovery of a new
nestful of victims: "But you shall see me fettle 'em off. My word, but I *will*
wallop 'em! See if I don't now! By gum! but there's rare sport for me in
that nest" (48). The governess herself is also a frequent target for Tom
and his siblings' violent tendencies. She suffers, for instance, from the
boy's "violent manual and pedal applications" (28) and from sister Mary
Ann's "loud, shrill, piercing screams, that [go] through [Agnes's] head like
a knife" (31). Even the three-year-old Fanny is an "intractable little creature, given up to falsehood and deception, young as she [is], and alarm-
ingly fond of . . . spitting in the faces of those who [incur] her displeasure"
(34). The other distinguishing trait of the Bloomfield children, while perhaps not quite as disturbing as their sadistic propensities, is nevertheless
more interesting because, aside from being a fault in its own right, it covertly suggests that Agnes's supposedly "sheltered" upbringing is *not* to
be considered the "mistake" it has hitherto been painted. Tom, it turns
out, acts unnervingly old for his age, presiding at his parents' tea table till
well into the evening, interrupting and correcting the conversation of
adults, and speaking to Agnes with the diction of a suitor rather than a
pupil. (As before, the younger Mary Ann mimics her brother's habits.)
Tom is encouraged in this unnatural precociousness by his Uncle Robson,
who continually gives Tom sips of liquor, telling him that drinking is proof
of "a bold and manly spirit," and who applauds his various breaches of
schoolroom discipline: "Curse me, if ever I saw a nobler little scoundrel
than that! He's beyond petticoat government already:—by G—, he defies
mother, granny, governess, and all" (49)! The result of all this is that the
youngsters live through a kind of twilight existence somewhere between
childhood and the world of adults, where they can only appear as prematurely knowing ruffians. Thus, while the heroine may bemoan her "always [being] regarded as the *child*" in the parsonage, the text sees the
matter quite differently, for a diametrical policy has been pursued at the
Bloomfields with appalling results.

Agnes can make no headway with the children, and the reasons she
herself gives for this failure further reveal those bourgeois commitments
of Brontë's that ensure Tom and Mary Ann's incorrigibility. At first it
seems that the governess's progress is impeded only because she is forbidden by the Bloomfields from spanking her pupils, and that "a few sound
boxes in the ear . . . might have settled the matter easily enough" (28).

Now, if this were the only means of correction denied her, we might be justified in seeing the text's primary tendency as narrowly and overtly instrumental rather than broadly and covertly ideological. However, this particular restriction upon her powers actually concerns Agnes much less than another and very different one, a restriction not mandated by the parents directly but brought into being indirectly nonetheless by their deficient familial practices. What the governess soon discovers is that she cannot get the children to do their lessons by either bestowing or withholding approval and affection, for their souls have been so deadened that such a "deprivation" has no effect: "With me, at her age, or under, neglect and disgrace were the most dreadful of punishments; but on her they made no impression" (31). This absence within the children truly shocks the heroine and moves her to wonderingly compare their situation to her own experience as a child. But notice: even here *Agnes Grey's* insistence on its heroine's relentlessly exemplary upbringing forces any discussion of her mother's *use* of such a tactic—the withholding of affection—into a pious and saccharine detour:

In vain I expressed my sorrow; in vain I lingered for some symptom of contrition; she really "didn't care," and I left her alone, and in darkness, wondering most of all at this last proof of insensate stubbornness. In *my* childhood I could not imagine a more afflictive punishment, than for my mother to refuse to kiss me at night: the very idea was terrible; more than the idea I never felt, for, happily, I never committed a crime that was deemed worthy of such a penalty; but once, I remember, for some transgressions of my sister's, our mother thought proper to inflict it upon her; what *she* felt, I cannot tell; but my sympathetic tears and suffering for her sake, I shall not soon forget. (32–33)

Thus when Agnes comes to sum up her troubles at the Bloomfields, it is not the staying of her hand that she mentions but the rebuff directed at her heart, telling her mother that it was "very unpleasant to live with such unimpressible, incomprehensible creatures. You cannot love them, and if you could, your love would be utterly thrown away; they could neither return it, nor value it, nor understand it" (55). "Unimpressible" and "incomprehensible"—these are the words that get to the core of the ideological stance that Agnes's failure illuminates. Children raised outside the benignly shaping pressures of the bourgeois hearth are not pressed into some *different* (and perhaps equally valid) shape, but rather are rendered "unimpressible" altogether, as if only a middle-class upbringing ensured the very humanness of its living products. "Incomprehensible" seconds this sense of the absolutely alien nature of different parental regimes, as well as of the fatal and far-reaching consequences of the childhood envi-

ronment. What Agnes inadvertently does here by employing such terms is
to give the lie to the first section's promise of a bildungsroman, for among
the unimpressible there can be nothing to teach, and from the incomprehensible nothing can be learned. What we have been subjected to instead
is an object lesson in comparative hearthsides showing the dangers in-
flicted upon future generations of the middle class when parents attempt
to emulate the practices of the gentry (again, as seen through bourgeois
eyes)—a lesson that can be imparted only by sacrificing any hope for genuine character development on the part of the novel's protagonist.

Eventually, Agnes is dismissed by the Bloomfields for making too little
progress with the children, a charge that, given the novel's conflicting intentions, she must both refute and agree with by insisting that "as far as
their learning went" she "*had* instilled *something* into their heads, and . . .
had at length brought them to be a little—a very little—more rational
about getting their lessons done in time to leave some space for recreation"
(Brontë's italics). Her subsequent feelings as she packs for the journey
home are hopeful, but in a way which again expresses the narrative's self-
contradictory desire to insist that Agnes has matured amid a household so
depraved that it has no lessons to offer or goals to reach: "I knew all parents were not like Mr. and Mrs. Bloomfield, and I was certain all children
were not like theirs. . . . I had been seasoned by adversity, and tutored by
experience, and I longed to redeem my lost honor in the eyes of those whose
opinion was more than that of all the world to me" (51–52).

In saying all of this I do not mean to maintain that one cannot learn
from failure; I am insisting, however, that the text, despite its sporadic
rhetoric about progress and growth, does not send Agnes to the Bloomfields
to learn or to help, but only to observe and report to us on the horrific
failure of domestic arrangements that do not conform to bourgeois standards. This is confirmed by the puzzled tone of several critics as they attempt to assess the episode's structural function in the book as a whole.
Tom Winnifrith, for one, remarks that it is "difficult to see what justification there is for making the novel so episodic" and that "in particular
the three chapters dealing with the Bloomfields are hard to explain," for
they hold the stage "in all their comic horror" only to "vanish without
further mention." He concludes by remarking that "one function of the
Bloomfield chapters is to show us a badly-brought-up family at an earlier
stage than we see the self-indulgent Murrays [the next family Agnes works
for]. What Anne appears to be saying is that the seeds of selfishness,

thoughtlessness, and wickedness are sown early." Obviously, I agree wholeheartedly with this assessment, though I would put it more forcefully: the text asserts that the family's role in moral pedagogy is so central and pervasive and irreversible that even a three-year-old can be ruined by a household that has turned its back upon bourgeois orthodoxy. Winnifrith goes on to say that "there *would* [italics mine] be sufficient reason for including the Bloomfield chapters if *Agnes Grey* was just a novel about the right and wrong way to bring up children" and that, though at times "it does seem to have this didactic aim," in the final analysis it is "no mere narrow pedagogic treatise."[12] My claim, of course, is that Brontë's novel *is* a pedagogic treatise of sorts, though the author herself doesn't fully realize it, and that the reason the text's true subject is so difficult to pin down is that its pedagogic concerns are not "narrow" at all, but vast. This argument will be strengthened as we turn to consider Agnes's next employers, the Murrays; for, contrary to what Winnifrith maintains, the Bloomfield chapters do not simply "vanish" from the book—rather, the pattern of fruitless effort against hardened depravity that they trace is strikingly repeated when the heroine arrives at her subsequent place of work.

Whereas the Bloomfields aspire to the squirearchy, Mr. Murray is "one of those genuine thorough-bred gentry" (58), whose wife is "anxious only to render [her children] as superficially attractive, and showily accomplished, as they could possibly be made without present trouble or discomfort to themselves" (64). As for the characters of the pupils, they too are variations upon the Bloomfield theme. The elder daughter, Rosalie, is sixteen and "something of a romp" (67), a girl whose prospects for improvement are, typically, both affirmed and denied: "upon the whole, I believe she respected me more than she herself was aware of, because I was the only person in the house who steadily professed good principles, habitually spoke the truth, and generally endeavoured to make inclination bow to duty; and this I say, not of course in commendation of myself, but to show the unfortunate state of the family to which my services were, for the present, devoted" (66). In truth, though, the girl's fate is sealed, and within a year Rosalie succumbs to her "ruling passion" and "all absorbing ambition": "to attract and dazzle the opposite sex" (67). This aspect of her personality betrays the same anxious exaggeration present in Tom Bloomfield's characterization, for her career as a coquette and heartbreaker soon moves through megalomania to outright sadism. While she is at first content merely to "coquet with all the world" (82), Rosalie winds up intentionally encouraging the hopes of the local rector for no other purpose than to issue a humiliating refusal when he finally proposes.

The younger sister, Matilda, also displays the effects of her deficient upbringing in behaviors bordering on—to Brontë's eyes—derangement and perversion. "As an animal, Matilda [is] all right, full of life, vigour, and activity," but "as an intelligent being, she [is] barbarously ignorant, indocile, careless, and irrational, and consequently very distressing to one who [has] the task of cultivating her understanding" and "reforming her manners" (68). The girl's real problem, however, is that her family has, through indifference and indulgence, allowed her to grow up overly masculine: "she ha[s] learnt to swear like a trooper" (69), and her conversation centers almost exclusively upon horses, dogs, guns, and hunting. True, once Rosalie is married, Mrs. Murray belatedly begins "to turn her attention to the younger, and [to be] truly alarmed at the roughness of her manners," forbidding her to enter "the yards, stables, kennels and coachhouse" (158–59). As we have now come to expect, however, it is a case of too little too late—she has already and irrevocably been stripped of her femininity by an upbringing uninformed by middle-class virtues and practices, and all Agnes can really do is to draw our attention to that fact by way of her failures and by reminding us that it is a "pity [her mother's authority] had not been exerted before" (160–61). There are a pair of younger brothers as well; but as we learned at the Bloomfields, even the tenderest age is far too late for remedial action, and young John Murray is, at age eleven, "unruly, unprincipled, untaught, unteachable" (69).

Agnes, of course, persists, but at the Murray household she does so in a strikingly passive way. Whereas at the Bloomfield's we saw the heroine in a state of continuous movement, trying to put out fires (literally) and put down rebellions, here she gradually settles into a routine in which her role is merely that of the patient, if still disapproving, observer. The Murray children are older, of course, and this in part accounts for the change, but one can also feel in these chapters the novel's central pretense dropping away from sheer exhaustion at keeping up appearances and Agnes's true role as a commentator on—rather than as a corrector of—the parsonage's social competitors coming to the fore. She does not object, for instance, when her pupils crush and suffocate her in the family coach, nor when they habitually insist upon doing their lessons outside in weather that gives Agnes a cold, the governess "foolishly choosing to risk the consequences, rather than trouble them for [her] convenience" (73). As we can see, here a newly exaggerated meekness seems to coincide with an abandonment of all attempts at moral instruction. Indeed, Agnes's reprimands are now directed chiefly at her own person, as she seems intent upon transforming herself into a middle-class martyr forced to suffer a kind of Babylonian captivity with stoic endurance: "I sometimes felt myself degraded by the life I led, and ashamed of submitting to so many indignities; and sometimes I thought myself a precious fool for caring so much about them, and feared I must be sadly wanting in Christian humility" (74). This effacement of the will is carried to incredible lengths when Rosalie, discovering that Agnes has fallen in love with the new curate, Mr. Weston, determines to ensnare him out of spite and a desire to once more display her erotic powers, a scheme that involves making Agnes a veritable prisoner in the house for six consecutive Sundays. To all of this the heroine responds with saintly silence: "It was no use beginning to dispute with such indulged, unreasoning creatures; so I held my peace" (152).

What is happening here is that *Agnes Grey*'s misleading depiction of itself as a bildungsroman is coming apart as its focus shifts from the twisted products of deficient households to the impeccable result of the parsonage's bourgeois hearth. And now at last we can see how hollow were the worries previously expressed about the heroine's home-bred passivity; for as the Murray section unfolds, passivity emerges as the female virtue that middle-class dicta insist it must be. Agnes can sit back and quote Scripture about the virtues of patient endurance while she and we watch Rosalie and Matilda fall ever deeper into the Sodom and Gomorrah of coquettishness and unnatural masculinity. In addition, the heroine's sense of class rivalry, which, at the height of the text's masquerade as a novel of education, was always its *unspoken* subject, now breaks into the open—that is to say, the reader hears directly about it, if none of the Murrays do. One example of this new candor occurs during a return walk from church, when Agnes is ignored by Rosalie and her friends, prompting her to complain that "it was disagreeable . . . to walk behind, and thus appear to acknowledge [her] own inferiority; for in truth [she] considered [her]self pretty nearly as good as the best of them, and wished them to know that [she] did so, and not to imagine that [she] looked upon [her]self as a mere domestic, who knew her own place too well to walk beside such fine ladies and gentlemen as they were" (111). It is important to stress here that, despite this rhetoric, Agnes always *does* hang back on this and all subsequent walks, her genuine attempts at changing her student's behavior having been given over in favor of more private exertions of mind.

But what is to prevent us from seeing Agnes's altered attitude as evidence that the significant dangers to bourgeois virtue promised at the novel's beginning are now commencing to menace the heroine in earnest? It may be that her exaggerated passivity and class-conscious barbs are corruptions she has inhaled from the antibourgeois atmosphere that surrounds her—perhaps her real time of trial is only now beginning? Certainly the text would have us believe that such hazards continue to represent a clear and present danger to its protagonist, for Agnes worries that since she "could not make [her] young companions better," they might "gradually bring [her] feelings, habits, [and] capacities to the level of their own. . . . Already, [she] seem[s] to feel [her] intellect deteriorating, [her] heart petrifying, [her] soul contracting. . . . beneath the baleful influence of such a mode of life" (102–3). The extent to which such assertions, combined with the text's other evasions mentioned above, can lead readers to take a straw danger for a real one is revealed by P. J. M. Scott's declaration that while "Agnes Grey is not utterly corrupted by her experiences . . . they do set fair to wreck her life. In a girl who started out guileless, ingenuous and open-minded, they have induced a sense of human incompetence and insufficiency that all but precludes marriage for her."[13] Again, this is no doubt the false scent that the novel means to have its readers follow because then the signal lack of character development mandated by its ideological underpinnings would be conveniently obscured as we trembled for Agnes's moral welfare; but in truth Brontë's heroine is in as little danger of putting a foot wrong as Austen's Fanny Price. The protagonist's new tone toward the Murrays signals no looming fall, but is rather an overt acknowledgment of what *Agnes Grey* has been saying covertly all along, an act of honesty sanctioned by the fact that by this time a decent interval has passed. Her passivity and class consciousness show not that she has succumbed to the gentry's tainted ethical environment, but that she has now tested it sufficiently to denounce it without making the text she inhabits sound so obviously like the *roman à thèse* it really is. W. A. Craik, speaking of the relative brevity of the Bloomfield episode, says that Brontë "recognizes . . . that the grotesque is incapable of growth, and so moves her heroine away forthwith from a household of grotesques."[14] The fact is, however, that both the Bloomfields *and* the Murrays have been on cautionary display, like apes in a zoo, from the very beginning; and it has only been by declaring, for a while at least, that the cages constituted schoolrooms in which progress might be made that the text has been able to disguise the schematic rigor of its own political assertions in both familial settings. As Winnifrith too tentatively puts it, "at times *Agnes Grey* appears not to be saying that governesses should be treated as human beings, but that there should not be governesses."[15]

This new and open recognition of the incorrigible nature of nonbourgeois households is amplified by a pair of chapters that are even more blatantly "episodic" than those covering the Bloomfields and can thus exist for no other reason than to drum the message home a final time. Some months after her dismissal from the Murrays, Agnes is invited by Rosalie, just returned from her honeymoon year abroad, to come to her home at Ashby Park and sign on as her new infant's governess "as soon as it can speak" in order to "bring it up the way it should go, and make a better woman of it than its mama" (181). The heroine accepts the invitation for a visit, though she has no intention of taking the job, and arrives at Rosalie's new seat only to find her former pupil locked into a disastrous marriage in which both parties already detest each other. During the course of the next few days, Agnes is forced to watch—and to record for our benefit—the inevitable continuation of deficient domestic attitudes into the next generation, for Rosalie's issue is "a small delicate infant of seven or eight weeks old, whom its mother seemed to regard with no remarkable degree of interest or affection, though full as much as [Agnes] expected her to show" (184). The heroine soon departs, leaving those households outside the bourgeois pale to their inevitable, irredeemable, and self-perpetuating fate. If we now recall Bakhtin's assertion that, for a text to merit the title of bildungsroman, "changes in the hero himself [must] acquire *plot* significance,"[16] we can see how the promises of Brontë's earlier chapters have been broken; for what we in fact witness is not the blossoming of the heroine but the decline and fall of the families who employ her—it is they alone who can be said to have a genuine "trajectory" in the novel, Agnes herself remaining the still-point of moral judgment.

The heroine's unsuccessful career as a governess now at an end, Brontë moves her fairly quickly toward the founding of a bourgeois home of her own in partnership with Weston. These final chapters are, in general, quite predicable; but there is one aspect of the novel's closing section that might give pause: Agnes and her mother are not idle at their new home by the seashore (Mr. Grey having died) but are in fact running a school, educating "such young ladies as [their] friends and the public [choose] to commit to [their] charge" (196). In light of the poor record of professional pedagogy in the novel, doesn't such a development run counter to the ideological polemic of the text as outlined above? Not really, once we recall

the sterling bourgeois credentials of both women. And it so happens that
Mrs. Grey's are conveniently reinforced just previous to the seaside move
by one of those episodes (it is assigned a chapter of its own) whose presence
is, once again, hard to account for if we only look at what it contributes
to the plot; however, when scrutinized for its ideological import, its function becomes clear. After the Reverend Mr. Grey's funeral, Agnes's mother
receives a letter from her father, the squire whose wishes she disobeyed so
long ago, inquiring whether she has "repented" of her middle-class marriage and offering—if she will only "confess" her folly and admit that she
has "justly suffered for it"—to "make a lady of [her] again" and "remember [her] girls in his will"—that is, if moral reclamation is still possible after her "long degradation" (168). Calling for her pen, Mrs. Grey
fires off a heated defense of her partnership of rational affection, her state
of middling sufficiency, and the pleasures of her plain but loving family
circle, a manifesto that both daughters applaud. No more is heard from
the squire, but the reader leaves the scene newly convinced that Agnes's
mother is the novel's untinctured font of middle-class orthodoxy; thus
when we hear that she is an "active, clever, and kind" teacher at the seashore, we are to understand that her pupils are, so to speak, as safe as if
they were in their mothers' arms. The ending is, then, in terms of the text's
own political commitments, a hopeful, if a contradictory one, for the "considerable addition [of] . . . pupils" Agnes and her mother have recently
seen and the "further increase" (199) expected soon point to a future in
which the soul-molding practices of an exemplary bourgeois home will be
made available to the community at large, however inconsistent the notion
of a pedagogic hearth outside the immediate domestic circle may be to the
broader middle-class orthodoxies the novel champions.

Terry Eagleton has asserted that *Agnes Grey* is, in the final analysis,
"ambivalent about how far morality is *class*-morality" and that, whereas
on the one hand the book proclaims that "in principle, any class may see
the light," on the other it suggests that "there is a clear and close bond
between class and morality," and that virtue and happiness "can thus be
realized only in a commitment to the values of piety, plainness, duty and
sobriety, which the novel shows to have obvious petty-bourgeois roots."[17]
I would refine this statement by locating the two positions in different parts
of the book. During its first half, where such pains are taken to persuade
us that we are reading a novel of Agnes's education and personal development, the myth of ethical enlightenment open to all classes is promulgated forcefully. Indeed, it is precisely by providing the reader with the

false trappings of a bildungsroman that the hope of Agnes's succeeding in her moral mission is kept alive and that her values are made to seem "universal" rather than class-bound. In the second half, however, the feints toward moral transformation drop away, and the text's actual position comes to the fore: Agnes has nothing to learn and nothing to teach because her pupils are from a different social stratum, and the middle-class hearth—because only it is free from "error"—can alone ensure the moral rectitude of the prospective adult. Thus, although it is true that Anne Brontë is "hardly taking the line that only the petty bourgeoisie will enter the kingdom of God,"[18] it is also correct to say that she sees no *secular* redemption outside the sacrosanct walls of the bourgeois family circle. The text may want to disguise this fact by having us believe that Agnes's life once she leaves the parsonage will be a sort of Pilgrim's Progress, but in truth Brontë's heroine is a Christian who need not earn her entry into Beulah Land because, being its sinless product already, she never really leaves it even when laboring among the heathen. And neither can she give aid and comfort to those unfortunate beings less favored by the secular Grace she enjoys, since, under Brontë's rigorously bourgeois dispensation, those unlucky enough to be born in the City of Destruction will find that the gate is not merely strait, but altogether shut.

II

Like *Agnes Grey*, *Oliver Twist* is also a text shaped by anxieties about the transmission of bourgeois values from one generation to the next. Unlike Brontë's protagonist, however, Dickens's has no exposure whatsoever to the formative middle-class hearth, for Oliver, raised in the brutal workhouse and then victimized by Fagin, knows only the iron hand of a caricatured Benthamism and a melodramatic underworld. Indeed, it is the fact that this horrific upbringing has no power to pervert even one of the impeccable bourgeois characteristics, which the hero appears to possess *ad ovo*, that has exposed both Oliver and his creator to a torrent of abuse. The former, for example, is said to be "impossibly untouched in soul and speech by his vicious companions"[19] and has been labeled "a complete cypher, quite unbelievable in his genteel speech and adamant innocence,"[20] as well as a creature who "might have come from another world"[21] and a walking contradiction who eventually "disintegrate[s]." The latter, meanwhile, is accused of lacking both a sound "intellectual grip" and "the courage to treat Oliver realistically in terms of his environment."[22] There are a few critics, of course, who are willing to let Dickens set the terms of his own fiction and to swallow Oliver's improbabilities without complaint, but most seem to agree with Grahame Smith that "to raise the [exculpatory] cry of fable at any aspect of Dickens's work which is unattractive to the modern sensibility seems an evasion of critical responsibility."[23]

It is this last point I wish to take up and expand, for it does seem to me that one in fact prematurely closes off discussion of the novel by merely informing the reader that Dickens's imagination was imbued with fairy tales, that he simply chose a protagonist resembling the heroes of romance and fable, and that it is no use repining or waxing wroth over such a decision. What these pronouncements seem to ignore is the fact that there is a politics behind every choice and that it might be worthwhile to investigate that politics and to determine if and how it shapes the remainder of the text. Now, of course, not all choices are equally interesting or equally open to this type of interrogation, but Dickens's deliberate decision, in 1837, to so blatantly endow his hero with that "inert nobility" characteristic of the archaic novel of ordeal surely asks to be investigated more thoroughly than it has been. The deliberateness is not in doubt: Dickens's famous pronouncement in the Preface of 1841 that the story of Oliver was designed to depict "the principle of Good surviving through every adverse circumstance, and triumphing at last" (33)[24] leaves us little room to complain that he somehow betrayed his own artistic intention by producing a character who changes not a whit over the course of the novel. As if to underscore this resolve, Dickens dropped "The Parish Boy's Progress" as the subtitle in the edition of 1846 and renamed his text "The Adventures of Oliver Twist." This alteration can be seen as the author's conscientious removal of a possibly misleading phrase, for, as has been pointed out, the idea of a "Progress" suggests "that a character can become something different from what he was at the beginning, as presumably in Bunyon's allegory," whereas "the conception of life as adventure (as chance encounter, for example) implies that change, real change, is not an issue."[25]

The main reason that "crying 'fable'" won't do, however, is that the origin of Oliver's virtues is not merely a *donée* offered up without explanation; rather, one of the text's most frequently reiterated *implicit* assertions is that Oliver is a model of bourgeois citizenship from the cradle upward because he has *inherited* his parents' middle-class traits. Every reader feels this is so, yet Dickens seems extremely shy about saying it out loud, fobbing us off instead with ambiguous passages like the following, in which the narrator informs us that "nature *or* inheritance [has] implanted a good sturdy spirit in Oliver's breast" (49, italics mine), or in which Rose maintains that "that Power which has thought fit to try him beyond his years, has planted in his breast affections and feelings which would do honour to many who have numbered his days six times over" (370). This attempt to obscure the issue of just how such traits make their way into the protagonist are doomed to fail because, since "nurture" is ruled out by the workhouse, once we begin to discover the identities of Oliver's parents, "nature"—in the sense of a physical and moral inheritance—becomes the only explanation we, as readers of a novel, can plausibly accept. Oliver physically resembles his parents, and the unmistakable implication of this likeness to Brownlow's pictures and memories is that his middle-class personality comes from the same source. Blind chance and divine intervention are hard things to fit convincingly into a genre so committed to secular causality as the Victorian novel, and even in the misleading passages cited above Dickens cannot escape the metaphors of sowing and generation.

But why should *Oliver Twist* be so reticent about admitting what is so obvious? After all, innumerable fictional characters, like innumerable people in the real world, resemble their parents to some degree in body and mind; it is a literary commonplace. I would suggest that the answer lies in an involvement with the same beliefs and fears we encountered in Brontë. Dickens attempts to obfuscate the obvious origins of his hero's character because his decision to render him that way is no unproblematic, free-floating "choice," but the spinning out of a perilous political fantasy fraught with anxiety. The text's insistence on the utter inviolability of Oliver's moral fiber—its insistence that he cannot be corrupted even by a childhood environment diametrically opposed to all of his inherited mores—can most profitably be seen as the product of ideological wish-fulfillment. Here, quite illogically but very comfortingly, we have a child thoroughly imbued with bourgeois virtues even though his contact with his parents is *the most tenuous imaginable*—a dead father and a mother who perishes in childbirth. By creating a protagonist who absorbs all of the needful habits and maxims from an older generation whose tie to him resembles "gold to airy thinness beat," Dickens symbolically banishes the fear that even the requisite years of incessant and inerrant upbringing beside a wholly orthodox hearth will prove insufficient—the stuff of dreams, surely, but politically potent for precisely that reason. However, this fantasy of a supremely durable middle-class ethos, of a rising generation carrying the hearth's "vestal temple" within, is not without its embarrassments. As stated above, because it appears in a novel, it cannot help but carry as its corollary the notion that Oliver's "blood" is responsible for his sterling character, and the truth of the matter is that the whole notion of inherited character traits is, to some extent, both antinovelistic *and* antibourgeois. The result of even the passive endorsement of such an explanation for Oliver is therefore a text that is not only constructed of materials at odds with the genre's very structure, but one that is also politically at odds with itself.

As to the former of these tensions, it should first be pointed out that if Oliver had experienced anything like a normal childhood, his resemblance to the previous generation would not be nearly so vexatious. However, the fact that his inheritance wins such an easy victory over the competing environmental influences of the workhouse and Fagin's gang means that we must see it as constituting a kind of genial *determinism*, and this is what places it in conflict with the enabling constraints of the novel. That such a label has rarely if ever been applied to *Oliver Twist* is due in part, I think, to the fact that most of the novels we conventionally label as "deterministic" or "naturalistic" are anything but cheery and usually profess contempt for middle-class values.[26] But consider: it is undeniable that Oliver's personality is the direct result of his parents' genetic bequest—that throughout his incarcerations under Bumble and Fagin he remains "the avatar of his father"[27]—and thus the text is laid open to the kind of attacks listed above, all of which indirectly spring from a tension between verisimilitude and certain forms of naturalism, as W. J. Harvey explains:

The *purer* the variety of naturalism, the more a novelist stresses *one* kind of determining force, the greater this strain [on our credulity] will become. The danger is that we shall attend less to an imagined fictional world and more to some dogmatic philosophy of life which engages us in an area of controversy entirely outside the world of art [italics mine]. . . . The extreme naturalist is, metaphorically, a Rousseau rather than a Montesquieu in that he tends to narrow down the multiplicity of . . . determining factors to a few, or even to one factor. This we tend to reject; we know that not *everything* is explicable in terms of our genetic make-up or our Oedipus complex or the nature of the class struggle. In other words, the naturalist strains our sense of mimetic adequacy because he offers too *simple* an explanation. We perceive many effects and conceive of many causes; unlike the [extreme] naturalist we are reluctant to trace all phenomena back to a single cause [Harvey's italics].[28]

The variety of "vulgar naturalism" outlined above clearly does occur in *Oliver Twist*, for, to repeat, there is no explanation in the text that can seriously compete with that of his blood inheritance in explaining the hero's immunity from ethical infection. And not only is there a lack of rivals, but the best potential candidate for a competitor—his environment—is waved continually in our faces, only to be discounted at every turn, making the insistence upon "blood" seem all the more strident. Dickens gets into trouble not because of his desire to depict an immaculately bourgeois child but because he appears so anxious to affirm that such virtues can be handed down the generations by a nature completely unassisted by nurture. We may not like his sentimentality in the person of either Oliver or Rose, but it is only in the depiction of the former that the author's anxieties over the durability of middle-class mores lead him to postulate a triumphant geneticism that struggles against the culturally mandated tendencies of the genre.

The second problem with Oliver's inheritance is that it is an attempt to graft onto middle-class characters and contexts an essentially upper-class means of explaining the conservation of valuable personality traits over time. As we have seen so starkly in *Agnes Grey*, bourgeois ideology denominates the well-conducted familial hearth as the necessary and sufficient explanation for the moral orthodoxy of each rising generation. Furthermore, aristocratic notions of immaculate bloodlines are routinely discounted in bourgeois discourses as a mystification employed to perpetuate the unearned privileges of a morally suspect ruling class. In Disraeli's *Coningsby*, for instance, the "Saxon" industrialist Millbank claims that he does not understand "how an aristocracy can exist, unless it be distinguished by some quality which no other class of the community possesses." And as for England's peerage of blood, he finds them no "richer . . . , better informed, wiser, or more distinguished for public or private virtue" than himself and his fellow businessmen.[29] Thus, while Dickens may attempt to suggest that Oliver is *Nature's* nobleman, the protagonist's physical and moral resemblance to his parents in the face of physical and moral brutalization cannot help but appear to endorse a way of conceiving character that is at odds with the author's own overarching bourgeois convictions. The message of Oliver's life is that "breeding will tell," a moral anathema to several middle-class habits of mind expressed not only in Dickens's other fiction but even elsewhere in *Oliver Twist*.

As a number of critics have shown, the rest of the characters in the text reveal the author to be fully committed to the idea that environment shapes character. Nancy, for instance, says to Rose: "Thank Heaven . . . that you had friends to care for and keep you in your childhood, and that you were never in the midst of cold and hunger, and riot and drunkenness, and—

and—something worse than all—as I have been from my cradle" (362). This emphasis upon formative surroundings is also present in the depictions of Noah Claypole and even Sikes, with the result that "Oliver and the thieves represent incommensurate kinds of reality and opposed standards of truth,"[30] a contradiction which renders the text as a whole "a curious exercise in double-think in that it mixes static (non-developmental) and developmental modes of treating experience."[31] It is for this reason that one part of Harvey's thesis seems *not* to apply to *Oliver Twist:* we are *not* led to "some dogmatic philosophy of life" or an "area of controversy entirely outside the world of art" because Dickens in no way believes in the geneticism his protagonist—and only his protagonist—implies. In general, and outside the realm of the text's political fantasy, Dickens is typically Victorian in his belief in the molding power of environment and circumstance.[32] *Oliver Twist* is thus determinist not by design, but by default, another reason it has not generally been recognized as such. Clearly, anxiety over the "survivability" of Oliver's virtues leads Dickens not only to create the kind of static protagonist ill-suited to a novel, but to butt his head against his own political presuppositions.

One hesitates to put forward any biographical specifics to account for Dickens's deliberate decision to render inheritance immune from the forces of environment in this novel; but as the members of the Bakhtin circle repeatedly point out, ideology and psychology are not separate and opposed; rather, they always intermingle. Ideology is always personal, and psychology is forever social, for our psyches exist on the borderline between our own organism and the outside world and mediate between the two.[33] It may therefore be germane to raise the well-worn issue of the blacking warehouse in this instance. Without belaboring the episode, one can point out that the childhood trauma that apparently shaped so many aspects of the author's imagination dovetails with the political anxieties discussed in this chapter. The young Dickens, feeling as though he had been wrenched from his proper sphere and unjustly consigned to the fate of a "little labouring hind,"[34] most likely did entertain both fantasies and fears about "blood" proving stronger than circumstance. If *Oliver Twist* is in part an autobiographical novel, then we can see in the protagonist's situation a repetition of the author's own juvenile hopes that some immanent manifestation of his middle-class parentage would serve to set him apart from the low company to which he had been relegated, and that his bourgeois birthright would somehow be brought to light in a manner able to effect his return to a world resembling that of Brownlow's and the Maylies'.[35] According to such a view, Oliver's characterization can be seen as "a hymn to the purity of the middle-class soul,"[36] prompted at least in part by an experience of social dispossession from which the author never fully recovered.[37]

In addition to the passages quoted earlier in this section, there are several other signs that Dickens himself is embarrassed by his choice of "blood" as the guarantor of Oliver's middle-class orthodoxy; and though none of these efforts to undo the havoc wrought by his political wishful thinking represents more than a token atonement or a feeble apology, they deserve attention because they cast light upon aspects of the text otherwise difficult to account for. The first of these countermoves involves the unusual prevalence of quasi-Wordsworthian discourse in the novel.[38] At several points the protagonist evidences psychic states that appear to owe much to the Intimations Ode,[39] and these, I would suggest, are designed to hedgingly account for Oliver's virtues in ways that distract attention from his implicit genetic inheritance. When he is first ensconced at Brownlow's, for instance, he opines that "perhaps [his mother] does see [him]" and that "perhaps she has sat by [him]," for he "almost feel[s] as if she had," admitting that he has "dreamed of her" (126) and beheld her face. These hints of Wordsworthian preexistence are reiterated more strongly when Oliver is taken in by the Maylies, in a passage whose self-contradictory constructions recall nothing so much as Wordsworth's half-remembered "heaven" that "lies about us in our infancy," and which suggest that Oliver has arrived in the world trailing clouds of middle-class comfort:

The boy stirred, and smiled in his sleep, as though these marks of pity and compassion had awakened some pleasant dream of a love and affection he had never known. Thus, a strain of gentle music, or the rippling of water in a silent place, or the odour of a flower, or the mention of a familiar word, will sometimes call up sudden dim remembrances of scenes that never were, in this life; which vanish like a breath; which some brief memory of a happier existence, long gone by, would seem to have awakened; which no voluntary exertion of the mind can ever recall. (268)

The covert argument of these and similar scenes has been precisely pinpointed by J. Hillis Miller, who demonstrates that while the passages obviously derive from Wordsworth's great ode, they seem to imply a state of affairs beyond anything suggested in "Intimations of Immortality." That is, although there clearly exists in the novel "a form of memory . . . which seems to connect the present with a supernatural paradise . . . anterior to

all Oliver's present life, but which the present seems somehow to reveal,"
this "orthodox" reformulation of the Romantic doctrine is accompanied
by a much more peculiar suggestion—that "one may [also] find signs in
the present of a secret past life which existed *on this earth* before one was
born. When those signs are understood, their revelations may be accepted
as a definition of what one really is. Then it will be possible to live ever
afterward in a kind of paradise on earth, a paradise regained which is the
present lightened and spiritualized because it is a repetition of one's pre-
natal earthly past" (Miller's italics).[40] This notion, when spelled out, seems
too outlandish to emanate from Dickens but does in fact silently undergird
other scenes in the text, and we can perceive the difference between it and
the more familiar Wordsworthian idea of preexistence by comparing Oliver's good-bye to Little Dick with his attack upon Noah Claypole. In the
former scene, Dick says the doctors' prognosis of his death must be true
because he "dream[s] so much of heaven, and angels, and kind faces that
[he] never see[s] when [he is] awake" (96–97). Oliver's own "shadowy
recollections," however, are (as in the passages above) usually of a more
personal cast. When Noah insults the mother that Oliver has never heard
described as anything but evil, not only does the protagonist react in a way
that suggests he possesses some hidden certainty about his parent, but the
act of defending her honor seems to transform him into a wholly different
person—the person he would have been in the undeprived bourgeois life
he was apparently meant to lead:

A minute ago, the boy had looked the quiet, mild, dejected creature that harsh
treatment had made him. But his spirit was roused at last; the cruel insult to his
dead mother had set his blood on fire. His breast heaved; his attitude was erect;
his eye bright and vivid; his whole person changed, as he stood glaring over the
cowardly tormentor who now lay crouching at his feet; and defied him with an
energy he had never known before. (88)

Notice how the movement here is still away from environment—he is
no longer the "dejected creature that harsh treatment had made him"—
but not toward the only obvious alternative. This violent epiphany (as well
as the more peaceful ones cited previously), though definitely linking
Oliver to his deceased parents, in fact muddy the issue of his blood inheritance by their vaguely mystical suggestions, depicting a transformation and a recollection of middle-class security no mere link of "blood"
could possibly account for. In short, all such quasi-Wordsworthian passages can be read as an attempt to transform the monochromatic determinism behind Oliver's character into something resembling a rainbow.

To explain why Dickens, consciously or unconsciously, might profitably pursue such a strategy, we can turn again to Harvey:

> Our sense of conditional freedom depends upon a combination of factors which, considered singly, may seem to determine us, but which in association tend to liberate us. When one considers the multiplicity of everyday experience one is, so to speak, a Montesquieu rather than a Rousseau. That is to say, one views the conditioning factors of self and non-self as an incredibly complex system of checks and balances; freedom lies in the interstices of this system, one force qualifying or negating another.[41]

The "hyper-Intimations" episodes thus partially absolve the text of its troubling reliance on a single explanation for character without having recourse to the familiar—but forbidden—expedient of environment. If the logic of such scenes is embarrassing, that is little matter, for anyone who doubts that quasi-supernatural determinants of character can be successfully "added in" to make a deterministic novel credible—even when the whole concept of the supernatural is supposedly incompatible with the author's expressed views—need only take up a copy of *Tess of the d'Urbervilles*. Oliver's recollections of a middle-class preexistence, fantastic as they are, distract from the doubly embarrassing situation Dickens forced himself into when he decided to render "The Parish Boy's Progress" no progress at all. And furthermore, if the credibility of such scenes is questionable, their politics is immaculate, for by calling Wordsworth to his aid in supplementally constructing Oliver's goodness, Dickens is invoking an explanation of innate virtue that has nothing to do with aristocratic genealogies and that pointedly insists upon such inner beauty's availability to the middling and even the lowliest run of mankind. Among the English Romantics, the middle-class mind discovered Wordsworth to be the most congenial to its outlook and the most applicable to its purposes, and thus the protagonist's intimations cannot help but heal the ideological rupture his "lineage" has heretofore introduced into the novel.

The other indication of Dickens's discomfort with his explanation of Oliver's virtues can be found in the text's eleventh-hour attempt to redefine moral and physical inheritance as an exclusively upper-class phenomenon. This effort to restore a bit of bourgeois political orthodoxy is undertaken largely through the character of Monks, about whom two objections have traditionally been raised: (1) that he starts off as a villain with promise, only to peter out toward the end, and (2) that he gets off, legally speaking, quite easily.[42] But however disappointing Monks's final disposition may be to the causes of gothicism and equal justice for all, it does play its part in shifting our attention away from Oliver's hitherto exceptional resemblance to his bourgeois parents, for in the novel's final pages the protagonist's half-brother is suddenly revealed to be the very embodiment of all the previous generation's *upper*-class *vices*.

As Brownlow spins out the tale, we learn that Monks's and Oliver's father was, before meeting the hero's mother, party to "a wretched marriage, into which family pride, and the most sordid and narrowest of all ambition forced [him] when a mere boy." This abandonment of his own class for an "ill-assorted union" with a wealthy but immoral woman led swiftly to a state of mutual "loathing" and to a separation, whereupon the unnamed wife, reverting quickly to the decadent ways of her kind, adopted a manner of life "wholly given up to continental frivolities" (435). Monks, we soon learn, is almost exclusively his mother's child—*her* avatar, if you will—for between his and Brownlow's accounts, a rough outline of his childhood and subsequent development is laid before the reader. What is most interesting about this revelation of character and motive, however—and what ties it all the more strongly to Dickens's seeming uneasiness over Oliver's inherited immunity from evil—is its own meticulous *balancing* of nature and nurture. On the one hand, the text insists that specifically upper-class vices can be passed along by means of "blood" to the next generation, while on the other, it accompanies each invocation of a tainted inheritance with a seconding, environmental cause, as if discounting the "genetic" explanation with the same breath that nominates it. Brownlow, for instance, recalls the father speaking of "the rebellious disposition, vice, malice and *premature* [italics mine] bad passions of . . . his only son" while at the same time asserting that the boy had been "trained [by his mother] to hate him." Thus, when we are told that Monks has "from an infant, repulsed [his father] with coldness and aversion" (458), it is difficult to tell with any certainty whether this is due mainly to nature or to nurture. This same crucial ambiguity is reiterated when Monks takes up his own story: " 'There she died,' said Monks, 'after a lingering illness; and, on her death-bed, she bequeathed these secrets to me, together with her unquenchable and deadly hatred of all whom they involved—though she need not have left me that, for I had inherited it long before' " (459).

This issue of "inherited" versus "acquired" is even blurred in as apparently straightforward a matter as the villain's venereal disease, for observe how the diction waffles: "you, who *from your cradle* were gall and bitterness to your own father's heart, and in whom all evil passions, vice, and profligacy, festered, til they found a vent in a hideous disease which has made your face an index even to your mind" (439, italics mine). This seems not so much an example of Victorian euphemism as an attempt to nominate both the cradle *and* the brothel as the origin of the disfiguring malaise. Now, none of these passages is crucially important (except as they work the levers and pulleys of the denouement), but their studied balance is striking. In my view, such attempts to paint ethical inheritance as a primarily upper-class phenomenon while contradictorily refusing to admit that blood alone can determine character at all can best be seen as a strategy whereby *Oliver Twist* may attempt to atone for its antibourgeois and antinovelistic aspects simultaneously.

It only remains to point out that an anxiety over the durability of middle-class values in a morally corrosive world seems to have shaped *Agnes Grey* and *Oliver Twist* in roughly similar ways. In the former, recall, the same concern that, almost against the author's will, prevents any genuine character development also ensures that the bourgeois realm and that of the Bloomfields and Murrays never enter into dialogic relations—the two discourses merely speak past each other, and Agnes can neither teach nor learn. In the case of *Oliver Twist*, critics have understood for some time that there is a connection between the protagonist's immunity from his environment and the fact that the criminal and middle-class realms never seem to influence or reflect each other. Oliver, bounced back and forth between two hermetic worlds of virtue and vice, never gets his bearings, for such "static dualism is alien to any systematic notions of personal growth."[43] This is so, I think, because, especially for a young hero like Oliver (or Agnes), character development must almost necessarily entail a receptivity to the varied languages of social life and an ability to dialogically transform them into what Bakhtin terms an "internally persuasive discourse," which could then begin to speak to and influence others on equal terms. But when an ideological position mandates that a text's youthful protagonist must spring forth onto the world's stage with his ears shut and his lines already memorized, it will likely be dangerous to depict the world at large as more willing to listen, learn, and grow, for a hero who is less receptive to dialogism than the society that surrounds him announces his spiritual poverty in too obvious a manner—no, if he is reified, his novel had better be so as well.

Certainly we can point to Dickens's subsequent development as a novelist and observe how a growing interest in the process of Bildung was paralleled by an increasingly skillful ability to dialogically interilluminate the various languages of his society. In his later texts, the protagonist typically engages in a process wherein "the movement toward a constructed unity is unending," while the character who "refuses to reinvent himself imaginatively" falls prey to "the conservative tendency to repeat the past, to deny the need for change because such change is always threatening," a conception that brings us Copperfield and Pip on the one hand, and Havisham, Headstone, and Jasper on the other.[44] At the same time, the novels of Dickens's maturity show the social languages of his society influencing and feeding off each other in a way that *Oliver Twist* does not. Bumble's workhouse, for instance, "is not established as representative of the society that has produced it in the way that the Court of Chancery and the Circumlocution Office are," for "the structure of the novel, with its polarized worlds, cannot accommodate such an effect." In the later texts, however, "the institutions that are attacked function as the foci of multifarious worlds that radiate from them,"[45] and no supposedly respectable drawing room or department of government is unaffected by, or free from responsibility for, the enormities committed among the crowded warrens of the poor. In this manner are the discourses of middle-class "virtue" and underworld "vice," to use Bakhtin's phrase, "put within quotation marks," as the similarities between, and the hidden conjunctions of, society's official and criminal languages are brought to light. It is very much to the point, of course, that accompanying both of these developments was Dickens's growing estrangement from the bourgeois orthodoxies that shape—or misshape—so much of *Oliver Twist*.

II

Dialogic Enactments

CHAPTER FIVE

Foucault, Neo-Marxism, and the Cultural Conversation

*

The impact of Michel Foucault upon the field of cultural poetics has been a decidedly mixed blessing. On the one hand, his genealogies of modern discursive formations and his rejection of a wholly repressive theory of power have made it all the more difficult to speak of the relationship between politics and literature in reductionist terms. After *Discipline and Punish* and *The History of Sexuality*, it is impossible to conceive of hegemonic structures as merely negative or inhibiting, for those texts compel us to understand the practices and vocabularies that traverse our lives not as limits pure and simple, but as a set of enabling constraints that open certain possibilities of freedom precisely by closing others off, and that sharpen our vision in some directions (and those not necessarily trivial or "distracting" or unprofitable ones) by their discreet placement of blinders about our eyes. Furthermore, Foucault has dealt a fatal blow to the notion of ideology as a collection of discoverably false ideas that masks an equally discoverable deeper truth, offering in its stead a conception wherein each discourse, including Marxist hermeneutics, produces its own set of "truth-effects," nominating some statements as true and others as false in a manner that is always, in an absolute sense, arbitrary, but that, on a local level, remains coherent and instrumentally useful. On the other hand, Foucault's interventions have fostered a literary-critical practice characterized by a sophisticated variety of defeatism which insists that the raised fist of revolt is indistinguishable from the iron heel of repression. This seems due chiefly to his descriptions of "power" as an entity resembling a fine mist which it is difficult to see, harder to grasp, and impossible to avoid, and to his corollary that our supposed acts of resistance are in fact a diabolically subtle charade staged by hegemony itself to disguise its virtual omnipresence. These accounts of the cultural landscape, though far more open to contestation than those mentioned above, have nevertheless been enthusiastically integrated by certain new historicists and other neo-Foucauldians[1] into a number of learned and ingenious readings of literary texts, readings which either imply or assert that any claims for the presence of effectual oppositional energies within the works concerned can only be the result of a hermeneutical naiveté, and that if one scrutinizes such *apparent* challenges to the status quo armed with a proper sensitivity for power's complete saturation of the social field, the formal patterns and rhetorical tropes that undergird and perpetuate bourgeois-liberal assumptions will always be detected masquerading as incitements to riot. The result is a criticism that is deaf to the contests of social voices that inhabit and energize the novel and blind to the manner in which the depiction of such struggles implicates the genre in the mechanisms of social change.

If Foucault's redescriptions of ideology and the will to truth have proved fruitful, while his overarching visions of power's ubiquity and unanswerability remain pernicious, there exists in the social and literary theory of Bakhtin much that, while broadly in accord with the former aspects of Foucault's legacy, offers important alternatives and refinements to the latter. Once Bakhtinian conceptions of the workings of hegemony, the limits of political domination, and the relationship between cultural forces and novelistic discourse are brought to bear upon the question of oppositional structures within the literary text, they will be seen to embody a cultural poetics that avoids the reductionist and foundationalist aspects of various Marxisms, while at the same time acknowledging the genuine potentials for resistance and dissent within the novel that Foucauldian strategies of reading seem willing to deny. Indeed, the attractiveness of much of Bakhtin's work lies precisely in its combination of freshness and familiarity, for that isolated intellectual's theories appear at once sui generis and yet uncannily anticipatory of many developments in neo-Marxist and poststructuralist thought.[2] As we shall discover, Bakhtin's theories of the novel— tough-minded yet determined to credit the efficacy of human voices—will allow us to rediscover within that genre a margin of hope that cannot be mistaken for the product of sentimentality or wishful thinking.

As the argument of this chapter will, in general, move from an overview of cultural totalities, through questions of social psychology, to conclude with a consideration of certain formal potentials within the novel, our first task is to delineate the important divergences between Bakhtinian and Foucauldian conceptions of how hegemony operates, a task we can best begin by scrutinizing what many neo-Marxist critics object to in Foucault's conception of "power." In broad terms, they are disturbed by the fact that his descriptions of the social field, while cognizant of endemic inequalities, postulate a network of relationships so multifarious and omnidirectional that large-scale structures of oppression and liberation, such as classes, political hierarchies, and cohesive social movements, become obscured:

> . . . power is not to be taken to be a phenomenon of one individual's consolidated and homogeneous domination over others, or that of one group or class over others. What, by contrast, should always be kept in mind is that power, if we do not take too distant a view of it, is not that which makes the difference between those who exclusively possess and retain it, and those who do not have it and submit to it. Power must be analyzed as something which circulates, or rather as something which only functions in the form of a chain. It is never localized here or there, never in anybody's hands, never appropriated as a commodity or piece of wealth. Power is employed and exercised through a net-like organization. And not only do individuals circulate between its threads; they are always in the position of simultaneously undergoing and exercising this power. They are not only its inert or consenting target; they are always also the elements of its articulation. In other words, individuals are the vehicles of power, not its points of application.[3]

Frank Lentricchia complains that such passages "suggest that power has no predominant direction, no predominant point of departure, no predominant point of terminus. Like the God of theism, it is ubiquitous; unlike God it has no intention." Furthermore, these and similar accounts seem to drain political questions of much of their urgency, since "to say that power [frequently] moves from bottom to top is to promote the misleading understanding that anyone at any time can grab a piece of the action."[4] What Lentricchia and like-minded critics are in effect saying is that Foucault cannot see the forest for the trees and that his discovery of individual branches pointing in all directions distracts him from noticing that the species as a whole invariably grows from the ground up. For Marxists of any stripe, this is a fatal lacuna in social vision, for how can one hope to seize power or even to correctly identify one's political adversaries if one adopts a view which denies that power congregates anywhere in particular? And how is solidarity to be inculcated if we allow ourselves to conclude that, as far as exploitation is concerned, we all appear equally guilty?

Considered from a Bakhtinian perspective, the problem with Foucault's "micro-physics of power"[5] is not so much that it sacrifices a clear perception of large-scale structures in its desire to faithfully represent details (though this too is a concern), but rather that it purports to sensitize us to the variety and multiplicity of the cultural field while in fact reintroducing a monolithic apparatus as paranoid and falsifying as anything produced by the vulgarest strain of Marxism. The problem can be approached by scrutinizing Foucault's characteristic employments of the term "power," for in his hands this word becomes the synoptic transliteration of all of the varied discourses ongoing within a given culture. He may grant that, at any particular time, significant discursive practices will be making unrelated, diametrical, or even mutually hostile assertions, but these contentions are ultimately recouped under the overarching sign of "power," which, conceived as a kind of enveloping gas whose very form and stability is constituted by the colliding atoms of social entities in conflict, consigns "resistance" to the status of an internal mechanism that serves only to increase the mass and extend the volume of the whole: "power needs resistance as one of its fundamental conditions of operation. It is through the articulation of points of resistance that power spreads through the social field."[6] Thus, the plenitude of conflicting voices becomes, in his final (and finalizing) analysis, a single voice chanting a mantra designed to ensure its own perpetuation, and what appeared at first to be so many instances of heteroglossia are exposed as merely the tonal inflections of a complicated but essentially monoglossic utterance, all conflict and dialogue being reduced to the status of vowels and conjunctions within power's Proustian sentence—paraphrasable as "I am that I am"—to which there is no answer and from which there is no appeal.

Were Bakhtin ever to have been confronted with Foucault's formulations of power, he would undoubtedly have characterized them as a particularly unfortunate example of "theoretism," that restless desire to completely account for and systematize *all* of the phenomena in a given field—a rage for order that inevitably falsifies the particular instances it is so desperate to organize and rationally align. Foucault frequently claims that he proffers no "theory of power," but his pronouncements about it leave little doubt that he believed such a theory would have been a desirable thing to possess, and that he ventured as far as he could toward formulating one. What this will to theory ends up doing, though, is blunting the force of Foucault's riveting genealogies of particular discourses,[7] for by pulling back from the specific and attempting a universal description— which he then labels "power"—of all the discursive practices operating within a culture, he presents us not with a template through which to better perceive and understand the patternings of social forces in conflict, but rather, and merely, with something very like the truism that human societies are always traversed by power relations. This result is embarrassing, not only because of its banality but because it also seems to posit something very close to a transhistorical feature of "human nature," something Foucault is usually at pains to avoid.

By contrast, investigating social configurations in a Bakhtinian mode enjoins one to continually avoid the seductive notion "that everything has a meaning relating to the seamless whole, a meaning one could discover if only one had the code," for such thinking is "totalitarian in its assumption that it can, in principle, explain the totality of things" and "semiotic (or cryptographic) in its approach to all apparent accidents as signs of an underlying order to which the given system has the key."[8] Thus where Foucault errs is in reaching too far toward a level of abstraction that cannot help but reify the disorderly columns and broken phalanxes of discourses that, in their loosely coordinated and intermittently interlocking way, constitute political hegemony. There is simply no point, from the Bakhtinian view, in looking beyond heteroglossia, beyond that

internal stratification of [the] single national language into social dialects, characteristic group behavior, professional jargons, generic languages, languages of generations and age groups, tendentious languages, languages of the authorities, of various circles and of passing fashions, languages that serve the specific sociopolitical purposes of the day, even of the hour (each day [possessing] its own slogan, its own vocabulary, its own emphasis)—[the] internal stratification present in every language at any given moment of its historical existence.[9]

It is on this level that discourse must be grappled with because it is on this level that the human subjects who constitute the social field are still audible—beyond lies only tautology, contradiction, and falsifying systematicity, as exemplified in the following: "In general terms, I believe that power is not built up out of 'wills' (individual or collective), nor is it derivable from interests. Power is constructed and functions on the basis of particular powers, myriad issues, myriad effects of power. It is this complex domain that must be studied. That is not to say that it is independent or could be made sense of outside of economic processes and the relations of production."[10] In abandoning such self-indicting formulations we need not fear that "stopping at" heteroglossia will inevitably mire our praxis within the business-as-usual channels of bourgeois liberalism and its self-proclaimed "toleration" of diversity, for among the welter of competing voices are discourses that Bakhtinian strategies of reading can identify as designed to perpetuate their speakers' monopoly on privilege. These strategies, as the following chapters will demonstrate, are adept at exposing false claims of universal competence, self-interested descriptions of social relationships, and attempts to terrorize others into silence. To do justice to a society's discursive diversity does not mean that we must accept at face value its descriptions of itself as broad-minded, lenient, and equitable.

Inseparably bound up with Foucault's conception of power is the idea of resistance—or rather that of its largely chimerical nature. Foucault himself, while at all times careful to claim that the adoption of his total-izing schematic need not usher in futility and despair, frames his argument in a manner that makes his disciples' dim hopes for oppositional efficacy quite understandable:

It seems to me that power *is* "always already there," that one is never "outside" it, that there are not "margins" for those who break with the system to gambol in. But this does not entail the necessity of accepting an inescapable form of domi-nation or an absolute privilege on the side of the law. To say that one can never be "outside" power does not mean that one is trapped and condemned to defeat no matter what. . . . [For] there are no relations of power without resistances; the latter are all the more real and effective because they are formed right at the point where relations of power are exercised; resistance to power does not have to come from elsewhere to be real, nor is it inexorably frustrated through being the com-patriot of power. It exists all the more by being in the same place as power; hence, like power, resistance is multiple and can be integrated in global strategies.[11]

Taken as a whole, Foucault's pronouncements on the prospects for ef-fective opposition to hegemony relay what seems to be a contradictory message. On the one hand, resistance is always the child of power—power spawns various challenges to itself in order to usher disruptive energies that might otherwise threaten it into channels from which power itself can draw nurture. This notion suggests that what we naively take to be op-positional practices—such as the youth "counterculture" of the sixties, to take a familiar but now sufficiently distanced example—are in truth dis-tractions which do not merely fob us off with symbolic or Pyrrhic victories (as a Marxist theory might hold), but actually serve to substantiate new distinctions, new categories and relationships that enhance the hold of power upon its subjects. (Why a power that is already everywhere would "need" to do this is left unanswered.) On the other hand, Foucault insists that resistance often does change the *nature* of power in some way, even if the margins of its dominion are never pushed back. These changes, though, are invariably described in cautious and qualified terms, rarely amounting to more than a nudge, a shove, or a temporary block.[12] Indeed, what undoubtedly frustrates Marxists about Foucault's conception is that it appears to argue that a kind of liberal reformism is all that is possible in the world, even when the outward political events (a revolution, a coup, a mass movement) suggest that a more radical break with the past has occurred. Still, Foucault must be given his due, for he does have at least a vague explanation for incremental change, and he does not declare that those who believe themselves to be resisting hegemony are *wholly* dupes of the system they oppose: "People know what they do; they frequently know why they do what they do; but what they don't know is what what they do does."[13] Alan Sheridan probably puts the best face on Foucault's view when he explains that "there is a plurality of resistances, each a special case, distributed in an irregular way in time and space. Sometimes a broad series of resistances converges to bring about a major upheaval, a 'revolution,' but, like power, and inextricably linked with it, resistance usually takes the form of innumerable, mobile, transitory points."[14] Perhaps a fitting label for Foucault's notion of resistance might therefore be "Lucretian," since, like atoms falling through the void, our isolated acts of resistance rarely swerve together into upheavals, revolutions, or anything else a Marxist would be likely to recognize as a genuine form of opposition.

Even this minimalist conception of the efficacy of resistance tends to disappear, however, when those who acknowledge (or merely exhibit) themselves in Foucault's intellectual debt apply his ideas within works of literary criticism. The result of this elision is a hermeneutic practice that relentlessly aspires to depict literary texts as carceral apparatuses incapable of any political result beyond the confirmation of the reader or spectator in her subject position—Tudor, liberal, or otherwise—where she is helplessly traversed by discourses that ensure that all her thoughts and actions will, whatever she believes to the contrary, do the state some service. Thus we find Stephen Greenblatt declaring that even as Marlowe's seemingly hypertransgressive protagonists attempt "to challenge the system," they can do naught but offer "unwitting tributes to that social construction of identity against which they struggle," imagining themselves "set in diametrical opposition to their society where in fact they have unwittingly accepted its crucial structural elements."[15] In like manner, Mark Seltzer informs us that "the novel secures and extends the very movements of power it ostensibly abjures," screening hegemonic discourses even as it exercises them with a beguiling discretion "achieved by modern technologies of social control," a discretion that "allows for the dissemination of power throughout the most everyday social practices and institutions, including the institution of the novel itself."[16] And so too D. A. Miller, who asserts in *The Novel and the Police* that while "no openly fictional form has ever sought to 'make a difference' in the world more than the Victorian Novel," the cultural work the genre actually performs is that of "confirm[ing] the novel-reader in his identity as 'liberal subject,'" a creature "who seems to recognize himself most fully only when he forgets or disavows his functional implication in a system of carceral restraints or disciplinary injunctions"—a forgetting the novel materially promotes by clandestinely collaborating with the structures of power it purports to oppose.[17] Why it should be that so often only half of the message gets through is an interesting question. In my view, it is likely due to the fact that if one finds something appealing in Foucault's depictions of power at all, then those of his pronouncements that emphasize power's ability to create and finesse supposed resistances for its own purposes simply seem more convincing than his hasty addenda (they do usually appear as such) to the effect that oppositional practices are not therefore necessarily futile. Like most examples of theoretism, Foucauldian "power" is better at describing stasis than at explaining change, more attentive to enumerating our fetters than to anticipating our acts of freedom.

Interestingly, one critic who is generally sympathetic to Foucault's enterprise but unconvinced by his assessments of the meager potential for meaningful resistance to hegemony is forced to supplement his vocabularies of power and opposition with those of Bakhtin (as well as with those of Raymond Williams, concerning whom more in due course). Peggy Knapp, writing of the social contest enacted in *The Canterbury Tales*, finds that Foucault's analysis of power relations are "enabling because they bring into focus a vast network of power working its effects beyond a conventionally 'political' arena and enforced at many social levels, rather than merely from above." At the same time, however, "his all-encompassing networks of discursive power . . . will not be taken as binding, because there must have been discursive tactics that escaped the effects of the most general coding." Some of Foucault's formulations about power's workings, she adds, "only allow confrontations whose end is foreordained, and cannot explain internally induced social change."[18] True, she finds in his notion of "subjugated knowledges" a reason to believe that a more realistic visualization of social struggle and historical development may be inferable from the pages of *Power/Knowledge*, even though Foucault touches only briefly upon these "naive," "disqualified," and "popular" knowledges, and states that they are "incapable of unanimity" and owe their force "only to the harshness with which [they] are opposed by everything surrounding [them]."[19] At any rate, rather than relying solely upon such an undertheorized conception, she seeks additional backing for her interpretation of Chaucerian struggle in Bakhtin's description of "internally persuasive discourses,"[20] a concept that allows her, and will allow us, to retain Foucault's antireductive articulations of hegemony while yet making intelligible the interactions of competing vocabularies that cast doubt upon new historicist prison houses of power.

According to Bakhtin, if we come to inhabit the subject positions hegemony marks out for us, we do so through a process of internalizing, in a modified form, certain discourses directed at us from the surrounding culture. At the same time, though, he insists that this process is an endlessly dynamic one, in which dominant social languages are to be seen as evolving rather than reified entities, and in which the subject's psyche is to be considered not as so much passive soil upon which ideology may spread its poisoned seeds, but rather as a battlefield over which both allied and contending linguistic battalions attack, retreat, re-form, reach truces, and occasionally switch sides. This dynamism flows directly from Bakhtin's most fundamental ideas about the relationship between language and culture. For him, the meanings of words are never stable or transparently self-evident because words are the locus of a chronic ideological warfare in which competing groups attempt to accentuate them to suit their various political purposes. Thus, "there are no 'neutral' words and forms . . . that can belong to 'no one,'" for language is always already "shot through with intentions and accents," and each word "tastes of the contest and contexts in which it has lived its socially charged life," existing "in other people's mouths" and "serving other people's intentions" in such a way that every phrase appears on the scene "overpopulated" with meanings and nuances, many of which will undoubtedly throw up obstacles to our own attempts at verbal appropriation.[21] With the meanings of words therefore continually at issue, it cannot be supposed that any discursive practice can maintain the stability, consistency, and aura of unanswerability necessary to effortlessly penetrate and thoroughly occupy the subject, for such discourses, no matter how hegemonic, are always involved in an ongoing struggle with other social vocabularies, a struggle which ensures that they will be forever modifying themselves, shifting their angles of attack, and throwing up defensive structures, all of which undermines their claims to be utterly "authoritative."

This ongoing external conversation is not, however, the only obstacle to the complete ideological saturation of the subject, for within each psyche the hegemonic discourses meet already-existing innerly persuasive discourses, which, though often harmonizing quite closely with prevailing cultural orthodoxies, never precisely mirror their exterior progenitors. Paul Smith comes close to Bakhtin's conception when he points out that "the subject/individual exists in a dialectical relationship with the social but also lives that relationship *alone* as much as interpersonally or as merely a factor within social formations: alone at the level of the meanings and histories which together constitute a *singular* history."[22] Innerly persuasive discourses are "half-ours and half-someone else's," for though "one's own discourse is gradually and slowly wrought out of others' words that have been acknowledged and assimilated,"[23] the multiplicity of discourses within the social field and the fact of their constant incremental mutation ensures that no two subjects can ever assimilate exactly the same ensemble of vocabularies in identical proportions. Furthermore, this process of absorption must not be taken to mean that the subject simply comes to parrot selected bits and pieces of exterior cultural languages like a schoolchild forced to learn scattered passages from the canon by rote; rather, the situation is reminiscent of that other, more complicated and challenging pedagogical exercise, "retelling in one's own words."[24] This must be so because the dialogic exchange between discourses in the culture at large continues unabated among all of the innerly persuasive discourses propagated within the psyche. Our interior conversation is just as potentially contentious as the one without and no less productive of at least incremental diversity:

Our ideological development is . . . an intense struggle within us for hegemony among various available verbal and ideological points of view, approaches, directions and values. . . . The importance of struggling with another's discourse, its influence in the history of an individual's coming to ideological consciousness, is enormous. One's own discourse and one's own voice, although born of another or dynamically stimulated by another, will sooner or later begin to liberate themselves from the authority of the other's discourse. This process is made more complex by the fact that a variety of alien voices enter into the struggle for influence within an individual's consciousness (just as they struggle with one another in surrounding social reality).[25]

Of course each subject's idiosyncratic retelling of the culture's hegemonic narratives will swiftly identify him or her as the member of a particular class, gender, profession, generation, or other social group, but within these groupings there can always be discovered a subtle variety and a continuous development—factors that our various synchronically-minded theoretisms find it convenient to ignore or disparage, but that must be recognized and worked through by any critical practice that wishes to understand, not merely dismiss, political resistance and social change.

For those who might object that Bakhtin's conception of how "consciousness awakens to *independent* ideological life" (italics mine)[26] cannot account for the existence of hegemony at all, a visual representation may prove helpful. If we conceive of the subject as a sphere and a culture's various discourses as so many arrows pointing toward it, we can represent the more or less "authoritative," hegemonic discourses as thick and darkly shaded and, moreover, as all approaching the individual from roughly the same direction, say from the top. As we move our way around to the sides and bottom of the sphere, we find the arrows becoming thinner and fewer, standing as they do for the weaker, less often heard vocabularies of dissent, resistance, and subversion. Inside the sphere itself are arrows that mark the subject's innerly persuasive discourses. Here the most important of these would resemble their exterior hegemonic progenitors in both direction and coloring—though not exactly—and thus they would be seen to strongly "answer" the incoming subversive vocabularies, but not in a perfectly efficacious, "head-on" formation. In like manner, some of the subversive discourses also have spawned innerly persuasive offspring, though, as one would expect, these must be represented with paler and thinner strokes than those of their more authoritative counterparts. They resemble the "orthodox" vectors, however, in having been themselves subtly changed in direction and composition by the dialogic exchange ongoing within the individual, to the extent that they now either meet the incoming hegemonic arrows at oblique angles or not at all—or perhaps in a configuration in which several of them converge upon the same target. Thusly can the existence of culturally dominant structures of feeling residing in the psyche be visualized without doing violence to the subject's unique "retelling" (i.e., reshading and redirecting) of those discursive practices.

The most important fact about this visualization, however, is that it must be conceived of as *merely one frame in a strip of motion picture film,* for the various arrows are to be understood as gradually swelling or shrinking, darkening or lightening, shifting their angle of attack either to the right or the left, all in response to the cumulative counterpressure created by their dialogic encounters with the innerly persuasive discourses of other similarly (though not identically) situated subjects across the culture generally. To quote Smith again, while "any 'subject's' motives and intentions are bound up with—indeed, in part built up by—a singular history" and thus "are to be seen as firmly implicated into a particular 'internal' constitution which is subvented by what is sometimes called 'the subject's self-narrative,'" the subject's actions "are also and equally engagements or interventions in everyone else's history and have real effects there. These two histories cannot be construed as separate, of course. They are mediated in a dialectical process as the 'subject' negotiates its self-interest in relation not only to itself, but to the world."[27] The only alteration necessary to bring this account wholly into line with Bakhtinian theory would be the substitution of "dialogical" for "dialectical," thereby emphasizing the fact that the various conversations between the individual's innerly persuasive discourses and those of the culture at large are not quasi-mechanical processes whose endpoint is synthesis, compromise, or accommodation, but a continuing series of encounters in which each utterance aimed at the subject causes her to shift her ground, however minutely, and in which her reply forces a similar reaccentuation of the hegemonic vocabulary. This is not done in a way that necessarily entails either increasing convergence or divergence between the two voices, but that does ensure that the nature of the exchange must change over time as a direct result of the subject and the cultural entity's conscious and unconscious reformulations of their speech in the face of resistance, misunderstanding, or even growing agreement. Another way to envision this process is as a variation on Althusser's notion that ideologies "hail" us in a way that fixes us in a particular subject position—as a worker, an intellectual, a "liberal subject."[28] Bakhtin would wish to modify such a description by insisting that this "hailing" never quite hits its mark, never discovers its target—the subject—to be residing precisely in the place it expected, and that the subject's answer to this hailing takes account of the perceived discrepancy, which in turn ensures that hegemony's hailing is never identically pitched on any two occasions. In short, "one's speech both reveals *and produces* one's position in class society, in such a way, moreover, as to set into dialogue the relations among classes."[29] The result is inevitable change, though in no inevitable direction.

This emphasis upon dialogism may well trouble some readers who will reasonably ask if it is so easy, or even possible, to *talk back to* a hegemonic discourse. By way of answer, one can first say that, in bourgeois society, most such vocabularies proceed not from loudspeakers but from one's family, friends, teachers, co-workers, and other, human agents, who can all be addressed in a more or less unproblematic way. As for those other, more "public" conduits of cultural hegemony, such as television advertisements, newspaper articles, political speeches, and novels, one must understand that the members of the Bakhtin Circle never abandoned the idea that cultural exchanges are most profitably thought of as conversations, even when, as in the cases above, indirection, mediation, and complication must inevitably intrude themselves. They repeatedly stress the point, however, that a conversational model of exchange between culture and subject makes sense only as long as we refrain from artificially separating ideology from individual psychology and remain mindful of the fact that all cognitive development, because it takes place *in* society, is at least partially dialogical (only partially, because children are especially prone to treat certain discourses as "authoritative" or unquestionable). Therefore, what we normally refer to as our private thoughts are, to a significant extent, a series of dialogues we pursue with ourselves because we cannot help but internalize the communicative process which links us to the world at large. We learn dialogically, says Voloshinov, and thus we think the same way, even when we are our own interlocutor:

Closer analysis would show that the units of which inner speech is constituted are certain *whole entities* somewhat resembling a passage of monologic speech or whole utterances. But most of all, they resemble the *alternating lines of a dialogue*. There was good reason why thinkers in ancient times should have conceived of inner speech as *inner dialogue*. These whole entities of inner speech are not resolvable into grammatical elements (or are resolvable only with considerable qualifications) and have in force between them, just as in the case of the alternating lines of dialogue, not grammatical connections but connections of a different kind. These units of inner speech, these *total impressions of utterances*, are joined with one another and alternate with one another not according to the laws of grammar or logic but according to the laws of *evaluative* (emotive) *correspondence, dialogical deployment*, etc., in close dependence on the historical conditions of the social situation and the whole pragmatic run of life [Voloshinov's emphasis].[30]

If, then, Bakhtin "imagines the self as a conversation, often a struggle, of discrepant voices with each other, voices (and words) speaking from different positions and invested with different degrees and kinds of *authority*,"[31] it follows that our personalities are genuinely social constructions—just as social as ideology—and that, likewise, ideology has no work to do unless it constitutes or at least colors a good measure of the conversations that define our "individual" psyche. Once we see our psyches not as strongboxes within our skulls that have been penetrated by the pickaxes of ideology but as "borderline" phenomena existing and developing at a place between our bodies and the outside world,[32] then the sense in which the discursive practices of hegemony must necessarily be "answered" every day becomes clear, even if one never writes a letter to the editor or does not possess the right to vote. Similarly, the necessity for cultural discourses to respond to the diffused, infrequent, or fragmentary utterances they provoke is also underscored, since if they fail to keep current with the ever-changing nature of the innerly persuasive voices they have been partially responsible for creating, their level of "impletion" within individual subjects risks waning to the point where they become irrelevant. No discourses, whether they originate in ourselves, in advertising agencies, or in government ministries, are sent into the world without an implied return-address label: the content of all utterances is invariably shaped not only by what the speaker wants to say but by his knowledge of whom he is addressing; for the act of giving life to an utterance is inseparable from the act of anticipating some sort of response,[33] and therefore a good portion of our dealings with the world at large—including those discursive practices that attempt to shape our ends—take the form of dialogues. We are less often passive auditors than active interlocutors with our culture.

But all of this, it will be remarked, makes it sound as if hegemonic discourses issued from *individuals.* Indeed it does, and this defines one of the Bakhtin Circle's clearest points of contention with certain Foucauldian and new historicist critics. Just as we cannot let fly an utterance without its being implicitly addressed to *some* listener, even if she is conceived of as a figure merely typical of a certain class or class fragment, so too do we receive every utterance as coming from *some* speaker, even if, after hearing the discourse, we can only conceive of her in approximate terms: "in the absence of a real addressee [or speaker], an addressee [or speaker] is presupposed in the person, so to speak, of a normal representative of the social group to which the speaker [or listener] belongs," and "even though we sometimes have pretensions to experiencing and saying things *urbi et orbi,* actually, of course, we envision this 'world at large' through the prism of the concrete social milieu surrounding us."[34] As Voloshinov here reminds us, even hegemonic discourses have speakers—not, to be sure, the shadowy kingpins of vulgar conspiracy theories, but subjects themselves subjected to the discourses of their cultures in ways similar (but again, never identical) to ourselves: "every ideological product bears the imprint of the individuality of its creator or creators," though, of course, "even this imprint is just as social as are all the other properties and attributes of ideological phenomena."[35] Thus where Foucault asserts that "power is not built up out of 'wills' (individual or collective), nor is it derivable from interests,"[36] a Bakhtinian perspective would insist that, after all, *someone* writes advertising copy, political speeches, product labels, and popular jokes, even though these people will never be known to us and even though their productions are shorn of all ostensible marks of individual authorship and mass-distributed throughout the culture. The fact that hegemonic discourses do not arrive on our doorstep with a signature at the bottom does not prevent us from conceptualizing our agreement or resistance to such vocabularies in broadly conversational terms and aiming our response toward an imaginatively constructed human speaker or speakers whose words have reassured or disturbed us.

If pressed, no doubt many cultural critics would admit that this is so but in the same breath insist that it is at best a trivial fact, since what really counts are the large-scale discursive structures that "speak" the subjects they traverse, not the fact that a biological entity named Jones or Smith puts pen to paper in an office somewhere. In practice, however, maintaining a clear recollection that some form of individual human agency is inseparable from the production of hegemonic discourses is vital, since the suppression of this fact seems inevitably to engender a vision of ideology as a structure that, because it was not *built* by human ingenuity, cannot be *resisted* by the same force. Recall that Foucault himself insists that "individuals . . . are not only [power's] inert or consenting target[s]" but "the elements of its articulation" as well, that "they are the vehicles of power, not its points of application." Yet because this realization is unaccompanied by an understanding of the essentially conversational structure of discursive exchange, the result is that impossibly diffusive "power," which, belonging to no one and thus "circulating" at the behest and direction of influences that must remain forever unnamed, resembles a natural rather than a cultural phenomenon, as if it were a plague visited upon us from afar rather than a yoke we have fashioned—however gradually, collectively, and unmindfully—with our own hands. One can readily grant that ideological structures frequently perpetuate themselves by inducing us to aim our responses at inappropriate or wholly imaginary agents and yet still maintain that abandoning the concept of a cultural conversation altogether will only further mystify the circumstances of our subjection.

It should be clear from what has been said that within a Bakhtinian vision of the social field, change is inevitable, and purposive resistance to hegemonic structures can and will produce genuine effects in the world. Opposition is here too the child of hegemony but in a manner very different from that outlined in *Power/Knowledge* and its progeny. For Foucault, "power" inevitably fosters resistances to itself because of its ubiquity and nearly flawless efficiency (one is tempted to say "omniscience" as well), throwing seemingly obstructive boulders in its own path merely the better to mark such territory as it has already subdued. For Bakhtin, however, hegemonic discourses breed resistance precisely because they are to some extent inefficient and can never attain the totalizing power they often claim for themselves. Ideology hails us, but because it always slightly mispronounces our name or throws its voice toward a space we inhabited yesterday rather than today, it gives the lie to its self-proclaimed "authoritative" power and leaves itself open to attack. Individuals, even when properly conceived of as "subjects," are never "finalizable"—that is to say, they always retain a measure of freedom, which springs not from some mystical essence within human nature but from the fact that human beings are dialogically involved with the world in a way that no supposedly totalizing system can completely explain and no discursive practice can fully shape, for the factors that determine the next step in any dialogic exchange are too multitudinous to make predictions possible. The writers of dialogic novels understand or intuit this aspect of social life, insisting that "as long as a person is alive he lives by the fact that he is not yet finalized, that he has not yet uttered his ultimate word," and they therefore represent a protagonist "at his point of departure beyond the limits of all that he is as a material being, a being that can be spied on, defined, predicted apart from its own will."[37] In monologic novels, by contrast, we can guess exactly what a character is going to do next, for he or she has been simplified to the point that the author's central ideological deduction can readily telegraph his or her every intention. Such novels are often described by readers as "flat" for the simple reason that life as a whole is rarely monologic and almost always provides avenues from which to escape the variously imperfect panopticons reared by bourgeois culture.

Bakhtin's view of the prospects for effective resistance are perhaps closest to those put forward by neo-Marxists such as Raymond Williams and Terry Eagleton, who take pains neither to underestimate the ability of hegemonic discourses to make contingent social arrangements appear perfectly "natural" nor to overlook the cracks that inevitably appear in these facades of normalcy and can often be exploited. Williams, for instance, describes hegemony as "a whole body of practices and expectations," dispersed "over the whole of living: our senses and assignments of energy, our shaping perceptions of ourselves and our world. It is a lived system of meanings and values—constitutive and constituting," which fosters "practices [that] appear . . . reciprocally confirming," and thus constructs "a sense of reality for most people in . . . society, a sense of absolute because experienced reality beyond which it is very difficult for most members of the society to move, in most areas of their lives."[38] At the same time, however, he delivers the following, which sounds like nothing so much as a chastisement of certain new historicists half a decade before their arrival in force:

> It can be persuasively argued that all or nearly all initiatives and contributions, even when they take on manifestly alternative or oppositional forms, are in practice tied to the hegemonic: that the dominant culture, so to say, at once produces and limits its own forms of counter-culture. There is more evidence for this view (for example in the case of the Romantic critique of industrial civilization) than we usually admit. But there is evident variation in specific kinds of social order and in the character of the consequent alternative and oppositional formations. It would be wrong to overlook the importance of works and ideas which, while clearly affected by hegemonic limits and pressures, are at least in part significant breaks beyond them, which may again in part be neutralized, reduced, or incorporated, but which in their most active elements nevertheless come through as independent and original.[39]

Like such neo-Marxists, Bakhtin never loses sight of the fact that it is inherently falsifying to view any culture synchronically, that no hegemonic structure can ever be perfectly fitted to the partisan task of the day because it at all times contains within itself "residual and emergent" elements as well as "dominant" ones.[40] Hegemony thus resembles a literary genre in the sense that it always presents itself to us in a form which, far from being tailor-made to the job of subjection at hand, has rather been haltingly evolved across long expanses of time, a situation that places limits upon the ability of its discursive practices to convincingly explain the status quo as "just the way things have to be."

If we now turn to assessments of which, and to what extent, literary texts can aid in fostering resistance to hegemony, divergences between the two methodologies begin to emerge. "Literature," suggests Eagleton, "is the most revealing mode of experiential access to ideology that we possess. It is in literature, above all, that we observe in a peculiarly complex, coherent, intensive and immediate fashion the workings of ideology in the textures of lived experience of class-societies. It is a mode of access more immediate than that of science, and more coherent than that normally available in daily living."[41] As Tony Bennett has pointed out, such a formulation does not quite avoid the charge of essentialism, for it still posits a transhistorical "literary effect" which literature always and everywhere exhibits, even though Marxist criticism must intervene before it can be fully exploited as an antihegemonic tool. Thus guilty of introducing an "invariant set of formal properties which establish an eternal, ahistorical distinction between 'literary' works and other forms of writing," Eagleton's view is revealed as simply a more skeptical and sophisticated version of the Romantic notion that literary works are *inherently* oppositional, that there is something about the mere presence of aesthetic form which throws up challenges to the powers that be. To avoid this pitfall, says Bennett, one would have to *historicize* that hitherto mysterious feature of the text or genre amenable to Marxist treatment, seeing it not as something all literature shares but as "the product of the formal properties of one form of writing that is distinguishable from others historically in terms of the forces and constraints which bear upon it."[42] Happily, this is precisely what Bakhtin accomplishes, for under his conception the subversive potential that Eagleton credits all literature with possessing is limited to the novel (or rather, to a particular subset within it), the specific cultural contingencies of whose birth and flourishing he is at pains to point out. The reasons that this particular genre's subversive potential is not fully shared by other forms can be briefly stated. Poetry, though fashioned like fiction from words that are always contested, always loaded with the accents and usages of diverse social groups, attempts to deny this fact about the language it employs. The poet, unlike the author of a dialogic novel, strives to make his words appear self-contained and self-sufficient, unproblematically equal to the task of conveying the one meaning he intends without the background noise of heteroglossia interfering. Thus, "the poet is a poet insofar as he accepts the idea of a unitary and singular language and a unitary, monologically sealed-off utterance" and insofar as he assumes "a complete single-personed hegemony" over the discourse he employs.[43] For excellent aesthetic—and historically explainable—reasons, poetry, especially lyric, disdains genuinely to acknowledge heteroglossia, a strategy that, whatever artistic advantages thereby accrue, causes it to resemble society's centripetal rather than centrifugal vocabularies, and thus limits its ability to reveal the ungrounded nature of all discursive practices, especially those that claim to be "natural" or "eternal."

Bakhtin, though less optimistic than various neo-Marxists when it comes to the *range* of literary works that can undermine dominant ideologies, remains much more sanguine than they about the *extent* to which those numbered texts can wreak subversion; for whereas critics of Eagleton's persuasion insist that the chinks in hegemony's armor must be sought within a work's elisions, evasions, and subtle silences, Bakhtin would have us believe that they are far more prominent and accessible for a number of reasons. In the first place, the novel is, historically speaking, a young and still-developing genre, and hence it "reflects more deeply, more essentially, more sensitively and rapidly, [social] reality itself in the process of its unfolding"[44] than do other literary forms, always maintaining a "zone of maximal contact with the present (with contemporary reality) in all its openness."[45] In the course of this effort to document the post-Cartesian world, the novel necessarily depicts the disparate languages spoken in society—that is, it not only represents objects in or aspects of the world in a particular language of its own, but takes other idioms, other patterns of speech, as its own object of representation: it depicts the heteroglossia endemic to modern societies. This task necessarily throws it into the midst of political conflict, for the various discourses thus depicted are never *merely* private or personal, as the above consideration of the psyche as a "borderline" phenomenon between the human organism and the ideological field makes clear. Rather, they are always the individual embodiments of ideological differences and political disputes, for "discourses cannot be tailored semantically to the expressive intentions of an individual without betraying the social fabric from which they have been cut."[46] Thus, every verbal exchange between two or more characters

sinks its roots deep into a fundamental, socio-linguistic speech diversity and multi-languagedness. True, even in the novel heteroglossia is by and large always personified, incarnated in individual human figures, with disagreements and oppositions individualized. But such oppositions of individual wills and minds are submerged in *social* heteroglossia, they are reconceptualized through it. Oppositions between individuals are only surface upheavals of the untamed elements in social heteroglossia, surface manifestations of those elements that play *on* such individual oppositions, make them contradictory, saturate their consciousness and discourses with a more fundamental speech diversity.[47]

This passage expands the assertion of Bakhtin's quoted in chapter 1 that "the speaking person in the novel is always, to one degree or another, an *ideologue*, and his words are always *ideologemes*.'"[48] Recall too from that discussion that, in "monologic" novels, one particular discourse— most often that of the narrator or of the author's fictional spokesperson— is presented as having a monopoly on truth, the other characters' languages being explained away as the result of some mental deficiency, biographical oddity, or other special circumstance. In dialogic novels, however, the differing idioms can interact in a mode of relative (though never complete) equality, whereby they begin to undermine each other's claim to be the only reasonable way of speaking about a particular subject.[49] In such a case, the mingling of perspectives demonstrates to the reader the cloaked weaknesses—and sometimes the unrecognized strengths—of the contending worldviews, exposing their hidden agendas and unstated presuppositions, and forcing us to recognize that the "meaning" of a discourse is as much dependent upon *who* speaks it as upon *what* is said. The dialogic novel thus accomplishes within a particular social class, class fragment, or occupational group what a thoroughgoing encounter with an alien culture does to a society as a whole, "undermin[ing] the authority of custom and of whatever traditions still fetter linguistic consciousness[,] erod[ing] that system of national myth that is organically fused with language, in effect destroying once and for all a mythic and magical attitude to language and the world."[50] The author who produces this kind of dialogic text—one that allows a number of the culture's disparate discursive practices to mutually interanimate one another—induces a skepticism about hitherto authoritative discourses and the unexamined boundaries of "acceptable" speech that simultaneously exposes the workings of hegemonic power and provides the reader with a sanction to add her own voice to the larger conversation that determines social change.

If Bakhtin is closer to the neo-Marxists than to Foucault or the new historicists in his evaluation of the *prospects* for resistance in the world at large, the *manner by which* dialogic novels supposedly undermine hegemony is nevertheless quite similar to the strategies pursued in texts such as *The Archeology of Knowledge* and *Power/Knowledge*. What Foucault there demonstrates is that ideology must not be envisioned as a tapestry that hides "the truth" from our eyes, a truth we will be able to discover once Marxism or some other form of the hermeneutics of suspicion has rent the folds of false consciousness and let in the light. Rather, we must abandon all notions about truth being "out there" in the world and instead conceive of it as being wholly produced by discursive practices. Hegemonic discourses do not hide the truth from us; they determine what *counts as* truth and falsehood in the world:

The important thing here, I believe, is that truth isn't outside power, or lacking in power: contrary to a myth whose history and functions would repay further study, truth isn't the reward of free spirits, the child of protracted solitude, nor the privilege of those who have succeeded in liberating themselves. Truth is a thing of this world: it is produced only by virtue of multiple forms of constraint. And it induces regular effects of power. Each society has its régime of truth, its "general politics" of truth: that is, the types of discourse which it accepts and makes function as true; the mechanisms and instances which enable one to distinguish true and false statements, the means by which each is sanctioned; the techniques and procedures accorded value in the acquisition of truth; the status of those who are charged with saying what counts as true.[51]

When discourses come into conflict, then, what ensues is not a battle between truth and falsehood but between differing sets of "truth-effects," differing ensembles of statements that are internally valorized by being labeled as "the truth." It is this kind of combat that Bakhtin seems to envision as occurring within dialogic novels, for not only does he insist that every character's speech reveals him as an ideologue—that "a particular language in a novel is always a particular way of viewing the world"—but also that a novel's plot records how each of these viewpoints "strives for a social significance."[52] That is to say, as the characters come into dialogic contact with one another, what we witness is a struggle to determine whose description of the world will prevail, whose collection of "truths" will become generally accepted. What Foucault thus calls the Platonic "will to truth" appears to be something close to a defining element in the dialogic novel as Bakhtin conceives it, for in the contest of words and wills that is played out between novelistic characters, the prize at stake is nothing less than the ability to remake the world in the image of one's own psyche[53] (itself largely a product of ideological determinants). And here the centrality of the distinction between dialogic and monologic texts for all questions of resistance comes clearly to the fore. In a monologic novel, the performance the reader takes in is much akin to that enacted when he reads a piece of Marxist criticism—"false" ideologies are gradually exposed and denigrated until, by the end, the one "true" view of reality, as embodied in the protagonist or the narrator, remains in unchallenged control of the social field. A dialogic novel, by contrast, is a much more Foucauldian affair, for even though the author may have a spokesperson in the text, "the author's consciousness does not transform others' consciousnesses (that is, the consciousnesses of the characters) into objects, and does not give them secondhand and finalizing definitions."[54] Here, the interpenetration and interillumination of social languages has exposed even the author's own viewpoint as interested, limited, and dependent upon its own blindnesses: its claims to knowledge, like those of all of the other viewpoints, have been revealed to be projections of power. Dialogic novels insist that there is always something more to be said, that all descriptions of reality can be challenged, and that the future is radically open—open because it cannot be predicted by any dialectical formula, only constructed through an ongoing conversational enterprise:

. . . the novel is not the bearer of a particular political content ("popular," "democratic," "progressive"); it is a means of imagining the truth that no rule is absolute. Its only politics is the insistence on the necessity of politics, of dialogical struggle, of power *as* struggle. To understand the radicalism of Bakhtin's thinking is to have seen that in his concepts the border of the sociopolitical has always already been crossed.[55]

But doesn't this vision of a social field wherein there are only interpretations and no facts lead inevitably to an extreme form of relativism, which in turn implies a political quietism? Bakhtin himself denies such a charge, insisting that the representation of dialogized heteroglossia "has nothing in common with relativism (or with dogmatism)," since "both relativism and dogmatism equally exclude all argumentation, all authentic dialogue, by making it either unnecessary (relativism) or impossible (dogmatism)."[56] Several things must be said, however, before this denial of dialogism's relativistic result can be reconciled with the account of its modus operandi given above. First of all, a dialogic approach is in fact *not* equivalent to relativism, if when employing the latter term one imagines a text that betrays *no* discernible preference for any of the various ideological positions it dramatizes. To claim that a novel is dialogic is not to declare that one could read it and remain unable to separate the protagonists from the villains, its mainly admirable from its mainly dubious characters. Were such a test required before a novel could be truly said to have dialogized its society's heteroglot languages, the number able to boast of the accomplishment might well be zero, as Wayne Booth, that relentless exposer of fictional rhetoric and admirer of Bakhtin, would undoubtedly attest.[57] Rather, what is required of a dialogic author is that she so structure her text that each of its voices, including her own, encounters the others in a manner that exposes its lack of a totalizing, unanswerable competence. And this operation does not entail artificially hobbling one's own horse before the race begins but rather extending sympathetic energies to the extent that, when each character speaks, we are able to understand his ideological perspective as if from inside his own head, not from some privileged point of spectation above the fray.

The above is a far cry from claiming that there is nothing to choose between the virtuous and the vicious (however the socially constituted psyche of the author conceives of those categories), for to assert that all viewpoints are, in both senses of the word, *partial*, is not to bar oneself from *preferring* one to another. Readers of dialogic novels may come to recognize that no character's moral-ideological ensemble is grounded in the fabric of the universe, but there will always be pragmatic reasons for choosing—often with violent emotions—one above another. For instance, it is not at all contradictory for someone holding to a Foucauldian or a dialogic or any antifoundationalist view of "truth" to object to a certain cultural practice or ideological position because it is "cruel," since to do so is to advance no claim about cruelty being an essential evil that nature shudders at or that the gods abhor, but rather to state that one would desire—perhaps passionately desire—to live in a society where kindness rather than cruelty was the rule, a disposition that could be justified by any number of arguments about public and private welfare. Surely this is a case, like countless others, in which our pragmatic preferences have life-and-death consequences. The knowledge that our truths are only perspectives does not therefore keep us from choosing among the latter, since they, being all the truth we have, will materially shape the world we must inhabit. The word "dialogic," then, far from heralding a polity in which all things are allowed, implies rather that there is always something genuine, frequently something crucial, to converse or argue about (though it would be a mistake to think that only disagreement can be dialogic);[58] and thus those who fear that Bakhtin's dialogism, like Foucault's archaeologies of discourses, will lead to paralyzing relativism, are most likely attempting to defend their own monologic and totalizing discursive practice, however dedicated to "liberation" they believe that practice to be. As Bakhtin well understood, relativism and dogmatism have more in common than is usually acknowledged.

Richard Rorty, in his discussion of those figures whose influence has helped steer twentieth-century philosophy away from the search for totalizing structures of thought, describes them as eschewing certainties and instead sharing an appreciation for "the power of redescribing, the power of language to make new and different things possible and important—an appreciation which can be attained only when one's aim becomes an expanding repertoire of alternative descriptions rather than The One Right Description." This open-ended process through which competing voices each offer their own articulation of reality, no one of which can claim to have pronounced the last word and no one of which is beyond being questioned, challenged, and subverted, describes quite closely what is alleged to occur when the differing social languages within a dialogic novel are put into play. Rorty himself sees many similarities between the practices of such figures and the activity of novelists, ranking Proust along with Nietzsche and Freud as representative figures in the shift of temperament he applauds. When it comes to explaining why the watershed occurred when it did, however, he seems strangely at a loss:

For it somehow became possible, toward the end of the nineteenth century, to take the activity of redescription more lightly than it had ever been taken before. It became possible to juggle several descriptions of the same event without asking which one was right—to see redescription as a tool rather than a claim to have discovered essence. It thereby became possible to see a new vocabulary not as something which was supposed to replace all other vocabularies, something which claimed to represent reality, but simply as one more vocabulary, one more human project, one person's chosen metaphoric.[59]

For anyone exposed to Bakhtin's thought, it cannot help but seem reasonable that one contributory factor in this change was the rise and triumph during the previous two hundred years of the novel, that genre whose intermittent but influential stagings of dialogism may well have helped direct Western thought in antifoundationalist directions. Not that this feature was spontaneously generated between cloth covers: the novel rose along with capitalism and urbanization in part because those historical factors forced together previously insulated social groups who possessed a myriad of differing ideological vocabularies, thereby creating the acute sense of heteroglossia upon which the novel draws its sustenance.[60] If, as some claim, capitalism carries within itself the seeds of its own destruction, it may not be too much to suggest that those seeds first began to sprout in the guise of that literary genre most closely associated with the rise of capitalistic formations. Rorty, at any rate, sees novels as an important tool in the building of a more humane society. Pain, he reminds us, is "non-linguistic," and for this reason "victims of cruelty" and "people who are suffering" do not possess "much in the way of a language. That is why there is no such thing as the 'voice of the oppressed' or the 'language of the victims.' The language the victims once used is not working anymore, and they are suffering too much to put new words together." Thus it falls largely to the novel, with its imaginative yet socially grounded redescriptions of the world, to perform the work that all of the now-untenable foundationalist conceptions of a common human nature were once supposed to perform—that is, to give a voice to those who go unheard, to "sensitize [us] to the pain of those who do not speak our language."[61] What Bakhtin allows us to appreciate with redoubled clarity is the fact that certain novels have been doing just this since the birth of the genre,[62] for his writings illuminate those formal potentials through which the novel consistently maintains "a deliberate feeling for the historical and social concreteness of living discourse, as well as its relativity, a feeling for its participation in historical becoming and in social struggle[, a focus upon] discourse that is still warm from that struggle and hostility, as yet unresolved and still fraught with hostile intentions and accents."[63] By dramatizing the battle between social languages, the novel allows the losers as well as the winners to have their say; by consistently pointing out that no ideological vocabulary is anything but contingent, it anticipates the day when the vanquished will rise again in strength; and by highlighting the dialogic nature of all social intercourse, it reminds us that cultural miscegenation is the rule and that no hegemonic claims of purity, originality, or totality are ever to be believed.

No doubt the linking of Rorty with Bakhtin has led some readers to definitively conclude what they have long suspected—that this chapter is nothing more than an attempt to reintroduce liberal humanism under an obfuscating guise of fashionable jargon. Rorty, after all, is a self-confessed liberal (though of a special, skeptical sort), and the affinities between his notions of the novel's role in social change and those I endorse are proof positive that I am, with the help of Bakhtin, promoting a variety of bourgeois reformism which cannot help but concede that novels are largely useless in undermining the liberal subject, if not chronically complicitous in constructing that gentleman—a charge I can imagine being leveled by both neo-Marxists and neo-Foucauldians. Indeed, those in the latter camp will no doubt point back to Bakhtin's heteroglossic catalog of "social dialects, characteristic group behavior, professional jargons, generic languages, languages of generations and age groups," and so on, and declare that they simply make fundamentally different assumptions about such a social panorama than do critics who work in the Bakhtinian mode. Whereas those who like to speak in terms of heteroglossia and dialogism wish to perceive actual diversity and conflict in this welter of voices, (some) new historicists understand that, whatever the surface turbulence, all of those vocabularies add up to the same unconscious panegyric to the notion of the autonomous bourgeois individual; and thus, whatever it is Bakhtinians think they've found in novels, it isn't any form of resistance worthy of the name. This, of course, is a popular rhetorical maneuver with a long pedigree: you think there is cause for optimism, but I see a level deeper and know there isn't, which means that you are naïve, unserious (pessimists being always more serious than optimists), and an unwitting dupe of the status quo.

The answer to this charge can lie only in the practical application of

Bakhtinian strategies of reading that constitute the following pair of chapters. In them I attempt to demonstrate that the dialogic energies within what are conventionally considered to be two of the most "conservative" Victorian novels are in fact capable of offering subversive challenges to central bourgeois orthodoxies, challenges that have implications somewhat beyond the usual parameters of liberal incrementalism. The chapter on *North and South* will show how the dialogue between the classes that Gaskell petitioned for so stridently in *Mary Barton,* when actually and honestly depicted, calls into question the possibility of interclass cooperation and even interclass understanding, both vital mainsprings of that cultural apparatus by which the bourgeois state perpetually defers radical political change. In the chapter dealing with *A Tale of Two Cities,* the entity put at risk by dialogism will be nothing less than the liberal subject himself, for we shall see that despite the novel's heated denunciations of revolutionary Paris, compared with bourgeois London, its intense concern with dialogue as the basis of a just civil society reveals both regimes as equally repressive, thereby subverting the central liberal assumption that the individual and not the group must remain the basic building block of a rational civilization. In presenting these interpretations, I will by no means be arguing that *North and South* and *A Tale of Two Cities* are, in defiance of long critical consensus, thoroughly radical documents. There is a great deal in both texts that is indeed conservative, that closely echoes the hegemonic discourses of their time; but they are not therefore *seamlessly* collaborationist, and as we shall discover, it is precisely in their enactments of those structural potentials toward which Bakhtin directs our attention that their oppositional countercurrents can be observed.

CHAPTER SIX

Interminable Conversations:
Social Concord in Mary Barton
and North and South

✳

It is a well-entrenched critical commonplace that of Elizabeth Gaskell's two industrial novels, *Mary Barton* (1848) is considerably more "subversive" of authoritative bourgeois discourses than is *North and South* (1855). Indeed, time and again one finds readers basing their preference for the former novel on frankly political grounds while in the same breath conceding that, formally, the later-written is clearly the more impressive example of narrative art. In a typical move of this kind, Raymond Williams declares that *Mary Barton* is, in its early chapters at least, "the most moving response in literature to the industrial suffering of the 1840's," a fact that makes it more "interesting" than *North and South*, even though "the integration of the [other] book is markedly superior."[1] Echoing these sentiments is Enid Duthie, who feels that *Mary Barton*, because it "interprets the cry of a submerged population, is more absolutely original" than *North and South*, though, again, "the latter is wider in scope and far superior in construction."[2] According to such readings, Gaskell's second tale of industrial life suffers in comparison to her first because it is less sympathetic to the plight of the workers and less critical of the Manchester "masters" and bourgeois political economy. Williams, fleshing out his complaint against *North and South*, finds that while "Margaret [Hale's] arguments with the millowner Thornton are interesting and honest, within the political and economic conceptions of the period," the "emphasis of the novel, as the lengthy inclusion of such arguments suggests, is almost entirely now on attitudes *to* the working people, rather than on the attempt to reach, imaginatively, their feelings about their lives."[3] Indeed, we know from Gaskell's own correspondence that in *Mary Barton* she had "represented *but one* side of the question"[4] and that in crafting *North and South* she

was in part responding to the accusations of bias toward the workers that
the earlier novel had occasioned. It would seem, then, that the more structurally coherent text is also the less oppositional—that, at least in the industrial portion of Gaskell's oeuvre, there is an inverse relationship
between novelistic craft and cultural subversion.

What I intend to argue, however, is that this generally accepted view
of the texts stems from an inadequate sensitivity to the dialogic nature of
North and South, as compared to its predecessor, and that this dialogism
in fact allows the later novel to undermine certain "authoritative" middle-
class discourses in a way that *Mary Barton* cannot, despite the earlier
book's admittedly more graphic depictions of working-class misery and
squalor. As we shall see, to throw a Bakhtinian light upon this pair of texts
is to expose an irony that in turn supports Bakhtin's descriptions of dialogism's ability to destabilize hegemonic social vocabularies. To put it succinctly, *Mary Barton* makes a desperate plea for dialogue between the
workers and masters, firm in the belief that this conversation will reveal
to all parties the truth of a central tenet of bourgeois orthodoxy: that the
interests of all classes are ultimately the same and that class conflict is
therefore always counterproductive. When, however, the characters of
North and South are represented as following this advice with enthusiasm,
the result is a genuinely dialogic encounter that calls the whole notion of
a concord among the social orders into serious question; once the contest
of conflicting voices begins in earnest, the possibilities for a cessation of
the class war come to seem more and more remote, and the middle-class
dream of all stations pulling together for a common good appears to recede
amid a welter of antithetical languages.

That important segments of the Victorian bourgeoisie conceived (or
wished to conceive) of class interests as so constituted that a gain for one
meant a gain—eventually—for all, can be seen in nearly every middle-
class imagining, fictional and otherwise, of the contemporary industrial
scene. From Dickens's dystopian Coketown to Carlyle's and Ruskin's
pseudomilitary conceptions of the ideal factory, cooperation among the
orders, not competition, is depicted as the road to national salvation; it is
the foundation upon which all of the particular schemes of Victorian liberal reformism are built. Class conflict, though it holds out the delusive
promise of immediate amelioration for the workers, will in the end only
lead to disaster by severing what, if properly understood, must be seen as
a single organism merely possessed of different parts, as a tree has its roots,
branches, and leaves, none of which can thrive alone. Gaskell, that "em-

inently bourgeois woman,"[5] is herself very quick to sound this fundamental principle of middle-class social thought, claiming in her preface to *Mary Barton* that the novel was born of her reflections upon the "unhappy state of things" existing "between those so bound to each other by common interests, as the employers and the employed must ever be" (37).[6] Later, the text's narrator, a being not overly given to direct intrusions, is willing to step forward in order to reinforce the point: "Distrust each other as they may, the employers and the employed must rise or fall together. There may be some difference as to chronology, none as to fact" (221).

Of course what makes this idea sound not merely naïve but suspicious to modern ears is our awareness both of the paternalism hidden within all the talk of teamwork (there is no question as to who will be captain and who will man the oars) and of how the coherence of the entire conception depends upon the unspoken assumption that the class system will remain pretty much in the same configuration indefinitely. My purpose, however, is not to chastise Gaskell with the scourge of historical hindsight but to illustrate the way in which her fidelity in reproducing the disparate and contending social vocabularies of Manchester ("Milton-Northern") leads her, in *North and South*, to create a text that is, with respect to the bourgeois ideal of an entente among the classes, less complicitous with her society's dominant discourses than it is generally given credit for being.

Any discussion of *North and South*'s cautious dialogism must begin with Gaskell's earlier novel of Manchester life because, according to *Mary Barton*, all that prevents masters and men from seeing the relationship between the classes in the proper bourgeois manner is, quite literally, a lack of verbal exchange. When, toward the middle of the book, a situation develops in which the millowners, feeling increased competition from abroad, attempt to get the workers to take lower wages, the hands balk at the suggestion and threaten a strike. The narrator, rather than chastising the masters' willingness to further stint their employees or questioning the larger principles of political economy that seem to demand such hard measures, fully endorses the manufacturers' offer, for while she admits that their purpose is to "beat down wages as low as possible," she also asserts that "in the long run the interests of the workmen would have been thereby benefited," since Manchester would soon enjoy a competitive advantage. What the industrialists *are* taken to task for is their unwillingness to communicate the workings of the marketplace to their underlings. Rather than stooping to the indignity of explaining themselves before rough and ignorant hands, "they stood upon being the masters" and "did not choose to make all these facts known." The result of the owners' determination not to "be bullied [or] compelled to reveal why they felt it wisest and best to offer only such low wages" is that "class distrusted class, and their want of mutual confidence wrought sorrow to both" (220–21).

When the strike eventually arrives, the Manchester capitalists are criticized once more—but again, *not* for their refusal to compromise on wages but for their aversion to stating "openly [and] clearly, as appealing to reasonable men, . . . the exact and full circumstances, which led [them] to think it was the wise policy of the time to make sacrifices themselves, and to hope for them from the operatives" (232). It is easy to see from such passages how well established the bourgeois ideal of a *concordia ordinum* is within Gaskell's imagination. The "fact" that all social strata share a common interest is so reasonable and self-evident that if the state of trade is merely explained properly, if all mistaken notions of a millowners' conspiracy are cleared up by frank discussion, the logic of class cooperation will then automatically take over and induce even the hungriest workers—and the text has already graphically described their distress—to accept even less. Under such a conception the problems of laissez-faire economic arrangements are shifted from primary to secondary sites—that is, the trouble with industrialism is not perceived to be the economic distance between masters and men, but the fact that this distance prevents them from communicating properly and thereby keeping the big picture—we all hang together or all hang separately—in front of everyone's eyes.

If the bourgeois masters are faulted by the text for remaining mute, the government seems, at the first encounter, to come under attack for being hard of hearing. When John Barton is picked by his union to travel to London as one of the delegates presenting the Chartist petition to Parliament, there arises "pure gladness" in his heart at the prospect of being "one of those chosen to be instruments in making known the distresses of the people" (127). His ears full of a Babel of advice from his fellow workmen, he replies that his only purpose will consist in "just speaking out about the distress, that they say is nought" (130). Upon his return, however, we are informed of "the political news of the day: that Parliament had refused to listen to the working-men" (141). Barton himself is fatally embittered at the treatment the delegation has received: "It's not to be forgotten or forgiven either by me or many another; but I canna tell of our downcasting just as a piece of London news. As long as I live, our rejection that day will bide in my heart; and as long as I live I shall curse them as so cruelly refused to hear us; but I'll not speak of it no more" (144–45). Every avenue of communication now choked off, Barton is driven to express himself through the barrel of a gun.[7]

This would all seem clear enough, were it not for the oddly ambiguous passage that inaugurates this section of the text, a passage wherein the genesis of the delegation's pilgrimage is recounted:

An idea was now springing up among the operatives, that originated with the Chartists, but which came at last to be cherished as a darling child by many and many a one. They could not believe that the government knew of their misery; they rather chose to think it possible that men could voluntarily assume the office of legislators for a nation, ignorant of its real state; as who should make domestic rules for the pretty behavior of children, without caring to know that those children had been kept for days without food. (127)

The tone here seems to insinuate that the hands are being naive in their estimate of the government's knowledge of, and implied complicity in, their plight. At first, this seems to darken the Parliamentarians even further, making them appear callous and cynical. I imagine, however, that Gaskell has just the opposite purpose in mind. When we recall that the millowners' sin is not the creation or perpetuation of a cruel system of economy but rather their failure to explain it adequately to the hands, we can more easily see the above as a nervous attempt to interpret the closed ears of Parliament as merely another version of the closed mouths of the manufacturers. Yes, they know of the workers' plight, but like the masters, they can't do anything about it; thus their refusal to *hear* becomes merely a symptom of their rank-proud refusal to *explicate*. This maneuver therefore has the double effect of blunting a potentially radical indictment of the government while at the same time diagnosing their behavior as springing from the same potentially curable lockjaw so prevalent in Manchester. Parliament's refusal of the Chartist petition was, after all, a historical fact, and Gaskell, having chosen to include it in her novel, must finesse it into a moral blunder that her liberal Christian outlook can number among the forgivable and correctable. The important point remains, however, that a lack of communication is again cast as the villain preventing the classes from perceiving and pursuing their mutual interests.

This diagnosis of political laryngitis can be seen nowhere so clearly as in Job Leigh's interview with the old industrialist Carson at the novel's end, for there—even though penury and wealth are brought into prolonged and vivid juxtaposition—conversation is the only coin the owners are urged to dispense more liberally. Job reminds the master of the suffering of the poor but insists that what "hurt [Barton] sore, and rankled in him," even more than his poverty, was the fact that the rich "kept him at arm's length, and cared not whether his heart was sorry or glad; whether he lived or died,—whether he was bound for heaven or hell. It seemed hard to him that a heap of gold should part him and his brother so far asunder" (456). Job is not really interested in disputing Carson's assertion that the business cycle "depends on events which God alone can control" (456), and readily admits that there may be no cure for starvation wages and sudden layoffs. What he insists *is* indispensable to maintaining social harmony, however, is some form of sincere speech: "If we saw the masters try for our sakes to find a remedy,—even if they were long about it,—even if they could find no help, and at the end of all could only say, 'Poor fellows, our hearts are sore for ye; we've done all we could, and can't find a cure,'— we'd bear up like men through bad times." Thus, it is not so much the *content* of the conversation as its mere *existence* that will speed the reconciliation of the classes, for, declares Job, "if fellow-creatures can give nought but tears, and brave words, [the operatives] will take [their] trials straight from God" (458).

Given this ability of verbal exchange to act as a balm irrespective of the message it delivers, it is little wonder that Job's interpretation of the conference he is then engaged in is much rosier than Carson's, since the latter is still a typical member of the class that, mostly due to misplaced pride, does not recognize the almost magical healing power—not to mention the practical utility—of a voice in dialogue: "You say, our talk has done no good. I say it has. I see the view you take of things from the place where you stand. I can remember that, [and] when the time comes for judging you, I sha'n't think any longer, does he act right on my views of a thing, but does he act right on his own. It has done me good in that way" (458–59). Job is "right," of course, for his words, in combination with Carson's continued suffering, eventually have their effect upon the elderly mill-owner, and he too comes to hope that "a perfect understanding, and complete confidence and love, might exist between masters and men; that the truth might be recognized that the interests of one were the interests of all." Note here that the *concordia ordinum* is to be brought about not by way of a tangible improvement in the workers' lot, nor by any burden-sharing on the part of the masters, but through a better circulation of information about the inevitable and irremediable brutalities of the system, through the "confidence and love" that only "educated" (460)—in the sense of "properly informed"—workers can feel toward their well-intentioned betters. Since such a view prevails, it is little wonder that Gaskell refuses to enumerate the "many . . . improvements now in practice in the system of employment in Manchester" which Carson has supposedly instituted since the time of the book's writing; for as we have seen, they really need have nothing to do with anything but ever increasing amounts of verbiage, even if this only takes the form of impotent apologies.

In light of all that has been said above, it might seem unfair to "accuse" *Mary Barton* of being less dialogic than *North and South*—after all, how can a text that sets out to depict a community suffering from a dearth of communication be expected to portray a "sufficient" amount of dialogue?[8] Such a question, however, confuses the conventional definition of "dialogue" with Bakhtin's much richer conception of the term. What renders Gaskell's first industrial novel less subversive of bourgeois dogma than her second is not its relative lack of represented speeches between characters of different classes, but rather the fact that the utterances of its workingmen are framed in such a way as to engender a one-time-only response rather than an ongoing social conversation. What I mean by this can be seen clearly from the above account of Job's meeting with Carson. In order for different social languages to interilluminate each other—a process in which those voices championing the *concordia* would be dialogically challenged, shown to be socially constructed rather than merely "natural" or "commonsensical," and thus rendered less "authoritative" (i.e., hegemonic)—the discourses involved in the exchange must be represented as meeting in an atmosphere of *contingency*, a fluid field of engagement where each utterance, whether a question, a demand, a panegyric, or a cry for help, moves the addressee to shift his ground and respond from a slightly altered ideological position. But we can see that this is just the kind of negotiation that *Mary Barton* has been insisting is not necessary, for both Barton and Job demand a merely *generic* reply—any answer will do as long as it is broadly sympathetic. If nearly any combination of soothing words will immediately end the social contest and usher in a general consensus, as both Job and the narrator insist it will, then all hopes of a truly dialogic exchange are stillborn. The same sort of short-circuiting is observable in the millowners' earlier refusal to explain market mechanisms to the hands, for there the narrator states precisely what it is they need to say in reply and how that reply will almost certainly put an end to any more speech that might make anyone uncomfortable or force one to rethink a habitual stance. The explanation of the business cycle, like the "poor fellows" declaration that Job yearns for, is not so much a genuine conversational answer as a formula or spell that it is necessary to utter only once because it carries within it an ungainsayable finality. Thus, what Gaskell presents us with is a situation in which something like "the ultimate word of the world and about the world"[9]—or at least about this corner of it—is well within the grasp of her characters, and the looming presence of this final and finalizing utterance alerts us that the depiction of dialogism, and the productively contingent exchanges that might spring therefrom, is not one of the text's priorities. Thus, while it is still true to say that *Mary Barton* is urging the residents of Manchester to engage in more frequent verbal parleys, it clearly envisions such exchanges as being easy, dovish, and short.

The monologic nature of the text also can be perceived in the about-face performed by John Barton. Originally intended as the work's central character, Mary's father is allowed to speak his mind freely in its first half, even when his sentiments run counter to those endorsed by the narrator. He is, for instance, permitted to sow doubts about the very raison d'etre of Gaskell's literary project by exclaiming, "Don't think to come over me with the old tale, that the rich know nothing of the trials of the poor" (45). Such outbursts, along with his powerful indictments of the squalor in which the operatives live and the obliviousness with which the rich daily pass it by, render him not only an articulate spokesman for his class but a decided voice of skepticism concerning the workability of any *concordia ordinum*, for his biblical rhetoric and bitter asides seem to presage revenge rather than reconciliation. If, however, the text Barton animates eventually fails to fulfill the promise of dialogism that he seems to embody, it is decidedly not because of the notable scarcity of his conversations with Carson and the other masters. True, his infrequent confrontations with the city's ruling class make for a stark contrast to the Higgins–Thornton relationship in *North and South*, but to emphasize this point would be to commit the double fault of again equating Bakhtinian dialogue with the sheer number of words exchanged and of not allowing Gaskell to dramatize her chosen theme: the lack of communication between masters and men. It is important to recall that in a dialogic novel it is not necessary that the characters themselves understand or even perceive the mutually enriching contest of social languages they each help to create (though this often occurs and increases the dialogic quotient by its presence); it is only required that the reader perceive it, for we are usually privy to more voices in a text than any one character ever can be. No, what goes far toward rendering Gaskell's book monologic is that we readers must endure the spectacle of Barton's unique and oppositional voice merging with that of the bourgeois narrator's as the end draws nigh, a process that also qualifies the text for a place in Lennard Davis's list of "normative" novels wherein protagonists move from being "one of them" to "one of us."

As Gaskell fashions her final act, Mary's father is not only physically debilitated by the murder he has committed—returning to Manchester a "wan, feeble figure," a "haunting ghost" (412), and an "automaton" (422)—but his characteristic social accents have been exchanged for those of a man far less destabilizing to middle-class conceptions of the social contract. In the novel's concluding chapters he asserts that both "masters and men, all alike cared no more for minding [biblical] texts, than [he] did for th' Lord Mayor of London," and that the union's call of "Stand up for thy rights, or thou'lt never get 'em" (440) is as far from the true prescription for a better life as the callous indifference of the millowners. As Igor Webb puts it, "the character who returns to the stage of the novel with Barton's name is not John Barton but a cardboard imposter: the Barton who returns, drained and repentant, is wholly Gaskell's puppet and no longer a voice with its own integrity."[10] Recall that Bakhtin emphasizes how difficult, almost contradictory, the challenge is for an author who would keep her narrator and characters in dialogic tension with one another, claiming that it entails finding one's own discourse "in intimate contact with someone else's" while "yet at the same time not fus[ing] with it, not swallow[ing] it up, not dissolv[ing] in itself the other's power to mean," for only thus will the other's voice "retain fully its independence as a discourse." He then adds: "To preserve distance in the presence of an intense semantic bond is no simple matter."[11] The paradox Bakhtin speaks of is that of a writer granting relative autonomy to her own literary creation, a maneuver easier to perform and sustain in a novel's first chapter than in its last, where the pressures encouraging ideological closure operate at full force. Gaskell wishes us to see the purgatory of Barton's guilt and repentance as sufficiently scourging to work a sea change, but the new tack he takes is too patently convenient, and the resulting harmony of voices seems thin and forced, exposing quite clearly the political temptation to which the author has succumbed. Things will be different in *North and South*, for there we shall discover that the voices of the protagonists remain, relatively speaking, their own to the last, and that we exit the book with the sound of lively contention still fresh in our ears.

Mary Barton's monological qualities assume their true importance only when we understand how intimately they are tied to the text's endorsement of the middle-class notion of a *concordia ordinum*. What both the demands of the workers for a merely generic reply from the masters and the swift conversion of the once implacable Barton implicitly proclaim is that a reconciliation of the classes is a consummation potentially near at hand and decidedly easy to come by. Consider: if the only sacrifice demanded of the owners is that of the pride of rank that stops their mouths, and if the simplest act of explanation or expression of sympathy will almost immediately extinguish the operatives' anger, then the reconciliation of the classes is not, to invoke Wordsworth, "A history only of departed things, / Or a mere fiction of what never was" but rather "a simple produce of the common day," which merely requires that the masters "speak of nothing more than what [they] are."[12] A new Manchester—one whose class relations are characterized by organicism rather than antagonism—hangs poised every minute above the angry streets like a ghostly double, awaiting only the "Open Sesame!" that will bring it rushing into the full flower of being. Thus we can say that characters' speech in *Mary Barton* is at the same time peculiarly powerful and yet radically unanchored; it is almost magically endowed with the ability to transform the world, although— and perhaps because—its own roots in the reality of Manchester's power relations are ultimately portrayed as nonbinding. A good way to describe *Mary Barton*'s conception of one language's ability to influence another is to label it catastrophist, since at almost any moment a single utterance can wipe out the existing world of discourse and replace it with a new and better one; to insist that *North and South* is infused with a more evolutionist view of the word's potential force is another way of saying that the later novel is the more responsibly dialogic of the two.

Given this study's general focus on the tensions between ideology and novelistic form, it may strike some as odd that nothing has been said about the infamous cohabitation within *Mary Barton* of a novel of social realism and a domestic melodrama. This split between the first half's preoccupation with the industrial milieu and the second half's "escape" into Jem's trial, with its last-minute rescue and sentimental clichés, has been a source of readerly dissatisfaction for decades. In recent years, however, several powerful feminist readings have begun to rehabilitate Mary's struggle toward domestic happiness by insisting that, after all, nothing is quite so political as the hearth, and that Gaskell's investigation of supposedly "private" issues may be seen as the heart of her attack on the the public weal of Manchester.[13] I find such readings largely persuasive and would locate *Mary Barton*'s most jarring discontinuity not in the radical differences between the plots of its first and second halves, but in the incompatibility of its vivid representations of working-class misery with the static, *merely* verbal remedy that is supposed to both usher in and then constitute the reconciliation of the masters and hands. After witnessing such scenes as those that occur in the Davenports' cellar or being told of Barton's ravenous encounter with Mrs. Hunter on her shopping trip, the purely semantic solution Gaskell proffers cannot but seem grossly inadequate.[14] Such suffering cannot be balanced by words that issue in no deeds, and explanation and sympathy are bound to seem like cold comfort after the text's reiterated juxtapositions of the millowners' abundance with the workers' destitution. As one critic puts it, Gaskell "is literally seeing more than she can finally declare in her role as mediator between the classes. Sympathy, observation, imagination is at war with all of the inherited, half-considered attitudes by which one class regulated its conduct to another."[15] I bring this up because it is precisely *Mary Barton*'s convincing representations of squalor that are cited when readers pronounce it more "subversive" than *North and South*. One understands what motivates such claims, but still they are troubling in that they seem to suggest that the strongest link in a novel may be synecdochically expanded to stand for the whole, instead of being seen as embedded in a larger narrative context by which it is constituted and which it in turn helps to construct. The scenes of starvation in *Mary Barton*, however masterfully depicted, are surrounded by a work which attempts to convince us that the remedy for such calamities is a quasi-magical verbal exchange that will instantly change every mental attitude while leaving every material structure intact (one is tempted to call it a "neutron-bomb solution," though one might as easily label it a typical Victorian "change of heart"). Thus, although it is true that Gaskell's later novel contains fewer and less harrowing set pieces of distress, it is worth investigating whether the engagement of voices that is also depicted as possessing the ability to ameliorate misery in *North and South*'s Milton-Northern may not in the end seem less frivolous and falsely comforting than that which promises instant deliverance in Manchester.

In 1850, a date falling between the publication of her two industrial novels, Gaskell writes to a friend that "we all *do* strengthen each other by clashing together, and earnestly talking our own thoughts and ideas. The very disturbance we thus are to each other rouses us up, and makes us more healthy."[16] This notion of verbal exchange, when compared to that put forward in *Mary Barton*, is most notable for its failure to posit any sort of quick resolution, for its implication is that explaining ourselves will not be enough to end any given dialogue, that most interlocutors are more likely to be "disturbed" than convinced by our divergent views. The phrase "makes us more healthy" also seems to argue against speedy victories for one side or the other, since it suggests that opposition will lead one to rethink and therefore strengthen one's own position rather than to capitulate to the unanswerable arguments of an opponent. All in all, the passage intimates that dialogue, though intrinsically improving, is no cure-all for dissension or incompatible ways of viewing the world; it will have its effects, but it will constitute an ongoing, perhaps interminable process. It is this new note of skepticism that will ring out all the louder in Gaskell's second attempt to dramatize Manchester's labor relations, though at times the author will seem unaware that she is sounding it.

At first encounter, *North and South* appears purposefully designed to put *Mary Barton*'s recommendation about the salutary effects of men and masters speaking plainly to each other into effect. We can say this because the novel is saturated with talk between representatives of different social strata, discussion following discussion, argument succeeding argument, in a debate that pits the different languages of workers, millowners, and the genteel middle class against one another in a multisided battle of contradictory outlooks. However, it is precisely in this great *volume* of conversation that we can begin to see how dialogue between the economic orders in *North and South* conforms more closely to the conception put forward in Gaskell's letter than in *Mary Barton*; for if the debates never let up, then clearly the earlier novel's prophecy of easy compromise and quick consensus is not being fulfilled. And it is not that the citizens of Milton-Northern fail to listen properly to one another—indeed, the characters frequently lend an ear more patient than the reader's—but that when they have finished listening, they almost always answer back with objections, countervailing views, and expressions of dissatisfaction, which in turn prompt yet more attempts at persuasion. W. A. Craik approximates the later text's crucial difference from its predecessor when he states that "most of the conflicts in the novel are . . . unresolvable. Just as in *Mary Barton* [Gaskell] saw her duty to pose the problem honestly, but not [to] provide the answer, if she saw no practicable answer, so here she goes further, presenting problems that are not even reducible to questions."[17] Throughout *North and South* the middle class utters the magic incantations that the author's earlier novel assured it would move mountains, only to discover that their reputedly wondrous properties have fled.

We can begin to appreciate Gaskell's shift from a facile to a tough-minded view of the social conversation by examining an exchange between Mr. Hale and William Higgins, a parley that begins in a manner designed to bring the goal of a *concordia ordinum* readily to mind. The prospects for the dialogue seem ideal: for his part, Hale treats "all his fellow-creatures alike," and so "it never enter[s] his head to make any difference because of their rank," an attitude that in turn draws out "all the latent courtesy" (227)[18] in the millhand. Their talk begins on the topic of religion but soon passes on to the relations between labor and capital. Higgins, as an avid union man, believes that strikes are an effective tool for raising wages, which draws a demurral from Margaret's father: "About the wages. . . . You'll not be offended, but I think you make some sad mistakes. I should like to read you some remarks in a book I have." It appears as though Higgins is about to receive the irrefutable explanation of political economy which *Mary Barton* advocated, but it is then that we learn the surprising news that he has already heard it, that a former employer once gave him a book setting out "how wages find their own level, without either masters or men having aught to do with them; except the men cut their own throats wi' striking, like the confounded noodles they are" (229). Higgins asserts that he was not convinced, though Hale insists that if the text informed him "that the most successful strike can only force [wages] up for a moment, to sink in far greater proportion afterwards, in consequence of that very strike, the book would have told [him] the truth" (230). The workman's objections, however, go beyond the tome's central thesis, for the treatise spoke of capital and labor "as if they was vartues or vices; and what [he] wanted to know were the rights o' men, whether they were rich or poor." Higgins says he is "not one who think[s] truth can be shaped out in words, all neat and clean, as th' men at th' foundry cut out sheet iron," for "some bones won't go down wi' every one. It'll stick here i' this man's throat, and there i' t'other's." Thus, whereas Hale takes the book's message as gospel, the workman will concede only that "it might [tell the truth], or it might not" since "there's two opinions go to settling that point" (229–30). Just previously, during their talk on religion, Hale responded to Higgins's question of whether his religious skepticism had given offense in the following manner: "None at all. You consider me mistaken, and I consider you far more fatally mistaken. I don't expect to convince you in a day,—not in one conversation; but let us know each other, and speak freely to each other about these things, and the truth will prevail" (227). The same tentative, unresolved atmosphere adheres to this conversation as well, and the talk soon turns to other aspects of unionism with no man the clear persuader of the other.

This episode undercuts *Mary Barton*'s claims of an easily attainable reconciliation of the classes in two ways. In the first place, Higgins's deep doubts concerning the supposedly immutable truths being promulgated makes it clear that simple clarity is not enough, or rather that "clarity" is a word which means different things in different social languages. Implicit in the earlier novel's immanent *concordia* is the notion that all classes speak basically the same tongue and that any utterances of truth and sympathy the owners can formulate, provided they are clear and sincere by middle-class standards, will be sufficient to satisfy even the most brutalized denizens of Manchester. Thus *Mary Barton*, which on the whole is no less faithful to the actual rhythms and sounds of working-class speech than is *North and South*, somehow forgets its own orthographic rigor when promoting the singular act of explanation that is to end all strife, for it frames that class-bound utterance as appealing to all ears equally. Here in Milton-Northern, by contrast, even the most eloquent and heartfelt speech may need to be thoroughly transposed before it can cross class lines, for, as Carol Landsbury remarks, "understanding" in *North and South* "is dependent upon circumstance and individual vision, and what is reality for one is fiction for another."[19]

To pursue this first point a little further, we can turn to the odd encounter of the millowner Thornton with Higgins over the idea of installing a common kitchen at the factory, for there too we observe the text's recognition that the different social languages of the industrial city may not be immediately mutually intelligible. The master, stopping by his workman's dwelling on a trivial matter, sees him preparing a "greasy cinder of meat" for dinner and comes up with a plan to buy food wholesale and let the hands pay a fair price for a decent meal at facilities of his own providing. As he explains to Mr. Bell, the proposal is "accepted" in a very roundabout way:

So I spoke to my friend—or my enemy—the man I told you of—and he found fault with every detail of my plan; and in consequence I laid it aside, both as impracticable, and also because if I forced it into operation I should be interfering with the independence of my men; when, suddenly, this Higgins came to me and graciously signified his approval of a scheme so nearly the same as mine, that I might fairly have claimed it; and, moreover, the approval of several of his fellow-workmen, to whom he had spoken. I was a little "riled," I confess, by his manner, and thought of throwing the whole thing overboard to sink or swim. But it seemed childish to relinquish a plan which I had once thought wise and well-laid, just

because I myself did not receive all the honour and consequence due to the orig-
inator. (361)

It might be tempting to dismiss this as a small piece of comedy meant
to illustrate the pride and stubbornness of Higgins and perhaps of his employer too, but, given Gaskell's increased sensitivity in *North and South*
to the acutely differing angles from which the various social groups observe
the same objects and events, we can more properly see this as a practical
illustration of how any word's meaning in Milton-Northern is largely a
function of who speaks it. One way to describe the difference between this
conception of language and that prevalent in *Mary Barton* is to say that
Gaskell has, in her later novel, come to recognize something like the Bakhtinian distinction between a "sentence" and an "utterance."[20] Sentences
are both repeatable and largely detachable from their speakers, so if the
masters in *Mary Barton* will only explain themselves plainly, the workers
will immediately understand. In *North and South*, by contrast, the characters are depicted as producing utterances—that is, words whose meaning is shaped as much by the social position and strategic context of the
speaker as by the abstract rules of the language system. As far as Gaskell
is concerned, both the advice that Higgins gets from the book on political
economy and the suggestion he receives about the common kitchen may
be "true" and "good"; but the text insists that, because they are utterances
issuing from the ruling class and aimed at the ruled, they cannot be expected to mean the same things to their auditors that they do to their
speakers. Nor is this a simple matter of an "uneducated" working class
not yet understanding the Queen's English, for in order for Thornton to
make the slightest headway toward convincing his men that the classes'
interests are identical, he must do so in the neutral ground of the factory
dining room and employ some of the workers' own vocabulary: "If any of
the old disputes came up again, I would certainly speak out my mind next
hot-pot day. But you are hardly acquainted with our Darkshire fellows.
. . . They have such a sense of humour, and such a racy mode of expression!" (362). *North and South* has not by any means given up on the
concordia, but it admits on every page that the owners' task of effectively
communicating it to their hands will be a matter not just of earnest speaking, but of mastering a foreign tongue.

The second way in which the initial interview between Hale and Higgins
does its part to reimagine and defer *Mary Barton's* goal of a general reconciliation is by depicting social dialogue as a struggle in which political

positions are abandoned reluctantly if at all and in which movement toward agreement is incremental at best. Hale is the middle-class spokesman
that Higgins finds most palatable, and Higgins is the worker most ready
to listen; and yet the latter exits not just that particular encounter but the
book itself still suspecting that what the former calls religious and political
"truth" is merely a convenient excuse under cover of which those who
possess capital can oppress those who must sell their labor, that "state o'
trade" is "just a piece o' masters' humbug . . . to frighten naughty children
with into being good" (134–35). In this respect, the Hale–Higgins encounter is only one of many similarly constructed verbal duels throughout
the novel. Indeed, one of the most striking aspects of *North and South* is
that it is a book with many arguments but few winners, for time and again
the contest of voices ends on an ambiguous note that keeps the question
at hand in suspension.

Consider, for instance, the central discussion of paternalism between
Margaret and Thornton in chapter 15, which pits the latter's self-serving
concern for his workers' "independence" during their off-hours against
the former's more intrusive vision of Christian duty, and which also ends
with no clear victor and no changed minds. Now, anyone who has read
the whole of *North and South* plainly understands that the narrator's (and
the implied author's) views are much closer to Margaret's than to Thornton's, but this fact does not interfere with the text's dialogic fairness, as
Catherine Gallagher attests: "we are repeatedly given other versions of the
action . . . foreign to Margaret's point of view. Some of these other viewpoints, moreover, subvert the assumptions shared by Margaret and the
narrator. . . . Indeed, as we survey Gaskell's integrating techniques, we . . .
see that the novel provides a running ironic commentary on its official
ideas."[21] And not only does the millowner hold his own ground, but the
doubts he sows about Margaret's ignorance of industrial concerns are allowed to stand unchallenged, in part because the narrator refrains from
making any partisan remarks, but also because the heroine has been depicted from the very first page as a character who, as a stranger from the
South suffering under a good many erroneous opinions about Darkshire
life, has a great deal to learn. Furthermore, tone of voice and physical
carriage are frequently colored in ways that nurture dialogism. Here and
elsewhere, for instance, the heroine's petulance and unearned assumption
of right lend the opinion Gaskell would endorse—the owners' obligation
to act as stewards toward their men—no help at all. Thus, according to

Rosemarie Bodenheimer, "it would be a mistake to read these dialogues as abstract position papers which are meant to be 'won' by one view or another. The social dialogues are dramatic—that is, truly novelistic—scenes in which the pressures of personal history can be heard, and the contradictions inherent in positions felt. The coalescence of personal and social vision is, in fact, closer to the point of the dialogues than is the content of the abstract statements."[22] Gaskell lays out Milton-Northern not as a lecture hall in which her heroine stands behind the podium but as a level playing field that yields unfair advantage to none and occasional hard knocks to the cherished opinions of all.

Some readers might protest that the Margaret–Thornton debates—as well as the later one between the millowner and the Oxford don, Mr. Bell—represent but poor examples of dialogism because, after all, they take place between fellow members of the bourgeoisie and never wander out of recognizably Victorian-liberal bounds. The truth is, though, that the number and frequency of *North and South*'s intraclass disputes does as much to defer the *concordia*'s arrival as those in which Higgins takes on his betters. Recall that in *Mary Barton* the middle class is entirely represented by the masters, who are individuated only by being placed into groups of soft- or hard-liners as regards the strike. This nearly monolithic cast is important to the book's great bourgeois hope because if Carson—presumably, like his son, one of the "violent party" (234)—can be transformed into an industrialist who sympathizes and explains, then a similar experience is implicitly within the grasp of one and all. *North and South*, by contrast, posits a polyvalent rather than a monolithic notion of class attitudes, depicting the bourgeoisie as split between characters associated with its more "domestic" virtues and those embodying its economic dynamism, with Margaret's liberal Christianity and Thornton's muscular gospel of toil frequently chafing against each other. Thus the heroine and her suitor's relationship is rightly described as "one continued series of opposition[s]" (197), which even in its calmer moments can only merit the name of an "antagonistic friendship" (239). The novel's title does not, of course, point to the most important division within the book, but it does show up Gaskell's admission that there are subdiscourses within each class and that no one person or group can speak wholly and adequately for the panoply of bourgeois values. To the extent that the overall class positions of *North and South* are internally riven by argumentative dialects, the larger reconciliation between the middling orders and the workers is represented as an increasingly distant prospect, and any social progress as dependent upon a *series* of agreements or compromises or understandings, rather than—as in *Mary Barton*—just one.

Perhaps the most convincing instance of Gaskell's dialogism undermining her bourgeois convictions, however, involves the volatile topic of the union's tactics. Given Gaskell's well-known view of combinations, we fully expect to see vindicated Boucher's complaint that the unionists "may be kind hearts, each separate; but [that] once banded together, [they have] no more pity for a man than a wild hunger-meddened [*sic*] wolf" (155), or Margaret's assertion that their practice of shunning their uncooperative workmates is a "slow, lingering torture" that can only be described as a "tyranny" equal to that imposed by the masters (232). But surprisingly, once Higgins engages his voice in debate, the "fact" (by the book's lights) that union methods are unnecessarily cruel is swamped amid rhetoric that paints coercion as a justified and inevitable response, *not* to the local issue of the owners' silence, but to the more global and intractable one of the workers' degradation.

"Nay," said Higgins, "yo' may say what yo' like! The dead stand between yo' and every angry word o' mine. . . . And it's th' masters as has made us sin, if th' Union is a sin. Not this generation maybe, but their fathers. Their fathers ground our fathers to the very dust; ground us to powder! Parson! I reckon, I've heerd my mother read out a text, 'The fathers have eaten sour grapes and th' children's teeth are set on edge.' It's so wi' them. In those days of sore oppression th' Unions began; it were a necessity. It's a necessity now, according to me. It's a withstanding of injustice, past, present, or to come. It may be like war; along wi' it come crimes; but I think it were a greater crime to let it alone. Our only chance is binding men together in one common interest; and if some are cowards and some are fools, they mun come along and join the great march, whose only strength is in numbers." (232–33)

This impassioned and honestly self-critical reply (which all but ends the chapter that contains it) is not a direct denial of Boucher and Margaret's charges, but it seems to partially absolve the union all the same by shifting the ultimate blame for such cruel measures to the economic system as a whole, and by concomitantly historicizing a state of affairs elsewhere described as inevitable and immutable. Whereas John Barton ceases to speak halfway through his novel and then returns mouthing Gaskell's own sentiments, Higgins never ceases to be one of those creations who, in Bakhtin's words, are "not only objects of authorial discourse but also subjects of their own directly signifying discourse." Thus *North and South*, unlike *Mary Barton*, can claim to present "a plurality of independent and unmerged voices and consciousnesses, a genuine polyphony of fully valid voices."[23] Mr. Hale, paying tribute to the power of Higgins's argument, admits that "the Union in itself would be beautiful, glorious,—it would be Christianity itself—if it were but for an end which affected the good of all, instead of that of merely one class opposed to another" (233). This is a telling concession on the text's part, for if an organization that, in Victorian eyes, is *synonymous* with class conflict can so nearly approach the Irreproachable, then the voices that counsel struggle rather than reconciliation cannot be written off as emanating *entirely* from the caves of "error" or "ignorance" and therefore cannot be silenced by even the most thorough explanation of the dismal science. The subversive nature of Gaskell's refusal to show Higgins's pro-union stand decisively bested in argument is illuminated by John Lucas's remark that "what is unbearable to [the middle-class liberal] is the implication that the object of his sympathy himself knows what is for his good, because this entirely destroys *the calming vision of a single nation* [italics mine] which gives his belief in progress its moral justification."[24] As we shall see, by the end of the novel Thornton is listening to Higgins as often as he is telling him something—and listening not as an act of sympathy, but in order to be instructed himself.

Of course, Gaskell never consciously abandons the attempt to dramatize a reconciliation of the classes, and as the text nears its end, Thornton and Higgins are shown to be gradually coming together in a manner that the larger society is meant to take as a model for attaining the *concordia*. But even here the author avoids the political temptation succumbed to in *Mary Barton*, for these final dialogues are by no means "compromises" that dramatize some swift narrowing of class positions; rather, they are instances of the still-contending discourses interilluminating each other in ways that undermine the foundationalist pretensions of each without in any way homogenizing them. Master and hand do not agree on how power should be distributed or even on how to call things by the same names;[25] what they do begin to share is an ability to understand each other's vocabularies, exiting the book not as speakers of some universal social Esperanto but as polyglots who better understand the foreign tongue of the other without necessarily adopting that language's alien construction of the world. In other words, *North and South* is a truly *dialogic* novel—its endpoint being not facile agreement, but a hard-won mutual comprehension.

This process of tentative convergence gets under way when Higgins asks Thornton for work in order to feed Boucher's children; the former's bar-

gaining position is weak, since as a leader of the strike he has been black-
balled by the other millowners; but the only "concession" he makes almost
promises further confrontation: "I'd promise yo', measter, I'd not speak a
word as could do harm, if so be yo' did right by us; and I'd promise more:
I'd promise that when I see yo' going wrong, and acting unfair, I'd speak
to yo' in private first; and that would be a fair warning" (320). Thornton
at first refuses, but the lingering impression of the operative's unapologetic
self-respect leads him to change his mind. *His* offer, when made, sounds
almost like a firing in advance, but Higgins refuses to play down the tenets
of his unionism even as he accepts:

> "Yo' spoke of my wisdom this morning. I reckon I may bring it wi' me; or would
> yo' rayther have me 'bout [i.e., without] my brains?"
> " 'Bout your brains if you use them for meddling with my business; with your
> brains if you can keep them to your own."
> "I shall need a deal o' brains to settle where my business ends and yo'rs begins."
> (326–27)

As Bodenheimer remarks, the end of this conversation has "a tentative
openness"[26] about it, as do so many like it scattered throughout the novel.

From this point on, most of the "reconciling" dialogues between Thornton and Higgins are summarized rather than dramatized, but, interestingly
enough, *not* by the narrator, whose voice is seldom heard at any point in
the text, and who almost never indulges in the kind of explicitly partisan
"corrections" that appear in *Mary Barton*. ("I know that this is not really
the case" (60) begins a gloss upon John Barton's accusations against the
rich.) Instead, the two characters themselves recount to third parties what
is said, a technique that manages to keep the social distance between their
two discourses before the reader's eyes even though we don't hear the individual words. Higgins, for instance, offers the following synopsis to Hale:

> "And I reckon he's taken aback by me pretty much as I am by him; for he sits and
> listens and stares, as if I were some strange beast newly caught in some of the
> zones. But I'm none daunted. It would take a deal to daunt me in my own house,
> as he sees. And I tell him some of my mind that I reckon he's ha' been the better
> off hearing when he were a younger man."
> "And does he not answer you?" asked Mr. Hale.
> "Well! I'll not say th' advantage is all on his side, for all I take credit for im-
> proving him above a bit. Sometimes he says a rough thing or two, which is not
> agreeable to look at at first, but has a queer smack o' truth in it when yo' come to
> chew it." (339)

Passages like this also point up another relevant difference between
Mary Barton and *North and South*. In the former text, the idiomatic ex-

pressions of the workpeople are communicated to the reader alone, with footnotes alerting us to their long literary pedigree. Throughout the latter, however, it is the middle-class characters themselves who puzzle out the hands' vocabulary and attempt to understand how their language shapes their view of the world and vice versa. We have already observed Thornton remarking over his operatives' "racy mode of expression," and Margaret's conversations come to include "vulgar" words such as "knobstick" (237) as surely as her brother Frederick's letters begin to incorporate the Spanish spoken by his fiancée. And here again we can see the text's avoidance of facile optimism concerning the *concordia ordinum*, for these newly acquired phrases are never fully integrated into the bourgeois idiom of the Thorntons and Hales, being always spoken within implied quotation marks. (Listen again, for instance, to Thornton's use of " 'bout" in talking to Higgins.) Rather—and more modestly—they are at best windows through which the characters can see into adjoining social rooms they are unable to otherwise enter, for unlike *Mary Barton*, *North and South* sees no particular utterance, no matter how sincerely and sympathetically spoken, as capable of effortlessly breaching the sturdy partitions set up between competing social discourses.

The novel's finale offers us a hopeful yet principled and cautious display of dialogism in action. On the one hand, Thornton and Higgins are both gripped by a kind of fascinated excitement over how the mental landscapes of their antagonists are being progressively revealed to them. On the other, this heady feeling is tempered by a clear-sighted recognition that increased appreciation of one's opponent's positions does not necessarily bring an end to disagreement and strife. As one critic pithily phrases it, "the understanding between Thornton and Higgins is not . . . a sentimental 'reconciliation' in the sense of a cessation of hostilities," but more like "a Geneva Convention aimed at minimizing civilian casualties."[27] Indeed, when the projected results of old Carson's conversion are compared to the fruits made available by Thornton's more gradual revelations, Gaskell's shift from wishful thinking to something resembling realism becomes apparent:

And by-and-bye, he lost all sense of resentment in wonder how it was, or could be, that two men like himself and Higgins, living by the same trade, working in their different ways at the same object, *could look upon each other's position and duties in so strangely different a way.* And thence arose that intercourse, which *though it might not have the effect of preventing all future clash of opinion and action*, when the occasion arose, would, at any rate, enable both master and man to look upon each other with far more charity and sympathy, and bear with each other more patiently and kindly. (420, italics mine)

Thornton, pursuing the bourgeois dream of "attach[ing] class to class as they should be attached" and "cultivating some intercourse with the hands beyond the mere 'cash nexus,'" is anxious to change Milton's industrial arrangements in ways that will increase "actual personal contact" between master and man, which he describes as "the very breath of life." And yet, while believing that the end result of such efforts might be a city in which the owners and the hands "should understand each other better" and "like each other more," he insists upon labeling his reforms as "experiments" and confesses that he is "not sure of the consequences that may result from them." And when the MP Colthurst asks him the crucial question—does he "think they may prevent the recurrence of strikes?"—his answer seems directed not only at his interlocutor but at the whole tenor of *Mary Barton*'s much different conclusion: "Not at all. My utmost expectation only goes so far as this—that they may render strikes not the bitter, venomous sources of hatred they have hitherto been. A more hopeful man might imagine that a closer and more genial intercourse between classes might do away with strikes. But I am not a hopeful man" (431–32).

If there is anything remotely resembling a last word in this novel that so scrupulously tries to avoid such a thing, it is Thornton's cautionary note concerning the future of industrial relations, for the brief remainder of the story is taken up with getting the millowner and Margaret engaged. And while it must seem that the text as a whole *ought* to be more hopeful than the industrialist it has so clearly labeled as overly dour, the contest of voices in which he has participated—and continues to participate—gives us no genuine grounds to refute him. Yes, at the novel's end he and Higgins are talking to and learning from each other, but a central assertion of Gaskell's about what *kind* of conversation they are having is continually undercut by her text's dialogic honesty. The narrator implies near the story's close that a reconciliation of the classes is near at hand because at last Thornton and Higgins have been "brought face to face, man to man . . . and (take notice) out of the character of master and workman," where they can "beg[in] to realize that 'we have all of us one human heart'" (419). The dialogues themselves, however, clearly belie this claim even in the final chapters, for millowner and operative depart the text still speaking very much from within their class positions, still very much *in* character, despite their progress toward mutual understanding. Thus, the narrator's effort at tidying up notwithstanding, *North and South* remains to the end a text in which "there are no definitive statements about faith and society. It is not a tract that is being preached but an experiential process in a situation where a number of variant and frequently contradictory opinions fluctuate and contend."[28] At one level, Gaskell may want to pretend that the dialogic novel she created has ceased to exist and that soon—very soon—all of the characters will be speaking the bourgeois language of social concord. But what Thornton and Higgins are actually saying as the last page is turned, the tones in which they are saying it, and the way in which their utterances are being received suggest that their projected exchange beyond the covers of the book will be a contentious and lengthy one, in which competition, conflict, and misunderstanding will long impede that perfect reconciliation which the novelist so ardently wishes to bring about.

Now it is true that Gaskell felt rushed and cramped toward the end by the exigencies of publishing in *Household Words*, but this sense of inconclusiveness, this feeling that only the *pen*ultimate word has or can be spoken, is undoubtedly due not to editorial deadlines (the finale we have being much revised from its magazine form) but to "the stubbornly open presentation of character and social change in the main part of the story," to the fact that the author "dared to venture so much that did not lend itself to the demands of 'resolution' in the conventions of serialized fiction."[29] Gaskell's narrator, so long an unobtrusive presence in the novel, speaks up at the end only to betray herself as one of those who cry "Peace, peace!" when there is no peace.

In the final analysis, what the dialogism of *North and South* accomplishes is to throw the waters of skepticism over a crucial utopian strain in bourgeois ideology. As Fredric Jameson explains, texts that produce "false consciousness" and that offer a "symbolic reaffirmation of this or that legitimizing strategy" must do so by mounting their own "complex strategy of rhetorical persuasion in which substantial incentives are offered for ideological adherence." His central point is that these incentives "are necessarily Utopian in nature" because they offer a vision of *some* form of solidarity and community, even if it is only among members of an already dominant class.[30] It is possible to see something resembling Jameson's "utopian incentives" in *Mary Barton*, where a proposed concord of *all* of the classes is the mechanism by which the status quo of middle-class hegemony will be perpetuated, and where this *concordia* is to be ushered in by a one-time verbal exchange conceived as universally comprehensible, universally applicable, and therefore all-sufficient. Bakhtin, of course, would argue that such a notion should sit uneasily within any novel, since for him the genre is marked by its special sensitivity to the always plural, chronically conflicted, and never completely adequate or finalizing nature of actual social discourses. Novels, when they utilize their inherent capacities to register dialogism, will represent a world where there are many languages forever engaged in a cross-fertilizing conversation and where there is always something more to say. For Bakhtin, "all forms of utopian thought are understood as denying openness and the importance of daily creative efforts," and thus "utopia and the realist novel are traditional enemies" that have "frequently parodied each other."[31] Such is certainly the case in *North and South*, where utopian discourse is to be sought only in the easily dismissible wishful thinking of the narrator, while the bulk of the text—that is to say, its many dialogues between the classes—offers us a world in which "daily creative efforts" are everywhere required because all progress toward understanding is presented as incremental and difficult. Gaskell's second and final industrial novel denies the transfiguring Word of its predecessor and, almost in spite of itself, places before us a vista of the many small words—conflictual, ambiguous, as yet barely comprehensible—that must each be uttered on the long road to civil harmony.

And so the conventional judgment that *Mary Barton* is, by virtue of its graphic depictions of misery, a more "subversive" text than *North and South* needs to be reconsidered in the light of Bakhtinian prosaics. Armed with a proper understanding of dialogic structures, we can now see the limitations of conventionally Marxist assessments of Gaskell's texts. Take, for instance, Lucas's assertion that "the great *North and South* is the novel that never got written" because, whereas the book *we* have ends in reconciliation, everyone who reads it is "inevitably struck by an awareness of how men ought to be forced apart *in spite of* their feelings for one another; that class interests *have* to wreck personal relations."[32] Such a criticism arises from a political and literary theory that is predisposed to see Gaskell fail at constructing a site from which oppositional discourses may genuinely sound because that theory itself fails to properly credit the oppositional dynamic present *in potentia* in the novel as a genre: had Lucas's ears been more attuned to the dialogic nature of the text, he would have found that the finer novel of his imagination was in fact before him on the page.

One feels justified in making such a claim because, if *North and South* is much more pessimistic about the attainability of the *concordia ordinum* than its predecessor, it cannot help but decisively affect our assessment of the texts' respective ideological effects, for it must be remembered that both books were written for the express purpose of *bringing about that very reconciliation.* If middle-class readers of *Mary Barton* are meant to be horrified at the sufferings of Manchester's wretched toilers, they are also clearly meant to be consoled by the notion that a good, clear explanation spiced with sympathy will defuse any potential for violence in the situation by immediately lifting the scales from all eyes everywhere. But readers of *North and South*, although coming away with a less urgent sense of the destitution of the workers, nevertheless receive a far more circumspect message about the quick arrival of that harmonious day when the bourgeoisie can stop worrying about class conflict. Moreover, at the end of the kind of conversation between the orders postulated by Gaskell's later novel, it is implied that the middle-class interlocutor may bear little resemblance to the all-sufficient speaker he thought himself to be at the beginning. Carson changes—at least we are told he does—but only into the good middle-class citizen he should have been all along, for what he comes to see is that "the interests of one [are] the interests of all" (460). What we actually witness Thornton coming to realize, however, is that there exists in Milton-Northern another language altogether for describing the world, that this language deserves to be understood rather than dismissed, and that it is just as dear to its native speakers as his own vocabulary is to him. *Perhaps* he and Higgins will one day properly and completely comprehend each other, and then perhaps they can resolve their differences and make Milton-Northern safe for bourgeois hegemony; but *North and South* insists that transformation can begin only after the exhaustive, exhausting—and perhaps interminable—work of translation is well under way.

CHAPTER SEVEN

Individual versus Collectivity in
A Tale of Two Cities

*

A Tale of Two Cities often seems to be a novel written for the express purpose of defending a central tenet of middle-class liberalism—or rather, for the purpose of denouncing its opposite. What most horrifies Dickens about the revolution he depicts is not its violence but its assertion that the group, the class, the Republic—and *not* the individual—comprise, or should comprise, the basic unit of society. The guillotine is horrible, but more ghastly still is the idea that all personal claims must defer to those of the polity as a whole, that the minds and hearts of citizens must be always and everywhere laid bare to the scrutiny of the community, and that virtues and crimes, rights and responsibilities, inhere in groups rather than in individuals. Dickens's revulsion is not mysterious, since an underlying assumption of nearly all bourgeois discourses is the presence of a discrete human subject, primary and inviolable, whose self-responsible actions constitute both the starting point and the ongoing focus of the vast majority of economic, judicial, and religious practices. It must also be remembered that the notion of the sovereign individual played a crucial role both in nurturing the infant genre of the novel in the eighteenth century and assuring its triumph in the nineteenth, a symbiotic relationship whose mechanisms have been well understood for some time.[1] With the collectivist doctrines of the Jacquerie thus calling into question so much that was, for a Victorian like Dickens, the indispensable constitutive categories of his lived experience and his vocation, the author's angry and even panicked depictions of revolutionary Paris are easily explained.

There is, however, a political subtext within *A Tale of Two Cities* that works against its comforting and conforming demonizations of those who would overturn middle-class assumptions. And just as the employment of Bakhtinian strategies of reading helped to recast *North and South* as a more subversive work than it is usually given credit for being, a similar optic directed at Dickens's novel will reveal much that undermines and even contradicts its counter-revolutionary thunderings. The crucial difference between the two texts will lie in the fact that, whereas Gaskell's novel weakens authoritative bourgeois discourses by representing heteroglossia and enacting dialogism, *A Tale* does so by quietly debunking the idea that bourgeois society is more hospitable to either of those processes than the polity ruled by the Jacobins. What may at first seem odd about such a pronouncement is that, as any reader will attest, the author's agitation over the squelching of dialogue most forcefully emerges in the text's politically orthodox passages. For instance, Dickens obviously wishes us to conceive of the Revolution's leaders as communitarian ideologues who, in their desire to profoundly transform society, are guilty of stifling the individual human voice, of turning what should be society's many-sided conversation into a monoglossal chorus. Hence, the attention lavished upon the disturbingly undifferentia*ted* cries of the mob and the undifferentia*ting* pronouncements of the Republican zealots, all part of the author's intent to highlight the Tribunals' coerced erasure of each discrete subject's personal and inimitable language. With respect to the moral chaos that ensues when the individual is not permitted to find, express, and dialogically modify his own voice, the Dickens of *A Tale of Two Cities* and the Bakhtin who suffered under Stalinism are in close agreement:

> The enormous significance of the motif of the speaking person is obvious in the realm of ethical and legal thought and discourse. The speaking person and his discourse is, in these areas, the major topic of thought and speech. All fundamental categories of ethical and legal inquiry and evaluation refer to speaking persons precisely as such: conscience (the "voice of conscience," the "inner word"), repentance (a free admission, a statement of wrongdoing by the person himself), truth and falsehood, being liable and not liable, the right to vote and so on. An independent, responsible and active discourse is *the* fundamental indicator of an ethical, legal and political human being.[2]

Where the novel's interest in the voice and its possibilities for enjoying dialogism becomes politically subversive is in its depictions of the English protagonists and the kinds of lives they lead. By way of a reassuring counterpoint to Revolutionary Paris, Dickens appears to offer us a quirky and decidedly unreformed London, a metropolis that, despite its many failings (and perhaps because of them), is home to a liberal multiplicity of idiosyncratic discourses. But even though England may be in some sense a genial Babel, I would contend that its freedom from monologic tyranny does not, in the eyes of the text, make it a land safe for beneficent heteroglossic frisson—that, on the contrary, *A Tale* repeatedly attacks bourgeois culture as a realm whose citizens are often mutually unintelligible and even hopelessly mute, a failing that renders the interillumination of languages that is necessary to civil society nearly as rare an event in London as it is on the banks of the Seine. And I would further argue that the novel represents this soundless state of affairs as arising precisely from a hypertrophy of the doctrines of middle-class individualism. What we shall discover in due course is that the Paris of choric collectivism has an equally hideous mirror image in a bourgeois City of the Dead, an urban graveyard in which human voices are unable to penetrate the sarcophagi that surround each and all of the discrete subjects there interred and, furthermore, that this dire state of affairs opens a space wherein the text can gaze with sympathetic and even envious eyes upon the Republican ideology its authoritative discourse finds repugnant.

There has been, of course, much thoughtful comment over the past few decades on the subject of Dickens's unmistakable ambivalence toward the Revolution he depicts. George Woodcock, for instance, sees in the "vigor" with which the author depicts the scenes of Revolutionary violence a kind of vicarious retribution against the society that betrayed him in his youth: "in one self [Dickens] is there, dancing among them, destroying prisons and taking revenge for the injustices of childhood."[3] Others have interpreted it as the result of the author's fitful attempts to work out an overarching theory of history, or to adapt Carlyle's ideas on historical necessity to the needs of his fictional genre.[4] Some critics have even pointed out parallels between the methods of the Jacquerie and the literary techniques employed by Dickens himself.[5] This chapter, however, seeks to go beyond such discussions by illuminating a double or even universal ambivalence, for once we accord due weight to *A Tale of Two Cities'* concern with what we would today label dialogism, we shall come to realize that there is really less to differentiate Jacobin Paris from bourgeois London than at first meets the eye, the former being viewed as an experiment offering real possibilities for perfected human communication even as its demands for monologic regimentation render them stillborn, the latter similarly depicted as a society holding out the promise of dialogic interaction while in fact promoting only estrangement and isolation. The result will be a novel that not only both loves and hates the Revolution, but attacks the very foundation of the liberal state its authoritative discourse attempts to promote as the stable alternative to all of France's wrongheaded social engineering. Of course Dickens's dissatisfaction with his own society is hardly news either, but then *A Tale of Two Cities* is an unusual Dickens novel. It is one thing to mount a critique of one's society from within it or from within some ideal conception of what it should and might be. But to equate it with a regime that is supposedly its *and* the author's detested opposite, to accuse it of perpetrating precisely the same violence by other means, is quite a different and more perilous affair. Nor does the Revolution's temporal distance from Victorian England defuse the situation:

> What is realized in the novel is the process of coming to know one's own language as it is perceived in someone else's language, coming to know one's own belief system in someone else's system. There takes place within the novel an ideological translation of another's language, and an overcoming of its otherness—an otherness that is only contingent, external, illusory. Characteristic for the historical novel is a positively weighted modernizing, an erasing of temporal boundaries, the recognition of an eternal present in the past.[6]

What *A Tale of Two Cities* winds up finding in the past is the present by another name, a discovery that goes far toward countermanding its myriad "official" endorsements of bourgeois individualism.

Before we encounter the novel's subversive subtext, we should glance briefly at its "authoritative" condemnation of the Revolution. Here Dickens's middle-class fears concerning the status of the discrete subject precipitate out as lurid scenes in which the Parisian radicals attempt to merge individuals into larger conglomerations, and to thus homogenize what should be the diverse plenitude of society's voices. One technique the text employs in this regard is that of taking the Revolutionary government's organization of Paris by supposedly homogeneous "sections" a step further and relentlessly anthropomorphizing the district of Saint Antoine. As a "character," of course, the section is almost always depicted as a villain capable only of enunciating threats and bloodthirsty howls: "The hour was come, when Saint Antoine was to execute his horrible idea of hoisting up men for lamps to show what he could be and do. Saint Antoine's blood was up. . . . 'Lower the lamp yonder!' cried Saint Antoine, after glaring round for a new means of death" (249). Indeed, all of the Republic's citizens seem to move from one place to another as a single entity, and each time they produce a sound that is horrible precisely because it *approaches* human speech while forever remaining undifferentiated, inarticulate, and therefore unsettlingly subhuman. Instances here come quickly to mind: the echoing footsteps that merge the tread of suffering individuals into the thundering of a vengeful herd,[7] the "sea" and "tide" of the Revolutionary mob breaking over the walls of the Bastille, and especially the dancing of the Carmagnole, which announces itself as "a troubled movement and a shouting coming along" in which "five hundred people" become "five thousand demons" dancing to "no other music than their own singing" and "keeping a ferocious time that was like a gnashing of teeth in unison" until they "swoo[p] screaming off" (307). Taking his cue from Carlyle, Dickens depicts this interminable and collective war cry of the Revolution as a long-suppressed reaction to the equally sinister silence of "Monseigneur"—that other hydra-headed "character" who helped sow the whirlwind in the first place. He too stands for an entire class, though unlike the mob he expresses his power through the absence of speech, leaving it to his quivering underlings to "discours[e] with spirits" and to consider "whether they should foam, rage, roar, and turn cataleptic on the spot . . . for Monseigneur's guidance" (137). What distinguishes both pre- and post-Revolutionary France, then, is the absence of humanly individuated voices and the unwillingness or inability of those in power to engage in dialogue, for the ancien régime is just as deaf to cries of suffering and whispers of impending doom as the Tribunals are to pleas for mercy.

When members of the insurrectionist camp do manage to hold a conversation, the result is an equally defective verbal exchange, for the text gets a good deal of political mileage out of the conspirators' habit of referring to each other by the code name "Jacques"—indeed, when more than two plotters come together in a scene, Dickens deliberately makes it difficult to remember who is speaking:

"How goes it, Jacques?" said one of the three to Monsieur Defarge. "Is all the spilt wine swallowed?"

"Every drop, Jacques," answered Monsieur Defarge. . . .

"It is not often," said the second of the three, addressing Monsieur Defarge, "that many of these miserable beasts know the taste of wine, or of anything but black bread and death. Is it not so, Jacques?"

"It is so, Jacques," Monsieur Defarge returned. . . .

"Ah! So much the worse! A bitter taste it is that such poor cattle always have in their mouths, and hard lives they live, Jacques. Am I right, Jacques?"

"You are right, Jacques," was the response of Monsieur Defarge. (64–65)

Although some of these exchanges verge upon the comic, there is, from the Victorian standpoint, always a palpable air of threat about them, for this blurring of personality and agency always takes place amid talk of a violent conspiracy, thereby undermining the middle-class faith that guilt and innocence can be doled out in just portions to discrete and self-responsible subjects. These plotters eventually receive numbers, but, with the exception of the overtly sadistic Jacques Three, the effect is just the opposite of endowing them with distinct voices. At the storming of the

Bastille, for instance, we get the following call to arms, ostensibly from Defarge: "Work, comrades all, work! Work, Jacques One, Jacques Two, Jacques One Thousand, Jacques Two Thousand, Jacques Five-and-Twenty Thousand; in the name of all the Angels or the Devils—which you prefer—work!" (245). This merging of what should be discrete subjects taking (or at least betraying) responsibility for distinct actions into an undifferentiated mob is portrayed as one of the Revolution's most fearfully pernicious effects, for in a world of merely generic entities, the discriminations upon which bourgeois law depends simply cannot be made—the idea that "we are all equally guilty" is anathema to middle-class habits of thought.

This brings us, of course, to Madame Defarge. What makes her so famously sinister is her propensity to utter the names of groups on those occasions when bourgeois readers expect to hear only of individuals. When Darnay is arrested and flung into prison, for example, his defense rests upon his assertion that he is not *personally* responsible for the crimes either of the aristocracy in general or of his family in particular. Madame, however, speaking not of Charles but only of the Evrémondes, says that "for other crimes as tyrants and oppressors [she has] this *race* a long time on [her] register, doomed to destruction and extermination" (370, italics mine). Halting the slaughter at those who can claim innocence only for themselves and not their class strikes her as unsound, a conception whose logical conclusion the text is eager to point out:

"It is true what madame says," observed Jacques Three. "Why stop? There is great force in that. Why stop?"

"Well, well," reasoned [Monsieur] Defarge, "but one must stop somewhere. After all, the question is still where?"

"At extermination," said madame.

"Magnificent!" croaked Jacques Three. The Vengeance, also, highly approved. (369)

It is interesting to note that at one point Lucy—apparently intuiting the bent of Madame's mind in the heat of distress—appeals to her for mercy as a "sister-woman" as well as a wife and mother. But this bit of rhetoric, meant to mask a personal appeal in collectivist diction, fails to take in Madame Defarge: "We have borne this a long time. . . . Is it likely that the trouble of one wife and mother would be much to us now?" As Madame makes her way through the streets on her way to kill Lucy and the child, the narrator sums up that blind spot in her moral vision that the champion of bourgeois individualism cannot help but abhor: "It was nothing to her, that an innocent man was to die for the sins of his forefathers; she saw, not him, but them" (391). It is this mote, even more than the "red hue" of animalistic violence, that the narrator perceives in the eyes of the mob gathered round the bloody grindstone—eyes he wishes to "petrify with a well-directed gun" (292).

Having sampled Dickens's politically authoritative passages, we may now turn to the text's muffled discourse of subversion, for if the frenzied dancing of the Carmagnole can be said to synopsize the state of the individual's voice and its opportunities for civilized dialogue in Revolutionary France, there is an image that can be read as doing much the same thing for bourgeois England. Interestingly enough, this image does *not* depict the latter as a nation in which an unfettered people enjoy the fruits of free speech and dialogic give-and-take, and no doubt this is the reason it has long been considered a merely "anomalous" or "digressive" fragment of the text. I refer specifically to the "Night Shadows" passage, a striking meditation upon the impenetrable barriers separating man from man that has proved perennially troublesome to readers.

A wonderful fact to reflect upon, that every human creature is constituted to be that profound secret and mystery to every other. A solemn consideration, when I enter a great city by night, that every one of those darkly clustered houses encloses its own secret; that every room in every one of them encloses its own secret; that every beating heart in the hundreds of thousands of breasts there, is, in some of its imaginings, a secret to the heart nearest it! Something of the awfulness, even of Death itself, is referable to this. No more can I turn the leaves of this dear book that I loved, and vainly hope in time to read it all. No more can I look into the depths of this unfathomable water, wherein, as momentary lights glanced into it, I have had glimpses of buried treasure and other things submerged. It was appointed that the book should shut with a spring, for ever and for ever, when I had read but a page. It was appointed that the water should be locked in an eternal frost, when the light was playing on its surface, and I stood in ignorance on the shore. My friend is dead, my neighbour is dead, my love, the darling of my soul, is dead; it is the inexorable consolidation and perpetuation of the secret that was always in that individuality, and which I shall carry in mine to my life's end. In any of the burial-places of this city through which I pass, is there a sleeper more inscrutable than its busy inhabitants are, in their innermost personality, to me, or than I am to them? (44)

The relationship of this passage to the major concerns of the novel has struck many a critic as problematic. Some have sought to link it with the rest of the text merely by pointing out its similarities to Carlyle's practice of dramatizing the miraculous hidden within the mundane, and thus to account for it as yet another example of the literary influence of Dickens's occasional mentor.[8] A more ambitious explanation of its thematic significance is attempted by Catherine Gallagher. She, claiming that Dickens depicts the Revolutionary ideology as ruthlessly inquisitive in order to make his own, novelistic invasion of the private sphere appear benign by comparison, sees the passage as a reassuring statement that novelists are needed by modern society to overcome a "perpetual scarcity of intimate knowledge," despite the lines' melancholy ring.[9] Most critics, however, follow the lead of Sylvère Monod in simply seeing it as an anomaly. Monod, who posits several distinct narrators for *A Tale*, asserts that he who speaks this address is employing "the philosopher's *I*" and that such a device "is used for general statements, not in order to convey any impression of the narrator as an individual person."[10] J. M. Rignall agrees, insisting that "the brooding, first-person voice is never heard again in the novel," that the passage is at best awkwardly related to the scene which immediately follows it, and that it cannot be said to illuminate "the general condition of life as it appears in the novel."[11]

It is Rignall's contention that I specifically wish to take issue with, for I believe that there is in fact a broadly thematic resonance to the passage, a resonance which is crucial to the book's tentative likening of bourgeois individualism to its revolutionary "opposite." To begin with, it is significant that all of the critics mentioned above, whatever their varying degrees of bafflement or insight, call attention to the passage's tone, for it is that aspect of the "digression" which, I believe, can most quickly lead us into its involvement with the novel's subversive currents of thought. Although the adjectives used to describe this supposed fact concerning contemporary social relations are not explicitly derogatory, the atmosphere of the paragraph as a whole is distinctly—nay, poignantly—that of a lament. What clearly comes across is a deeply felt sadness and frustration before the impermeableness of the barriers between self and self—a despairing desire to merge the discrete and opaque personalities dictated by *Gesellschaft* and to enter a state of dialogue, communal knowledge, or even communal being. Reflecting upon the iron-clad separation of souls within the "great city" may indeed provoke wonder and awe—but it also clearly elicits a wish that things might be otherwise.

The imagery employed in the passage is also pertinent if we remember that the working title of *A Tale* was "Buried Alive," for the passage continually attempts to blur the distinction between life and death, presenting a portrait of urban existence as a kind of living entombment. Not only does the incommunicability of souls have "something of the awfulness, even of Death itself . . . referable" to it, but the narrator, in his quest for communication with his fellow beings, speaks of himself as looking into

"depths" for "glimpses of buried treasure." Furthermore, the deaths of
his friend, neighbor, and love are described as "the inexorable consolidation and perpetuation" of their isolated, living states—as if these people
are most true to their nature only after they have ceased to breathe. The
final sentence, in which the corpses in actual graveyards are declared to
be "sleepers" no more "inscrutable" than the town's "busy inhabitants,"
completes the equation of the living community with that of the dead.
What the narrator has accomplished here is graphically to portray the
"great city" as a metropolis in which everyone is virtually "buried alive,"
to depict a condition of society in which each citizen goes about his everyday offices—and even endures his supposedly most intimate moments—
enclosed in a sarcophagus of impenetrable individuality. As we shall see,
this damning critique of modern life inaugurates the subversive subtext
that dares to equate, as far as their ultimate *effects* are concerned, the
coerced sloganeering of the Revolution with the stifled solipsism of middle-
class normalcy—and that even propels some of the novel's protagonists
into a mimicry of the Jacquerie as a means of escaping from the "solitary
confinement" mandated by bourgeois individualism.

This last-mentioned gesture, wherein English characters begin to sound
curiously like Republicans, can be observed in the discourse of Jarvis
Lorry, a man who, on the surface, appears to embody everything that
Robespierre's France is not. This is brought home by the physical description of the banker's beloved Tellson's, an institution that embodies un-
swerving allegiance to a fusty—and exceedingly English—traditionalism.
Indeed, its partners' unashamed pride in its "smallness," "darkness,"
"ugliness," and "incommodiousness" (83) links the bank with the decidedly unreformed England of 1780 and allows it to function as a specifically
Burkean counterweight to the programmatic rationalism of the Revolution. Moreover, banking is a profession that in some measure depends
upon secrecy and opacity—states of being proscribed by the Paris Tri-
bunals—and that often serves interests opposed to those of the state. When
Lorry is sent to France late in the book, for instance, he sets about saving
what he can of his clients' property from the Jacobins' program of confis-
cation and nationalization.

And yet there are odd echoes of the Terror cheek by jowl with the comic
"Olde England" trappings of Tellson's. Lorry, though nothing but satisfied with his surroundings, seems to abide in a kind of prison, for he labors
over "great books ruled for figures, with perpendicular iron bars to his

window as if that were ruled for figures too, and everything under the clouds were a sum" (172). More graphically still, Tellson's is linked to the Revolution by its alarming proximity to the corpses of those executed by the state and the consequent violent intrusion of the political sphere into a previously sacrosanct domestic realm:

Your lighter boxes of family papers went up-stairs into a Barmecide room, that always had a great dining-table in it and never had a dinner, and where, even in the year one thousand seven hundred and eighty, the first letters written to you by your old love, or by your little children, were but newly released from the horror of being ogled through the windows, by the heads exposed on Temple Bar with an insensate brutality and ferocity worthy of Abyssinia or Ashantee. (84)

If Lorry's place of business appears in some ways to reflect the carceral and ensanguined conditions of Paris, his view of the relationship between his supposedly discrete self and the surrounding world often sounds like a comic version of Madame Defarge's pronouncements, for throughout the novel the banker repeatedly attempts to deny his individuality, always insisting that he possesses no "buried life" whatsoever and that all of his aims and desires are perfectly congruent with those of the institution for which he labors. In his first interview with Lucy, for instance, he begs her not to "heed [him] any more than if [he were] a speaking machine" (54). He then goes on to explain that all of his dealings with Tellson's customers are devoid of private emotional entanglements:

His [Manette's] affairs, like the affairs of many other French gentlemen and French families, were entirely in Tellson's hands. In a similar way I am, or I have been, trustee of one kind or other for scores of our customers. These are mere business relations, miss; there is no friendship in them, no particular interest, nothing like sentiment. I have passed from one to another in the course of my business life, just as I pass from one of our customers to another in the course of my business day; in short, I have no feelings; I am a mere machine. (54)

In such capacity does Lorry claim to turn his "immense pecuniary Mangle" with "no time for [feelings], no chance of them." Goaded by Carton about the way his loyalty to Tellson's seems to take precedence over any personal proclivities, the banker testily reminds him that "men of business, who serve a House, are not [their] own masters" and "have to think of the House more than [them]selves" (113). Indeed, when Lorry shakes hands, he does so "in a self-abnegating way, as one who shook for Tellson and Co"—a trait "always to be seen in any clerk at Tellson's who shook hands with a customer when the House pervaded the air" (172). "The House," of course, is both the shorthand name for Tellson's as a whole and the only title ever bestowed upon its director—touches that heighten the sense of the bank as a single organism, staffed only by a host of un-differentiated cells.

Lorry's relentless assertion that he gladly subsumes his own will into that of the firm "whose bread [he has] eaten these sixty years" (266)—the fact that he claims (and at times truly seems) to have no desires which can be distinguished from the collective aims of "the House"—clearly suggests a parallel with the Jacquerie. The banker, like the model citizen of the Revolutionary Republic, defines himself first and foremost as part of a collectivity and only secondarily as an individual. He lives out, in a comic mode, the creed that the president of the Tribunal attempts to instill in Dr. Manette: "As to what is dearer to you than life, [i.e., his family] nothing can be so dear to a good citizen as the Republic" (346). Related to this is Lorry's contention that he is a completely *transparent* being, the entire contents of whose mind and heart can be effortlessly read because they are writ large upon the public aspirations of the collectivity he serves. Now, as Gallagher points out, it is precisely the Revolution's adamant "demands for transparency" and its practice of the "universal watchfulness" (275) needed to ensure it that "the narrator finds particularly abhorrent," since, as the novel purports to demonstrate, such a state of affairs can be guaranteed only by "a whole population practic[ing] surveillance on itself, a surveillance that ultimately destroys."[12]

Here, then, a paradox clearly arises: the parallels enumerated above would, if one were judging solely by the narrator's authoritative posture, all appear to denigrate Lorry, but of course the banker's career emerges as anything but sinister. Indeed, as Albert Hutter rightly notes, Lorry seems to gain mobility, strength, and even renewed youth from his un-swerving devotion to Tellson's,[13] and no one can dispute the fact that his subsumption of self into the collective enterprise of the bank endows his life both with a beneficent purposefulness and (for all his talk of heart-lessness) an unproblematic sociality which that of *A Tale*'s main protag-onist signally lacks. But with so many ties to the dogmas of Paris, why should this be so? The explanation, I think, can be approached by recalling the Night Shadows passage, for if Lorry's immaculate "citizenship" within Tellson's associates his service with the totalitarian aspirations of the Tri-bunals, it also exempts him from residence in the "great city" depicted by that striking segment. In other words, Lorry's devotion to "the House" renders him largely devoid of the terrifying and impenetrable secrets pos-sessed by the denizens of that bourgeois metropolis of the prematurely buried, where the most significant fact about individuality is the profound deafness and utter opacity with which it confronts all attempts at genuine dialogue and sufficient understanding. If the revolutionaries of Paris are blind and intoxicated in their frenzied hurtlings, the inhabitants of the Night Shadows city are frozen in ice; and to the extent that the elderly banker inclines toward the practice of the former, he avoids the paralysis of the latter, as if the only place where a socially useful existence could be safely pursued were a point of unstable equilibrium suspended halfway between the text's two monoglossic regimes. The enveloping shackles of bourgeois orthodoxy thus partially cast off, Lorry is free to act as the novel's factotum of beneficence until Carton awakes from his own uncommunicative lethargy. Already Dickens's "digression" on the unknowable nature of his silent fellow citizens begins to stand forth as the emblem of a truly subversive structure of feeling.

In turning our attention to the novel's protagonist, we must follow an escape from the coffin of bourgeois individualism that leads through tragedy rather than comedy, and that we follow step by step as the narrative progresses. Indeed, when we first encounter Sydney, he appears to be the very epitome of the secretive and unfathomable individual lamented in the Night Shadows passage.[14] Darnay, his outward double, feels as if he is in "a dream" in his presence (114), and in fact no one else—not Lorry, certainly, or even Stryver—has much of a clue as to what he is really about. The primary reason for this, of course, is that throughout the novel's first third he quite purposefully evades dialogue, intending always to be misunderstood. The bitter, self-depreciatory ironies that pervade his speech are really intended only for himself, and this chronic tendency to become his own audience lends his conversation a solipsistic air even when he is supposedly in the interrogative mode:

"Mr. Darnay, let me ask you a question."
  "Willingly, and a small return for your good offices."
  "Do you think I particularly like you?"
  "Really, Mr. Carton," returned the other, oddly disconcerted, "I have not asked myself the question."
  "But ask yourself the question now."
  "You have acted as if you do; but I don't think you do."
  "*I* don't think I do," said Carton. "I begin to have a very good opinion of your understanding." (115)

It is not until his love-stricken confession to Lucy, which contains truths she "know[s he] would say . . . to no one else," that a genuine exchange occurs. Previous to this, his words are almost literally the mask he hides behind.

The larger political implications of Carton's opaque character and self-referential speech come to the fore as soon as we recall the work he performs, for as Stryver's "jackal" he enacts what can almost be termed a parody of the division of labor that upholds bourgeois capitalism. He and Stryver, it should be remembered, divide between them what should rightly be the labor of a single person, and furthermore, this "division" is anything but equitable—Carton performs the labor, Stryver garners the credit. Moreover, the very nicknames "jackal" and "lion" seem to replicate the social practices of Victorian society at large, heaping opprobrium upon the faceless who sell their labor, lauding the famous who purchase it. As Rignall—pointing to this same connection between unreadable character and exploitative labor relations—puts it, Carton's "gloomy estrangement . . . suggests the neurotic price that may be exacted by the aggressive pursuit of individual success, by the bourgeois ethos of individual endeavor in its most crassly careerist form."[15] Carton, then, though distinctly odd, is in a real sense a typical citizen of Dickens's nocturnal city of unknowable individuals: the victim of alienated labor, he too is "buried alive." Thus, if we now recall Lorry's attitude toward his "business" at Tellson's, so fraught with Revolutionary connotations, and contrast it with Carton's view of his own labors, the following conversation between Sydney and the banker takes on a new significance despite the former's evasions:

"And indeed, sir," pursued Mr. Lorry, not minding him, "I really don't know what you have to do with the matter. If you'll excuse me, as very much your elder, for saying so, I really don't know that it is your business."
"Business! Bless you, *I* have no business," said Mr. Carton.
"It is a pity you have not, sir."
"I think so too."
"If you had," pursued Mr. Lorry, "perhaps you would attend to it."
"Lord love you, no!—I shouldn't," said Mr. Carton. (113)

Carton possesses "no business" and further confesses that he has always "fallen into" his proper "rank," which he describes as "nowhere" (120). Now, since in Lorry's case it is precisely "doing business" that beneficently makes him as one with the collectivity of the House, Carton's having *no* business can be taken as yet another marker of his perverse (but socially endemic) isolation from all larger communities, an isolation that renders his life and labor meaningless.

With all of this in mind, I would like to suggest a reading of Carton's name that will perhaps prove more useful than the various scramblings of the author's initials attempted in the past. "Carton," in nineteenth-century parlance, refers to layers of paper that have been treated and pressed until they have attained the sturdiness of cardboard or pasteboard; the related word "carton-pierre" denotes a kind of paper-mâché used to imitate much harder materials, such as stone or bronze. Even more suggestive is the term "cartonage," by which archaeologists signified the layers of linen or papyrus that were pressed and glued together to fashion the close-fitting mummy cases of the ancient Egyptians. In light of what has been said so far, it thus seems plausible to see the name as an anxiously hopeful comment upon the protagonist's enforced estrangement from his fellow beings. On the one hand, it is a label that draws attention to his predicament of isolation amid a society whose creed of acquisitive individualism goes far toward turning all of its citizens into self-enclosed enigmas—or if you like, mummies in the nocturnal City of the Dead. Simultaneously, however, it seems to hint at the original flimsiness and permeability of those barriers, reminding us that what encloses and separates is merely a superfluity of material actually translucent, or gossamer calcified. The name, then, is one that both diagnoses the protagonist's moral ailment and hints at the availability of a cure.

As it happens, Sydney does eventually puncture the "carton" walls that close him off from the world; he does finally emerge from his sarcophagus of "cartonage." This is accomplished through his remarkable verbal and sartorial commingling with Darnay on the eve of his execution, a evanescent escape from the constraints of bourgeois individualism that is prepared for by the fact that Carton and Darnay bear a strong physical resemblance to each other. It is important to remember, however, that up until the time when the novel's main characters are all assembled in Paris, Sydney is at best a radically defective doppelgänger of Charles. In fact, early on, the former's "doublings" of the latter serve merely to emphasize the distance that separates them. When first juxtaposed at the trial, they appear "so like each other in feature, so unlike each other in manner" (108), and soon afterward Carton admits that he resents a mirror image who only serves to remind him "what [he has] fallen away from" (116). In England, Darnay appears as a close-dangling but ultimately frustrating possibility, his and Sydney's twinlike appearance suggesting that closer communion between men *should* be possible, the pair's mutual unintelligibility underscoring how difficult it is to achieve under prevailing circumstances. It is only later in Paris, when Carton determines to sacrifice himself for Darnay and Lucy, that the doublings become nearly perfect. Indeed, "doubling" is too pallid a word to adequately describe what goes on, for such a term still implies two separate identities, two discrete selves, whereas what actually occurs is more properly described as a veritable *merging* of two individuals into one, a fantasy of all-sufficient communication far beyond the capacities of any real-life dialogue.

The central irony that emerges from Carton's successful commingling with Darnay in prison is that Sydney's "cure" is effected in the shadow of the novel's explicit condemnation of the very practice which heals him, for while he participates in a process whereby one man is able to transcend the suffocating barriers of the bourgeois self, the Revolution's insistence that the same is to be done for *all* men meets with nothing but scorn. And here one can anticipate an objection: the obvious fact that Sydney and the Jacquerie see the annihilation of the conventional barriers between individuals as the means to ends that are diametrically opposed does not weaken this irony to the extent that one might initially suppose. Yes, Carton abandons his personal claims for the protection of middle-class domesticity (one might even say for the Victorian hearth, since Sydney's figurative descendants are to recount his story for generations) while the Paris Tribunal demands that the individual subsume himself into the polity in order to speed the flourishing of a world in which only groups will matter. But my point is that the former cause rests upon the foundation stone of bourgeois individualism, whereas the latter is committed to its destruction, and that Carton can ensure the safety of liberal society (in the form of the Darnays, Manette, Lorry, and Pross) only by temporarily violating one of its fundamental tenets. To put it another way, Carton can make the world safe for discrete subjects only by temporarily ceasing to be one himself and thereby blocking the plans of a regime bent on abolishing the entire concept of the discrete subject forevermore.

This contradiction between what Sydney is trying to accomplish and the way he goes about accomplishing it has an analog in the sometimes contradictory vocabulary of the narrator, whose middle-class outrage at the Revolution's anti-individualism is intermittently shadowed by a less critical, dissenting register. Most often, of course, *A Tale* treats the discourse of the Jacobins in a thoroughly monologic fashion, depicting it as a kind of social pathology that the reader may shudder before but whose claims to express valid human aspirations he need not trouble himself to answer. Occasionally, however, we come across passages in which the "official" (and polemical) bourgeois discourse seems to stand cheek-by-jowl with expressions of calm understanding and even of sympathy directed at the Parisians. Among these must be counted those well-known, fair-minded assessments of the wretched social conditions that first brought the Revolutionary ideology into being and then chafed it into monstrous form. There are others too, however, and they often arrive at unexpected times. Consider, for instance, the abrupt change in tone that occurs as the narrator describes the trial at which Manette's own testament is used, over the doctor's protest, to convict Darnay. At first he recounts with biting irony how the president of the Tribunal suggests "that the good physician of the Republic would deserve better still of the Republic by rooting out an obnoxious family of Aristocrats, and would doubtless feel a sacred glow and joy in making his daughter a widow and her child an orphan" (362). One can clearly hear in this passage the revulsion of a good Victorian— and yet, when pulling back to explain the scene as a whole, he unexpectedly informs us that "one of the frenzied aspirations of the populace was, for imitations of the questionable public virtues of antiquity, and for sacrifices and self-immolations on the people's altar" (362). If we are to understand that the citizens of Paris have hitherto merely been practicing "questionable public virtues," then it appears that Monod may be right about *A Tale*'s having more than one narrator. Be that as it may, these halting feints toward an omniscient voice that could be said to embody genuine ambivalence—coming as they do amid otherwise orthodox denunciations—seem to betray, as do Sydney's methods of rescue, the text's fitful remembering of bourgeois society's own propensity to stifle dialogism, its reluctant admission that the Revolution may stand to middle-class culture not as anathema but as *antidote*. On such a view, the approving depiction of Lorry and Carton as they repeatedly mimic the practices they are ostensibly trying to discredit and foil is only the most protracted and significant of the anomalies caused by this ideological instability at the novel's core. What keeps the pair's behavior from becoming an intolerable contradiction within the narrative is, I believe, a crucial qualification: this mimicry is allowed to manifest itself only in the realm of the comic or in that of strictly private life. And since we have already discussed Lorry's risible similarities to the collectivist regime he battles, we may now turn to Carton's own moral pilgrimage from the City of the Dead toward the Republic One and Indivisible, a journey undertaken not because of any public commitment on his part, but because of a nearly secret passion.

As Sydney pursues his famous midnight walk before the final Parisian trial, his steps are dogged by religious images, and he repeats "I am the resurrection and the life" continually to himself as he wanders. At one point, though, he pauses to sleep and, in a moment obviously fraught with

symbolic meaning, awakes to find an analogue of his life in the motions
of the Seine:

The strong tide, so swift, so deep, and certain, was like a congenial friend, in the
morning stillness. He walked by the stream, far from the houses, and in the light
and warmth of the sun fell asleep on the bank. When he awoke and was afoot
again, he lingered there yet a little longer, watching an eddy that turned and turned
purposeless, until the stream absorbed it, and carried it on to the sea.—"Like me!"
(344)

When one considers that Sydney's sacrifice of himself for Lucy's happiness
will necessarily thwart the collectivist wrath of the Revolution, this passage
reads curiously indeed, for, cutting across the obvious message concerning
Carton's lassitude giving way to action, there is the further hint that to do
so involves subsuming himself in a larger entity. One could perhaps suggest that he is being "absorbed" into the greater life of humanity at large
or into the Christian dispensation were it not for the quite programmatic
way in which "tide" and "sea" have been associated throughout *A Tale*
with the Revolutionary mob. The "strong tide, so swift, so deep, and certain," which now appears as Carton's "congenial friend" and into which
his life is "absorbed," may not partake of the violence of that which breaks
against the Bastille, but the provocative choice of simile cannot help but
alert us to a parallel between Sydney's path to personal salvation and the
Revolution's recipe for a secular utopia beyond the constraints of bourgeois
individualism.

    This hint of a parallel between Sydney's desideratum and that of the
Jacquerie is reinforced by a strange blurring of agency and personality
within the protagonist's dialogues as his plan of rescue unfolds. On the
evening after Darnay has been condemned, Carton urges Manette to try
his influence with the judges one final time. Lorry, watching the doctor
depart, opines that he has "no hope" that the old man will succeed. Carton
agrees and explains why he has sent him on what must be a futile mission.
What is striking about this passage is that since Sydney has already made
up his mind to replace Darnay upon the guillotine, but has not told the
banker of his plan, he and Lorry have two different individuals in mind
when they employ the pronouns "his" and "he":

"Don't despond," said Carton, very gently; "don't grieve. I encouraged Doctor
Manette in this idea, because I felt that it might one day be consolatory to her.
Otherwise, she might think 'his life was wantonly thrown away or wasted,' and
that might trouble her."
    "Yes, yes, yes," returned Mr. Lorry, drying his eyes, "you are right. But he will
perish; there is no real hope."

"Yes, He will perish: there is no real hope," echoed Carton. And walked with a settled step, down-stairs. (367)

This sharing of pronouns, causing momentary confusion about who is being referred to, is reminiscent of nothing so much as those passages in which Jacques speaks to Jacques. It is as if Carton had already ceased to be a discrete subject, his personality commingling with that of Darnay as he approaches his salvational moment.

This process of merging reaches its climax during the scene in Charles's cell, where the two, having already exchanged boots, cravats, coats, and ribbons, write what amounts to a joint letter to Lucy, Carton dictating as Darnay holds the pen. As the latter scribbles, Sydney gradually applies his hidden narcotic, so that we see Charles's individuality diffusing itself too, his consciousness drifting beyond its normal boundaries as he attempts to record Carton's sentiments:

"What vapour is that?" he asked.
"Vapour?"
"Something that crossed me?"
"I am conscious of nothing; there can be nothing here. Take up the pen and finish. Hurry, hurry!"
As if his memory were impaired, or his faculties disordered, the prisoner made an effort to rally his attention. As he looked at Carton with clouded eyes and with an altered manner of breathing, Carton—his hand again in his breast—looked steadily at him.
"Hurry, hurry!"
The prisoner bent over the paper, once more.
" 'If it had been otherwise;' " Carton's hand was again watchfully and softly stealing down; " 'I never should have used the longer opportunity. If it had been otherwise;' " the hand was at the prisoner's face; " 'I should but have had so much the more to answer for. If it had been otherwise—' " Carton looked at the pen and saw it was trailing off into unintelligible signs. (381)

As any reader will attest, it is nearly impossible to read this passage without backtracking, for Dickens makes it especially difficult to keep the speakers straight for any length of time. And it is not only we who are confused as to who is being referred to, for soon afterward Basard finds Sydney's unorthodox use of pronouns disconcerting:

"Have no fear! I shall soon be out of the way of harming you, and the rest will soon be far from here, please God! Now, get assistance and take me to the coach."
"You?" said the Spy nervously.
"Him, man, with whom I have exchanged." (382)

Although Carton exchanges literal freedom for imprisonment in this scene, and although his semantic overlappings with Darnay are much closer to a fantasy of incorporation than to anything resembling dialogic communication, he does effect his escape from Dickens's solipsistic City of Dreadful Night, for the entombing barriers surrounding the discrete subject of liberal society have momentarily been shattered. Furthermore, the imagery and wordplay here associate Sydney with the self-subsuming Jacquerie at the very moment when he prevents the Tribunal from executing the man Madame Defarge defines as the last of the "race" of Evrémondes.

That Dickens was aware at some level of the parallels he had drawn can be deduced from the violent reaction which occurs in the novel's final pages, for there he takes pains to insist that although Carton is in one sense just another face among a crowd of the condemned—one more victim of what is essentially a mass murder—he nevertheless stands out as a distinct individual whose personality will remain intact even beyond the grave. This reaction begins as the narrator follows his protagonist from cell to guillotine. After emphasizing that the prison officials are exclusively concerned about the "count" in the tumbrils—that there be fifty-two bodies in it—he goes on to provide us with a catalog of the condemned's deportment which makes it clear that they are all quite discrete personalities:

Of the riders in the tumbrils, some observe these things, and all things on their last roadside, with an impassive stare; others, with a lingering interest in the ways of life and men. Some, seated with drooping heads, are sunk in silent despair; again, there are some so heedful of their looks that they cast upon the multitude such glances as they have seen in theatres, and in pictures. Several close their eyes, and think, or try to get their straying thoughts together. Only one, and he a miserable creature, of a crazed aspect, is so shattered and made drunk by horror, that he sings, and tries to dance. (400)

Carton's own possibly "prophetic" speech at the foot of the scaffold gives us a taste of individualism triumphant, with Sydney personally persisting through the generations. He sees Lucy "with a child upon her bosom, who bears [his] name," a child who eventually "win[s] his way up in that path of life which once was [his]" and who in turn fathers a "boy of [Carton's] name," to whom he "tells . . . [Sydney's] story, with a tender and faltering voice" (404). Chris Vanden Bossche sums up the tone succinctly: "The image of self-sacrifice created by this speech puts the authenticity of that very self-sacrifice into question by envisioning a future that nearly effaces Darnay (only portraying his death) and foretelling a line of sons named for Carton."[16] Indeed, Sydney's "cartonage" of middle-class individuality seems so firmly and solidly back in place that not even the worm can worry it, and this sense of the protagonist's "haunting" both the place of his death and future generations is very much to the point, for it cancels out several passages in which the Revolution's practice of mass killing threatens to endorse their anti-individualist ideology by sheer weight of numbers and frequency. We have been told, for instance, that "before their cells were quit" of the fifty-two, "new occupants were appointed; before their blood ran into the blood spilled yesterday, the blood that was to mingle with theirs to-morrow was already set apart" (375–76). Earlier, the narrator informed us that death under the Revolutionary regime had become "so common and material, that no sorrowful story of a haunting Spirit ever arose among the people out of all the working of the Guillotine" (343). Now haunting is the individualist pursuit par excellence—only individuals may haunt the living, not groups or classes. And thus Carton's death—and his subsequent life after death—stridently refute the collectivist ideology, insisting as they do upon the individual's persistent influence in secular history and hinting at the spiritual indwelling that is the religious sanction for the discrete subject of classical liberalism, a subject conceived of as retaining its individuality even beyond the grave. As the author of *A Tale of Two Cities* was well aware, serious contemplations concerning the obscuring walls of the bourgeois self have "something of the awfulness, even of Death" about them.

Having come to this point, it is important to make a distinction between the function, on the one hand, of the Night Shadows passage and Carton's early isolation and, on the other, of Lorry's and Sydney's adventures beyond the limits of the liberal self; for although all of these aspects of the text undermine *A Tale*'s authoritative discourse, the first ensemble takes aim at the novel's "official" valorization of London, whereas the second reaccentuates the thoroughly negative judgment pronounced upon Paris. The bourgeois city of silent and secretive individuals and the Jackal's unhappy career which it mandates both insinuate that England is not the benign antithesis to Paris that the narrator would often have us belive it to be. The anti-individualist speeches and actions of the banker and barrister, meanwhile, imply that Revolutionary France may in fact be a *superior* alternative to the night-shadowed metropolis of fatally discrete subjects. This subversive nibbling at both poles of the text's political axis must result not in a complete overturning of *A Tale*'s overt assessments of the two camps, but in a bleakly comprehensive ambivalence; for consider: whatever the novel's flirtations with communal modes of existence, Lorry's and Carton's comic and private excursions away from middle-class assumptions can never rehabilitate the Paris of the grindstone and the national razor. And conversely, whatever the triumphs of the English characters over Republican barbarism, they prevail only to return to their voiceless interment, as the otherwise seemingly gratuitous fate of Pross testifies. It is that lady, recall, who loudly reminds the assembled company that she is "a subject of His Most Gracious Majesty King George the Third" and that "as such, [her] maxim is, Confound their politics, Frustrate their knavish tricks, On him our hopes we fix, God save the King!" (318). It is she who, in the novel's penultimate chapter, vanquishes the Revolution incarnate in the form of Madame Defarge. And yet it is also Pross who, after her triumph, complains of a "stillness [that] seems to be fixed and unchangeable, never to be broken any more as long as [she] lives." Cruncher, driving her back to the presumed safety of England, is of the opinion "that indeed she will never hear anything else in this world," to which the narrator adds: "And indeed she never did" (399). It is fair to say, then, that *A Tale* can conceive of no viable positive alternative to the two ideologies, no middle ground in which the individual can remain discrete and yet avoid a deathlike incommunicability. At best, the novel halfheartedly implies that such a compromise may be available in a vague hereafter, where, the best of both worlds prevailing within the bosom of God, discrete souls will see each other face to face at last. The text's frustrating ambivalence toward its two earthly realms should not, however, lead us to underestimate its counterhegemonic force: after all, for an author on the "winning" side of history to rewrite the struggle between collectivism and individualism in such a way as to subtly imply that there have been *no* winners is to call a great many comfortable assumptions into question.

Dickens's novel of the French Revolution follows *Little Dorrit* in his canon, and much has been written about what attracted him to a subject that, on the face of things, seems rather distant from his usual literary milieu. Of course we have Dickens's own words in the Preface, explaining how he "conceived the main idea of the story" while acting in Collins's *The Frozen Deep*. The similarities between the central dramatic conflict of the play and the novel, however, tell us little as to why he chose to set his work mainly in Revolutionary Paris—after all, one may sacrifice oneself for a loved one and a rival in any number of possible situations. And then too, there is the problem of covering ground already pronounced upon—there is no other word for it—by his friend and mentor, Carlyle. The obsequious tone of the Preface, in which he states that "it has been one of [his] hopes to add something to the popular and picturesque means of understanding that terrible time" while simultaneously assuring us that "no one can hope to add anything to the philosophy of Mr. Carlyle's wonderful book" (29), betrays the awkwardness and risk inherent in his project. I would suggest that it is possible that the Revolution attracted him precisely because it allowed him to study, confront—and to some extent flirt with—modes of thought which claimed to offer a solution to what he, on some level, perceived to be one of the pervasive diseases of his own society, even if he was constrained to denounce such desperate remedies in the selfsame breath. To understand how clearly he did in fact see the endemic and secretive individualism that underlay his acquisitive culture as a blighting phenomenon, and how refreshing and perhaps intoxicating he may have found the whiff of collectivism he allows to Lorry and Carton, we need only glance back as far as his preceding novel. As Arthur Clennam walks the streets of London, his thoughts give rise to images that, as George Levine says, "speak with remarkable appropriateness as representative both of the plot(s) of *Little Dorrit* and of the texture of its world."[17] Notice again how in this passage, as in Sydney's case, silence and opacity of character are inseparable from acquisitive activity, how nefarious economic practices are protected by the obscuring partitions that mask self from self:

As he went along, upon a dreary night, the dim streets by which he went seemed all depositories of oppressive secrets. The deserted counting-houses, with their secrets of books and papers locked up in chests and safes; the banking-houses, with their secrets of strong rooms and wells, the keys of which were in a very few secret pockets and a very few secret breasts; the secrets of all the dispersed grinders in the vast mill, among whom there were doubtless plunderers, forgers, and trust-betrayers of many sorts, whom the light of any day that dawned might reveal; he could have fancied that these things, in hiding, imparted a heaviness to the air. The shadow thickening and thickening as he approached its source, he thought of the secrets of the lonely church-vaults, where the people who had hoarded and secreted in iron coffers were in their turn similarly hoarded, not yet at rest from doing harm; and then of the secrets of the river, as it rolled its turbid tide between two frowning wildernesses of secrets, extending, thick and dense, for many miles, and warding off the free air and the free country swept by winds and wings of birds. (596–97)[18]

Here again is the nocturnal metropolis of the Night Shadows passage, the city that stands as the mirror image of barricaded Paris, reversed yet identical, simultaneously antonym and synonym. Little wonder, then, that Dickens begins his tale by claiming that the era of the French Revolution resembles nothing so much as "the present period" (35). The graveyard and the scaffold are, of course, implied in one another, and both are equidistant from that sufficient public square that, after midcentury, he vainly struggled to discover or even to plausibly represent, where war cries and divisive secrets are both unknown, and voices in dialogue draw individuals together. Such an aspiration does not acquit Dickens from the "charge" (as many today would insist upon framing it) of being a bourgeois liberal. It does, however, allow us to recognize *A Tale of Two Cities* as a novel that challenges, even as it cannot help but reflect, the dominant discourses of its age.

Conclusion: Does Subversion
Make a Difference?

✳

The previous chapters have constituted an attempt to assess the politics—
and especially the subversive potential—of novelistic form. Since, in accomplishing this task, I have frequently employed Bakhtinian theories, it
seems incumbent upon me to say something about the politics of dialogic
criticism as well, for literary theories are no less implicated in structures
of power than the literary works they claim to illuminate. I will therefore
approach my final thoughts about the novel's ability to resist and subvert
bourgeois hegemony through a discussion of how Bakhtin's name is currently appropriated by literary intellectuals of differing political persuasions, and of whether there exists the possibility of arriving at any helpful
compromise between these contending voices. In the course of doing so I
will also attempt to clarify what I think we mean—or ought to mean—
when we use a term like "subversion," and how we who write profession-
ally about literature ought to conceive of our own enterprise's ability to
promote social transformation. My labor throughout will be to clear a
space in which, concerning the practical political effects of the novel and
of literary criticism, we may be tough-mindedly unromantic without abandoning a belief that both we and the texts we study can somehow make a
difference.

Currently, Bakhtin studies can be divided into a liberal camp and a
bivouac located farther to the left. In the hostilities ongoing between them,
the leftists accuse the liberals of emasculating what they see as Bakhtin's
potentially radical critique of bourgeois capitalist culture, while the liberals contend that the leftists are continually attempting to make Bakhtin,
explicitly or implicitly, into the full-bore Marxist or deconstructionist or
Foucauldian he decidedly wasn't. My own position, as has perhaps become
clear already, is the uncomfortable one of a redoubt midway between the
contending trenches, riven by sympathies for and disagreements with both

sides. In what follows I will attempt to explain how the critical discourse of one faction may fail to fully appreciate the oppositional potentials of Bakhtin's sturdiest conceptions, while that of the other occasionally leans too heavily upon some of his flimsiest.

What unites many, though by no means all,[1] of the left-Bakhtinians is their tendency to view Bakhtin's writings on carnival as being nearly as convincing as his theories concerning dialogism. Indeed, it is sometimes from the pages of *Rabelais and His World* that they draw evidence of Bakhtin's most radical challenges to the bourgeois order.[2] (Since Bakhtin's conceptions of carnival are the most widely disseminated and, in my experience at least, the most widely employed aspect of his corpus, both within and beyond literary studies, I will not attempt to synopsize them here.) For their part, the liberals see Bakhtin's pronouncements concerning the carnivalesque as contradicting the spirit of other—and to their mind more central—phases of his thought:

This carnival mode is the canonic base for a number of very peculiar appropriations of Bakhtin, from Marxist to deconstructionist, and, in our view, it has tended to obscure the larger and more consistent shape of his thought. Generally speaking, Bakhtin was much less concerned with millenarian fantasies and holy foolishness than with the constraints and responsibilities of everyday living. Carnival, while offering a provocative insight into much of Rabelais and some of Dostoevsky, ultimately proved a dead end. In his last period, laughter but not the idealization of carnival anarchy remained—and the functions of laughter were more closely specified.[3]

My own particular objections to notions of the carnivalesque and its reputed presence within literary works does not spring from its contradictions with Bakhtin's other writings, for it seems to me the most reasonable thing in the world that a dialogic thinker like Bakhtin would contest his own discourse and provide his internal doubts and rejoinders with a fulling signifying voice. Rather, my skepticism arises from the fact that the whole category of carnival—and especially its deployment as a means of explaining centrifugal discourses in eighteenth-, nineteenth-, and twentieth-century novels—appears idealist and unhistorical.

In defense of this position, I have no embarrassment about calling to aid Lennard Davis, whose objections to dialogism were found so wanting in chapter 1, for when Davis turns his attention to carnival, it seems to me that he hits the mark directly. Alarmed at the way Bakhtin uses one term to cover a multitude of social and writerly practices separated by great swaths of time, he points out that "just because there were saturnalias in Rome and May Days in Europe does not mean that *any* literary text of either historical period that includes the grotesque or laughter is somehow joined by the glue of carnivalesque continuity. . . . One becomes extremely uncomfortable with the way that Bakhtin leaps over 1300 years of history in a single page."⁴ Davis is speaking specifically here about a leap between ancient Rome and medieval Europe, but surely such a dissent becomes even more pertinent when one talks about "carnivalesque" energies arising in novels of, say, the Victorian era. If I myself was forced to take pains (which some have no doubt found insufficient) to differentiate what "bourgeois" might plausibly mean when applied to Goldsmith in 1766 from what it designates when referring to a text of the mid-1800s, surely many crucial differences are being papered over when the subversive energies present in Rabelais's works are all but equated with those at work in Thackeray or Joyce.

Indeed, Bakhtin at times seems more cautious on this score than many of his followers, for even in the midst of a passage asserting that "the popular festive carnival principle is indestructible" and that "though narrowed and weakened, it still continues to fertilize various areas of life and culture," he delivers the following caution:

During this period (actually starting in the seventeenth century) we observe a process of gradual narrowing down of the ritual spectacle, and carnival forms of folk culture, which become small and trivial. On the one hand the state encroached upon festive life and turned it into a parade; on the other hand these festivities were brought into the home and became part of the family's private life. The privileges which were formerly allowed in the marketplace were more and more restricted. The carnival spirit with its freedom, its utopian character oriented toward the future, was gradually transformed into a mere holiday mood. The feast ceased almost entirely to be the people's second life, their temporary renascence and renewal.⁵

Moreover, we are informed that "the peculiarity of comic imagery, which is one in spite of its variety and is inherent to medieval folk culture [is] generally foreign to modern times (especially to the nineteenth century)."⁶ Thus, "carnival," when applied to Augustan, Romantic, Victorian, or modern contexts, begins to take on the lineaments of an essentialist category—one of those often sentimentalized "eternal verities of the human heart"—rather than a historicized and historicizing tool of literary-critical investigation. As Robert Young complains, "Bakhtin is celebrated because he adds the missing element of history to deconstruction, but when this argument is rehearsed in detail it turns out that he offers an alternative only if carnival is, paradoxically, dehistoricized."⁷

Simon Dentith, a critic quite sensitive to this troubling aspect of Bakh-

tin's thought, rightly asks how "a carnivalesque disposition [can] be realized in periods of history when the social practices of carnival are
themselves all but extinct?" Focusing on Dickens, the one major Victorian
writer who would soonest leap to mind were one interested in proving the
persistence of genuine carnival energies, the conclusion he draws from
scenes of popular laughter and lower-class "unmaskings" of social superiors is cautious and cautionary: "though it certainly does seem . . . that
there are elements in Dickens which draw upon directly carnivalesque energies, these can only be realized in the particular accents or intonations
of the moment of writing. What begins as an epochal kind of explanation,
seeking the intelligibility of an aspect of Dickens' writing in the generic
roots of the novel, is pulled towards a more directly historical account."
Pulled hard, I would say, and to an extent that calls the usefulness of the
term "carnival" into more serious question than Dentith is, I think, willing
to admit. To drive the point home, let me describe an experience that must
be familiar to many who engage Bakhtinian issues: when one reads an
article or hears a paper on the carnivalesque in isolation, one can usually
be convinced that *some* kinship, however tenuous, between the oppositional discourses represented in a particular modern text and those described in the Rabelais book actually exists. Recalled en masse, though,
one quickly gets the uneasy feeling that "carnival" is being used as something very close to a synonym for centrifugal energies of any and all kinds.
Dentith seems aware of this discomforting sensation, for he is led "to ask
whether we ought not to seek those epochal carnival energies, not in the
particular scenes of rowdy popular laughter imagined by Dickens, but in
the novel's capacity to exploit and extend the heteroglossic diversity of
which it is made."[8] Reasonable enough, surely, but what is this "capacity"
except dialogism by some other name, and why should we then have recourse to notions of the carnivalesque when a better, more precise term is
at hand?

This is no mere quibble over semantics, for as I attempted to show in
chapter I, dialogism is a potential within the formal structure of the novel
itself (using "novel" in the conventional sense, not Bakhtin's extended
one), which was nurtured by specific historical conditions (i.e., middle-
class hegemony) gaining force at the beginning of the eighteenth century
and persisting in recognizable form through all of the nineteenth and into
the twentieth. Dialogism is thus a more historically concrete conception
with which to talk about the oppositional energies of the genre than one
that inevitably brings to mind historical practices that long predated

Daniel Defoe and that Bakhtin himself admits were in precipitous decline by the time Moll Flanders began shocking the bourgeoisie. If the only way to make carnival acceptable to a sufficiently rigorous historicism is to shift and attenuate its meaning until it is synonymous with dialogism, it seems to me we are better off just using the latter term and confining the former to a much more historically circumscribed set of cultural and literary practices.

Another problem with the carnivalesque is that, as has frequently been pointed out, its centrifugal credentials are open to serious question. Davis remarks in this regard that "the same peasants who subverted the hierarchical order on feast days went quietly back to the yoke at the end of the festivities. Rather than seeing the carnival as a liberating event, one could equally view it as the escape valve—the bread and circus—that allowed oppression to function."[9] Again, this criticism appears to be seconded by material that Bakhtin himself quotes in the Rabelais book. Here, for instance, is a document of 1444 justifying the feast of fools in a manner that must give scant encouragement to those who wish to see carnival as a wholly progressive and emancipatory force:

Wine barrels burst if from time to time we do not open them and let in some air. All of us men are barrels poorly put together, which would burst from the wine of wisdom, if this wine remains in a state of constant fermentation of piousness and fear of God. We must give it air in order not to let it spoil. This is why we permit folly on certain days so that we may later return with greater zeal to the service of God.[10]

Given the fact that, as Terry Eagleton reminds us, the medieval and Renaissance feast day was an "officially licensed affair, without the rancour, discipline and organization essential for an effective revolutionary politics,"[11] it follows that even if one could make a convincing case that recognizably carnivalesque energies are to be found operating within bourgeois novels, their ability to unseat or even discomfit the discursive powers that be is far from certain.

Diminishing our reliance on the notion of carnival, however, does not mean that one is left with a politically tamed Bakhtin, for, as I hope the second section of this book has begun to demonstrate, dialogism carries within it energies of subversion potent enough to deconstruct the "tolerant" and "disinterested" discourses of liberal reformism and to convincingly decenter the supposedly autonomous liberal subject. At base, this is so because of a fact about Bakhtin's thought that, paradoxically, looms so large in the forefront that its full implications can be easily underexplored and underappreciated: I refer to his radically *social* conception of the human condition. A passage from some of Bakhtin's last writings underscores how deeply he felt our existence to be an ineluctably communal affair:

Everything that pertains to me enters my consciousness, beginning with my name, from the external world through the mouths of others (my mother, and so forth), with their intonation, in their emotional and value-assigning tonality. I realize myself initially through others: from them I receive words, forms, and tonalities for the formation of my initial ideas of myself. . . . Just as the body is formed initially in the mother's womb (body), a person's consciousness awakens wrapped in another's consciousness.[12]

And not only awakens, but continues to live wholly within the osmotic field of others' discourse: "quests for my own word are in fact quests for a word that is not my own, a word that is more than myself; this is a striving to depart from one's own words, with which nothing essential can be said."[13] These and like pronouncements—which have struck so many of us as startlingly fresh and yet entirely apt descriptions of how we negotiate our word-constructed world—may hardly sound like a call to man the barricades but, properly understood, are nevertheless so many dialogic daggers aimed at the heart of bourgeois liberalism, for what can the crucial term "individualism" possibly mean after Bakhtin?

Here, if anywhere, one feels not the slightest hesitation in trumpeting the fact that Bakhtin's voice emphatically seconds and supplements that of Marx, extending the latter's critique of the solitary subject by showing such a figment to be not only the obfuscatory tool of a particular class at a particular phase of socioeconomic development, but a dangerous misprision of something akin to our biological inheritance. Of course, Marx would have little truck with notions of an enduring "human nature," but would he really quarrel with Bakhtin's wider vision of our species as always already communal by the very fact that we are implicated in—and by—language? And at any rate, the results of their demystifications are entirely complementary, since Bakhtin's critique of the autonomous individual gives the lie to what John Brenkman calls that "mythic moment in our understanding of consent," in which we convince ourselves that "only the individual, as individual, gives consent to the polis and receives its consent in turn," insisting instead that "individuals participate in the polis as culturally and socially shaped agents, just as they are barred from the polis on the basis of their group belonging."[14] For Bakhtin, then, certain discourses of the self central to bourgeois hegemony can be labeled "monologic" not only because they attempt to pass themselves off as the only natural and inevitable way of conceiving of the world, but because they also try to convince us that, when we ourselves speak, our own utterances are wholly monologic. In other words, a main thrust of middle-class ideology is to make us believe that we hourly accomplish the impossible.

Of course there have long been those on the deconstructive left who claim that Bakhtin is hopelessly soft on liberal humanism because he still believes in a self-responsible subject and a relatively "free" human voice that is more than simply an epiphenomenon of language speaking itself. He certainly *does* believe in such a being, but with crucial qualifications that will bring the liberal wing of Bakhtinian studies little comfort if their aim is, in fact, to dress up their mentor in the garb of conventional liberalism. The fact is that Bakhtin, in one of his by now familiar acts of seeming prescience, stakes out a middle ground between the positions occupied by the two sides in the "culture war" now raging within the American academy. To put his formulation simply, all of our words *are* inevitably the words of others and therefore of the sociolinguistic structures that inhabit us, but the ways in which those words are combined into the utterances we actually direct back at the world are the unpredictable results of a dialogic encounter between the vocabularies of others and our own unique melange of innerly persuasive discourses. Language speaks us, then, but what it winds up saying is always *partially* the result of the unfinalizable contribution of our own psyches, which are themselves always unfinalizable variations on a norm constructed by the dominant ideologies that imbrue them. As Michael Gardiner helpfully puts it, Bakhtin "conceptualize[s] human beings as neither entirely autonomous, self-directed entities nor as surface effects of a deep epistemic structure, but rather as reflexive agents embodying a range of socially-determined practical capacities, a repertoire of collective skills and resources."[15] This formulation, while decentering the autonomous subject from the chimerical eminence accorded him by middle-class hegemony, does not mean that our individual responsibility has vanished. Rather, it challenges us to arrive at a critical self-consciousness about our subject-position that bourgeois capitalism would just as soon we not bother about; for as Bakhtin asserts, "the better a person understands the degree to which he is externally determined. . . , the closer he comes to understanding and exercising his real freedom."[16] We are responsible, then, for our own utterances, and responsible also for social change, but in a manner fundamentally different from the mystifying "great man" theory of history promulgated by middle-class hegemony. Gardiner again: "Bakhtin *et al.* remain 'human-

ists' in the sense that they . . . continue to ascribe importance to the category of 'agency'—that is, a belief in the creative or active role of collective
human praxis vis-à-vis the making of history."[17] Surely the crucial word
here is "collective," for as we have seen, the very fact that we are language-
using beings dictates that there can be no Archimedean individual at the
crux of epochal or even hourly change. History, like the pyramids, was
built collectively (and, of course, coercively), a state of affairs that Bakhtin
insists provides us with "no alibi for being," though it may offer us a partial one for the inequities we daily suffer under and perpetuate.

It is coercion that really gets us to the heart of the dispute between the
liberal and left positions, for there is a hole in Bakhtin's writings on dialogics and sharp disagreements about how, or even whether, it should be
filled in. It is generally agreed that Bakhtin, though keenly aware of the
unequal distributions of power that characterize nearly all dialogic encounters, neither developed what could be properly called a "theory of
power" nor had much that was particularly incisive to say upon the matter.
Gardiner, for instance, complains that "he fails adequately to grasp the
social and institutional realities of power and domination—indeed, at
times Bakhtin seems to equate the whole machinery of class rule with the
suppression of unhindered dialogic communication."[18] Young agrees,
asserting that he "hardly explains how a dominant ideology manages to
operate successfully,"[19] while Robert Stam declares that one of the
"wrinkles" in Bakhtin is "his failure to deeply theorize power relations."[20]
Luckily for us, the one thing today's academy is in no short supply of is
theories of power, and thus the question becomes, How far, and with what
qualifications, is it appropriate to supplement Bakhtin with the likes of
Marx, Eagleton, Foucault, Gilbert and Gubar, and the like?

By describing the situation this way, I wish to exclude two extreme positions at once. On the one hand, all attempts to portray Bakhtin as being
himself an out-and-out Marxist seem to me to fly in the face of overwhelm-
ing evidence to the contrary, and even efforts to prove that he possessed
something akin to a labor theory of value fail to convince, as is shown by
Michael Holquist's endeavor to do just that in his Introduction to *Art and
Answerability*:

A new book by James Lynch, director of the Psychophysical Laboratory at the
University of Maryland's medical school, provides evidence that calling dialogue
"work" is not just a metaphor (or not only a metaphor): in a series of imaginative
experiments, Lynch has shown a direct corollary between blood pressure levels
and the activities of talking and listening. Since 1904, when the modern technique

of measuring blood pressure was developed, physicians have insisted their patients *not talk* while being tested, because talking had the effect of raising "normal" levels.[21]

This may facilitate every professor's dream of entering the proletariat while still giving university lectures, but it only underscores how little Bakhtin has to say on the relationship between toil and value. At the same time, it will not do to claim that because Bakhtin was not himself a Marxist, no aspects of Marxist or neo-Marxist thought may be appended to his corpus without fundamentally perverting it. Bakhtin is frustratingly silent on the subject of power, but it seems to me that his lacunae are best described not as ragged fissures but as concave edges to which a good number of current theories about the inequities of social distribution and the dynamics of cultural change can be readily married in a way that constructs an organic whole rather than creating some sort of intellectual griffin or satyr. Could not it be the case that those who, especially during the first rush of unconsidered Western enthusiasm over Bakhtin, expended so much energy refuting the genuinely inappropriate Marxification of that thinker are now too quick to conflate those who wish to appropriately supplement him with those who continue to fundamentally misrepresent him? Is it not all too easy, especially in the heat of a continuing battle against ignorance, to mistake those who merely mention Marx and Bakhtin in the same breath with those who attempt to make the latter into an obedient disciple of the former? To say that we must dig a protective moat around Bakhtin to protect him from infection by Marxists, Foucauldians, feminists, and post-structuralists of all types is just as much a failure to allow his discourse to "sound" as is painting him a Bolshevik.

One of the things I have attempted to do in the previous chapters is to suggest and then demonstrate how Bakhtinian thought can be—always with proper caution—melded with neo-Marxist and Foucauldian conceptions. If I have done so without distorting the first, it also seems to me that what has been jettisoned from the two latter intellectual structures represents no real loss, but rather the shedding of so much cumbersome baggage. At the present moment there is more than enough evidence issuing from both the academy and the evening news to entirely discredit Marxism's endless attempts to refine the base-superstructure model, its rigid prophetical dialectics, its wholly inadequate definitions of ideology, and the arrogantly finalizing tenor of its rhetoric. And, as we approach a new century in which the worldwide force that has so long represented itself as the only rational alternative to a rapacious capitalism will likely have vanished from the scene, Foucault's vision of an omniscient and unassailable Power is an excuse for passivity and despair in which we can ill afford to indulge. I should mention that, in choosing to deal mainly with these two particular systems of thought, I make no claim whatsoever to having exhausted the list of "isms" that can be profitably conjoined with dialogics. Indeed, the most obvious gap in this book is the absence of a chapter employing feminist prosaics, for much valuable work is now going forward that seeks to discover sites of subversion within the novel that arise from the conflict and interillumination of gendered rather than class-based social vocabularies.[22] In true dialogic fashion, neither Bakhtin nor the various strands of feminist criticism can expect to look quite the same after the implications of such a wide-ranging encounter are more fully revealed.

Having arrived at the no doubt unsatisfying conclusion that Bakhtin's proper place on the political spectrum is approximately halfway between the liberals and the left, I would like for a moment to turn away from the internecine squabbles of the present and cast an eye upon the future. Bakhtin, of course, strongly counsels against any attempt to predict the course of history, even within the relatively confined space of an academic discipline, so if I suggest that there is a logical next step to be taken in any dialogic investigation of the politics of novelistic form, it must be taken not as a prognostication but merely as a wish. Rather than continue to bicker among ourselves about who owns Bakhtin, it seems to me we ought to turn our energies in a direction designed to answer some of the strongest criticisms from those who continue to maintain that the methodology of dialogics is *tout court* naïve and sentimental. One such criticism centers around the question of silence. The most common result of oppression, say critics like Young, is the silence of the oppressed, and Bakhtin "assumes that there are no groups in society that are voiceless or silent, that none have been excluded from speech as such"; thus, he possesses no sensitivity "for what the book does not say, for things which must not be said."[23] Has dialogics, in fact, anything to offer concerning social languages that are not merely flattened by monologic authors but excluded altogether from texts that purport to be comprehensive social canvases? Can a dialogic interpretation look at a novel and uncover that speech which is not merely prevented from "sounding" but drowned out altogether? Although attempting to analyze the absence of voices may seem to carry all of the attendant risks of trying to prove a negative, it strikes me that discursive elisions committed for political reasons will probably tend to leave their telltale signs within the remaining languages of the text, as in astrophysics those significant absences called black holes are depicted as warping and stretching the fabric of space-time. In such cases, though, the trick will be in determining what discourses are both conspicuously available in the text's wider social field and thus *significantly and oddly* absent given the subgenre (that is, the chronotope, range of characters, and plot events) of the particular novel under consideration. To accomplish such a feat, it is likely that prosaics will need to draw heavily upon the techniques of the new historicism, an interillumination of methodologies that would no doubt benefit both schools, as well as improve the image of dialogics in the eyes of those who (with *some* justification) see Bakhtinians as a bunch of unhistorical Pollyannas.

The question of whether this relative cultural optimism, which does seem to pervade Bakhtian criticism, is justified or naïve allows us to shift our discussion from the current state of the Bakhtin Industry to the primary question of the subversive potential of the novel as a genre. Davis, clearly feeling exasperated with the implicit predictions of the Great Day of Dialogic Equality to be ushered in any moment now thanks to the cumulative influence of prose fiction, asks, "How many upscale corporate executives have recently read the quite dialogic *Bonfire of the Vanities* and come away carnivalized?"[24] The question is, of course, on one level quite unfair (and then too, one can argue about whether Wolfe's novel really is dialogic or not), but it also ought to give pause to all theorists of novelistic form who, like the author of this book, are even in partial and cautious agreement with Bakhtin's readings of social diversity, of the novel's representation of that diversity, and thus of the genre's ability to act as an agent of subversion and social change. Actually, such criticisms emerge not only from scholars as skeptical of things dialogic as Davis, for Gardiner also complains that Bakhtin's

conception of cultural politics seems to involve a somewhat questionable belief in the capacity of the "people" for self-liberation, insofar as he felt that the imposition of an official language and culture could be effectively countered by the spontaneous heteroglossic forces contained within popular culture and novelistic discourse without being translated into forms of specifically political organizations and struggle. In short, Bakhtin is keenly aware of the subjective dynamics of deconstruction as a transgressive social practice, but he tends to overlook the objective factors (particularly the possible mode or agency of social and cultural transformation) which are of equal importance.[25]

This is an important qualification, for if to the question "Can the novel alone save us?" we are even tempted to answer "yes," we must ask ourselves what separates dialogical criticism from the attractive but utterly exploded ideology of Romanticism, which posits the poetic imagination as a faculty potentially able to transfigure us without the aid of day-to-day political struggle? What is the use of our supposedly exacting historicism and attention to the novel's social situatedness if we wind up making the same exaggerated claims for prose fiction that Wordsworth and Shelley made for poetry? As Young suggests, no matter how dialogized a society's heteroglossia becomes between the covers of a novel, the novel will not "do our politics for us."[26] Political progress, it seems clear, will always require structures outside our politically ambivalent genre, and one should not shy away from the fact that they may need to be considerably less open to heteroglossic diversity than their literary ally. It would be an interesting thought experiment, for instance, to ponder what Bakhtin would think of a liberationist political party that necessarily possessed a *platform* in order to enlist members, identify opponents, and generally promote its vision. Since one has difficulty conceiving of Bakhtin strongly endorsing such an indisputably essential entity, one is led to admit that his seeming optimism about just how much the novel by itself can do toward constructing a more dialogic future is indeed at best naïve, and at worst contains the potential for leading sympathetic readers and critics into an aestheticist excuse for eschewing practical efforts in the nonliterary realms of cultural politics.

A problem arises, however, when one attempts to scale back Bakhtin's exaggerated claims for the novel's subversive potential, for at times there appears to be little stable middle ground between his overly sanguine position and the relentlessly negative one of Davis. Here, for example, is what I take to be a fairly typical attempt, in a Bakhtinian mode, to save the formal structures of the novel for the progressive cause while avoiding an overly rosy scenario:

As quintessential social document, the novel is thus able to underwrite most consistently a culture's fundamental activity of not only producing texts but of generating a set of texts that function to define the culture itself at its various stages of development. The novel, in effect, may be viewed ideally as affording a multitudinous series of nodal points within a culture's aesthetic sphere, by which the culture perceives and defines itself.[27]

It will be recalled that this formulation is similar in several ways to that put forward by neo-Marxists such as Raymond Williams and Terry Eagleton in their own attempts to define what role the novel can and cannot play in the political struggle, and it may help to introduce an uncomfortable question that could certainly be raised by any skeptical reader of this volume's previous chapters. Is there, after all, any genuine political result that can be traced to the novel's *merely representing* dissident, unofficial, and repressed social vocabularies, even if it portrays them as, in Bakhtin's words, "fully valid discourses"? If we go so far as to admit that the dialogic novel provides a particular culture with a uniquely detailed picture of its ideological geography, is that the equivalent of saying that it is bound to *alter* that geography in any measurable way, or for that matter in any particular direction? Why shouldn't such a portrait lead to a self-satisfied and narcissistic gaze rather than the panic of Balthasar's banquet?

To synopsize the argument made at the outset of this book's second half, it seems to me that over the past two centuries the novel *has* been responsible—precisely through a dialogizing of languages made possible by the kind of exemplary reflective ability noted above—for relativizing all social vocabularies, which in turn has been the first step away from an essentialist and toward a historicist conception of the world, and thus toward a society significantly more open to attacks on long-entrenched inequalities of power. But of course to invoke the long history of the novel's construction by, and construction of, the larger culture of which it is a part is to admit that the genre is one whose effect on political discourse has primarily been a liberal-reformist one. It is precisely here, though, that a Bakhtinian criticism secure in its moorings at a position between liberal reformism and left-utopianism can illuminate the novel's *rare and scattered* moments of truly radical decentering. Were, for instance, a dialogic reader of liberal persuasion to insist that the genre seems steadfastly antiutopian and therefore incapable of giving much aid and comfort to any system of thought enamored of teleology and hubristically certain of the precise shape the Good Life should eventually take, one could reply that bourgeois reformism is also in part a utopian ideology, and that novels will equally resist any attempt by middle-class hegemony to ventriloquize their heteroglossic accents. Along these lines Bakhtin himself makes reference to "the tragedy of a genre,"[28] by which he means those instances when an author attempts to force certain textual effects into a chronotope not historically conditioned to handle them, since "each genre is only able to control certain definite aspects of reality," and "each . . . possesses definite principles of selection, definite forms for seeing and conceptualizing reality, and a definite scope and depth of penetration."[29] As I have attempted to demonstrate, *The Vicar of Wakefield*, *Mansfield Park*, *Agnes Grey*, and *Oliver Twist* are all "problem novels" precisely because their authors undertook the "tragic" (i.e., doomed) enterprise of trying to make their works precisely recite certain scripted official discourses of their culture,

losing sight of the fact that the novel is, structurally, an inveterate im-
proviser. At the same time, dialogic critics on the left are, in my opinion,
obliged by much the same set of considerations to admit that those moments within novels in which the central foundations of bourgeois hegemony are called into question in a way befitting the title "revolutionary"
or "utopian," though undeniably present, are likely to be difficult to ex-
tract amid conservative counterthemes and counterdiscourses that go far
toward muting their resonance and mitigating their efficacy. Such, at least,
were the beleaguered conditions in which we found the genuinely radical
subtexts described in *North and South* and *A Tale of Two Cities*. This
hermeneutical middle way, though its formulations may strike some as
altogether too timid and unambitious, is no defeatist surrender to the status quo, for, as Stam remarks, "what the left badly needs" are "analytical
categories, such as those of Bakhtin, which allow for the fact that a given
utterance or discourse can be progressive and regressive *at the same time*"
(Stam's italics).[30]

   Bakhtin, says Morson, "eventually came to regard the novel—the great
realist novel of Dostoevsky, George Eliot, Goethe, and Tolstoy—as the supreme achievement of Western thought because the novel, more than any
other literary or non-literary form, respects the particularity of context,
the eventness of events, and the uniqueness of personality."[31] Agreed, as
long as "achievement" is understood to comprehend the phrase "radical
self-critique," for, under the proper dialogic scrutiny, the greatest novels
are capable of reminding us, as Benjamin would have it, that the civilization their very presence bespeaks is continually underwritten by daily
acts of barbarism. For my own part, I can think of no better passage to
illustrate the novel's endemic mixing of radical and conservative energies,
its leavening of middle-class commonplaces with an idealism that seeks to
transcend their inequities and meannesses, than that which stands as perhaps the central statement of the nineteenth century concerning the moral
charge, and the moral limits, of realism. I speak, of course, of the famous
moment within George Eliot's *Adam Bede*, where, as the chapter title informs us, "the story pauses a little," and the narrator defends her atten-
tions to the "merely" prosaic aspects of life from those who would urge
her to "touch [the world] up with a tasteful pencil, and make believe it is
not quite such a mixed, entangled affair":

But, my good friend, what will you do then with your fellow-parishioner who op-
poses your husband in the vestry?—with your newly appointed vicar, whose style
of preaching you find painfully below that of his regretted predecessor?—with the

honest servant, who worries your soul with her one failing,—with your neighbour, Mrs. Green, who was really kind to you in your last illness, but has said several ill-natured things about you since your convalescence?—nay, with your excellent husband himself, who has other irritating habits besides that of not wiping his shoes? These fellow-mortals, every one, must be accepted as they are: you can neither straighten their noses, nor brighten their wit, nor rectify their dispositions; and it is these people—amongst whom your life is passed—that it is needful you should tolerate, pity, and love: it is these more or less ugly, stupid, inconsistent people, whose movements of goodness you should be able to admire—for whom you should cherish all possible hopes, all possible patience. And I would not, even if I had the choice, be the clever novelist who could create a world so much better than this, in which we get up in the morning to do our daily work, that you would be likely to turn a harder, colder eye on the dusty streets and the common green fields—on the real breathing men and women, who can be chilled by your indifference or injured by your prejudice; who can be cheered and helped onward by your fellow-feeling, your forbearance, your outspoken, brave justice.[32]

There is a hauntingly mixed message dialogically unfolding here, one that is widely synoptic of the novelistic enterprise as a whole: the world isn't going to change, but novels can change the world. On the one hand it seems only wisdom to resign oneself to the fallible, familiar world in which we painfully—barbarously—muddle through, and yet at the same time the words themselves speak of a new and juster community waiting to be born if only the prosaic truths contained within the narrator's own double-voiced discourse could be absorbed by the readers who themselves comprise such a fallen community. The strength of dialogic criticism, and of a Bakhtinian assessment of the politics of novelistic form, is that it is uniquely sensitive to the ways in which the genre facilitates this ongoing conversation between society's progressive and regressive voices. This is not to say, of course, that such a sensitivity implies any untenable claims to disinterestedness or complete objectivity, for there is no point in denying that, as Stam reminds us, "Bakhtinian categories . . . display an intrinsic identification with difference and alterity, a built-in affinity for the oppressed and the marginal, a feature making them especially appropriate for the analysis of opposition and marginal practices."[33] It has been my argument throughout this book that, in the full knowledge of the political biases inherent in the critical tools I have employed, it can still be maintained that the affinity spoken of above, though contended against on every page, infuses the formal structures of the novel as well.

In closing, I must say a word or two about our own relationship to that alluring word, "subversion." Much of the increasingly bitter contention, within Bakhtin studies and elsewhere in the profession of literature, springs from an understandable yearning among us to make a palpable difference in the world, as well as to disagreements about how and to what extent this can be accomplished through the institutional practices of our discipline. Certainly anyone who takes the concept of dialogism seriously must believe that every utterance changes something in the world—sometimes profoundly, much more often incrementally. And, though the precise direction of this change must remain unpredictable, we are not left without a general guide by which to shape our daily intellectual labor in ways that may, however slowly, abet the kind of cultural transformations we so eagerly seek. Gardiner puts forward two propositions about the political beliefs of the Bakhtin Circle that, I believe, can find general agreement among those who participate in the much larger, much less homogeneous circle comprised by those of us who today label ourselves "Bakhtinians" of one stripe or another. First, "that any ruling class, concomitant with its general interest in centralizing and unifying the social world (in all its economic, political and cultural manifestations), attempts to fix meaning and univocalize the sign, and thereby to effect a form of ideological closure or homophony."[34] And second, that "Bakhtin's politics of culture can be characterized as the desire to understand and indeed encourage . . . the 'popular deconstruction' of official discourses and ideologies" coupled with "the staunch belief that the establishment of linguistic and cultural freedom is a necessary prerequisite to the emergence of a truly egalitarian and radically democratic community."[35] Most of us, I would hazard, share this insight about how our unjust society operates, this desire to deconstruct its perpetuating discourses, and this staunch belief about what must be encouraged if a better society is to take its place. And yet, what can *we* really expect to contribute to this contemporary enterprise, who write almost exclusively about the dead? Aren't we just fooling ourselves and laying our profession open to the charge of self-important silliness by claiming to lend a hand as we turn out yet one more book on Defoe, or George Eliot, or Virginia Woolf? We certainly are if our claims are not deeply tempered by humility and patience, and also by a profoundly Bakhtinian awareness that, in Patricia Yaeger's words, any "struggle against constraining ideologies is complicated by the fact that words may not submit easily to the writer's will," that furthermore "the limiting 'intentions and accents' of a language system can be inscribed to such a depth that words become difficult to reappropriate even in new dialogic contexts," and that finally "as linguistic and social patterns reinforce one another over time, language may change only to stay the same."[36] In other words, if language—and therefore culture—is forever fluid, it is also chronically inertial, and thus we will only make fools of ourselves by claiming, even implicitly, that next week's lecture or next month's article or next year's conference will "undermine" much of anything.

And yet there is reason to think that even an institution like ours, which our culture often takes pains to ignore, is not totally devoid of effect upon the larger discourses that order our lives. We can take comfort, I think, by joining Gardiner's description above of Bakhtin's and our own "politics of culture" with a kind of profession of faith recently articulated by Peter Hitchcock, who claims that "to render the past as dialogical is to make the future more so."[37] This credo becomes more than just a fantasy about the soaring influence of scholarly journals or progressive pedagogy if one ceases to pin one's hopes exclusively on discourses issuing directly from the university and glances in addition at the secondary channels occasionally responsible for carrying our practices off-campus. Take, as a not quite random example (and *pace* Davis), the novel. Who can doubt that the serious prose fiction of the past decade has been one of the more important conduits through which that varied collection of ideas and attitudes known as poststructuralism has begun—slowly, slowly, but at last noticeably—to permeate our wider heteroglossic society? The prospects for dialogism's wider cultural dispersal through similar "indirect" means are, I would argue, even better than deconstruction's. I say this because it has long been recognized that although Bakhtin uncannily anticipated many facets of Derridian, de Manian, and Foucauldian thought,[38] he did so without invoking terrifying aporias or hailing giddy liberations from meaning and responsibility. The word's always already appropriated nature, the fact that it is everywhere inscribed by power, and the knowledge that it cannot help but continually deconstruct all foundationalist claims to truth—these insights, he insists, lead neither to a prison house of language nor an inescapable panopticon nor a hermeneutical free-for-all. There is no reason to doubt that this maturer, less extravagant, more historical, more hopeful—and ultimately more radical—mode of poststructuralism will itself soon begin, if it has not already, to be registered upon the sensitive tissue of our culture's still dominant literary genre. It should not, therefore, be long before we are presented with what might be termed fully self-conscious dialogic novels, in the sense of works that, as part of their heteroglossic ensemble, include—and dialogize—recognizably Bakhtinian discourses.

It should be interesting to watch.

Notes

✳

Preface

1. M. M. Bakhtin, *Speech Genres and Other Late Essays*, ed. Caryl Emerson and Michael Holquist, trans. Vern W. McGee (Austin: University of Texas Press, 1986), p. 147.

2. See especially Michael Ryan, *Marxism and Deconstruction: A Critical Articulation* (Baltimore and London: Johns Hopkins University Press, 1982); Catherine Gallagher, "Marxism and the New Historicism," in *The New Historicism*, ed. H. Aram Veeser (New York and London: Routledge, 1989), pp. 37–48; and Mark Poster, *Foucault, Marxism, and History: Mode of Production versus Mode of Information* (Cambridge: Polity Press, 1984).

3. The phrase is Gertrude Himmelfarb's, from "History with the Politics Left Out," in *The New History and the Old* (Cambridge: Belknap Press, 1987), p. 16.

4. Fredric Jameson, *The Political Unconscious: Narrative as a Socially Symbolic Act* (Ithaca, N.Y.: Cornell University Press, 1981), p. 291. Jameson himself states that Bakhtin's theories may "hint at . . . articulating a properly Marxian version of meaning beyond the purely ideological" (p. 285). While I agree that neo-Marxism can profit greatly from Bakhtin, I am not sure that the end result of the dialogue I propose would still strike Jameson as *properly* Marxist, for he still seems intent upon rescuing some aspects of Marxism's prophetic and utopian discourses.

Chapter 1. Novelistic Form and the Limits to Cultural Collaboration

1. Ian Watt, *The Rise of the Novel: Studies in Defoe, Richardson and Fielding* (Berkeley and Los Angeles: University of California Press, 1957).

2. D. A. Miller, *The Novel and the Police* (Berkeley and Los Angeles: University of California Press, 1988); Nancy Armstrong, *Desire and Domestic Fiction: A Political History of the Novel* (Oxford: Oxford University Press, 1987); Lennard J. Davis, *Resisting Novels: Ideology and Fiction* (New York and London: Methuen, 1987); Jon Stratton, *The Virgin Text: Fiction, Sexuality, and Ideology* (Norman: University of Oklahoma Press, 1987).

3. Stratton, *The Virgin Text*, p. xi.

4. Ibid., p. xiv.

5. Gary Saul Morson and Caryl Emerson, *Mikhail Bakhtin: Creation of a Prosaics* (Stanford, Calif.: Stanford University Press, 1990), pp. 292–93. It is they

(pp. 45–46) who make the analogy between natural selection and the process by which, according to Bakhtin, cultures produce literary genres.

6. Terry Eagleton, *Marxism and Literary Criticism* (Berkeley: University of California Press, 1976), p. 26.

7. See especially the chapter "Discipline in Different Voices: Bureaucracy, Police, Family, and *Bleak House*," in Miller, *The Novel and the Police*, pp. 58–106.

8. Morson and Emerson, *Mikhail Bakhtin*, p. 46.

9. A project broadly similar in form, though different in content, is pursued by Terry Tanner in *Adultery and the Novel: Contract and Transgression* (Baltimore: Johns Hopkins University Press, 1979).

10. Mikhail Bakhtin, *The Dialogic Imagination*, ed. Michael Holquist, trans. Caryl Emerson and Michael Holquist (Austin: University of Texas Press, 1981), p. 34.

11. See Bakhtin, *Dialogic*, pp. 86–129.

12. See Bakhtin, *Dialogic*, pp. 130–46, quotation from p. 141.

13. One could, I suppose, point to Hardy's novels and claim that the auguries and prophecies that hector his protagonists seem much more than merely symbolic. This is true enough, but still, Hardy always allows us the option of taking such utterances and events merely as striking coincidences if we wish, a choice never tendered by the chivalric romance.

14. Bakhtin, *Dialogic*, pp. 151–58. For another discussion of the novel's preoccupation with the incremental effects of time as compared to other genres, see Eleanor H. Hutchens, "An Approach Through Time," in *Towards a Poetics of Fiction*, ed., Mark Spilka (Bloomington: University of Indiana Press, 1977), pp. 52–61.

15. See Watt, *Rise of the Novel*, pp. 13–27.

16. W. J. Harvey, *Character and the Novel* (Ithaca, N.Y.: Cornell University Press, 1965), p. 120.

17. Davis, *Resisting Novels*, p. 120.

18. Bakhtin, *Dialogic*, p. 7.

19. David Goldknopf, *The Life of the Novel* (Chicago: University Press of Chicago, 1972), p. 18.

20. Lionel Trilling, "Manners, Morals, and the Novel," in *The Liberal Imagination: Essays on Literature and Society* (New York: Charles Scribner's Sons, 1976), p. 211.

21. Bakhtin, *Dialogic*, p. 333.

22. Mikhail Bakhtin, *Problems of Dostoevsky's Poetics*, ed. and trans. Caryl Emerson (Minneapolis: University of Minnesota Press, 1984), p. 82.

23. Bakhtin, *Problems*, p. 7.

24. Morson and Emerson, *Mikhail Bakhtin*, p. 310.

25. Davis, *Resisting Novels*, pp. 165–71.

26. David Lodge, *After Bakthin: Essays on Fiction and Criticism* (London: Routledge, 1990), p. 22.

27. Bakhtin, *Problems*, p. 82.

28. Bakhtin, *Problems*, p. 83.

29. Davis, *Resisting Novels*, p. 117.

30. E. M. Forster, *Aspects of the Novel* (New York and London: Harcourt, Brace, Jovanovich), p. 78.

31. See Watt, *Rise of the Novel*, pp. 60, 179–80.

32. As Watt points out (*Rise of the Novel*, p. 71), "It is very likely that the lack

of variety and stimulation in the daily task as a result of economic specialization is largely responsible for the unique dependence of the individual in our culture upon the substitute experiences provided by the printing press, particularly in the forms of journalism and the novel."

33. Edward W. Said, *Beginnings: Intention and Method* (New York: Basic Books, 1975), p. 81.

34. Harvey, *Character*, p. 24.

Chapter 2. Wakefield's Vicar, Delinquent Paragon

1. Robert H. Hopkins, *The True Genius of Oliver Goldsmith* (Baltimore: Johns Hopkins University Press, 1969), pp. 166–230; Richard J. Jaarsma, "Satiric Intent in *The Vicar of Wakefield*," *Studies in Short Fiction* 5 (1967–68), pp. 331–41.

2. D. W. Jefferson, "*The Vicar of Wakefield* and Other Prose Writings: A Reconsideration," in *The Art of Oliver Goldsmith*, ed. Andrew Swarbrick (Totowa, N.J.: Barnes & Noble, 1984), pp. 17–32; Martin Battestin, *The Providence of Wit: Aspects of Form in Augustan Literature and the Arts* (Oxford: Clarendon Press, 1974), pp. 193–214.

3. For discussions of the signal differences between the text's first and second halves, see Michael Adelstein, "Duality of Theme in *The Vicar of Wakefield*," *College English* 22(5) (February 1961), pp. 315–21; Ronald Paulson, *Satire and the Novel in Eighteenth-Century England* (New Haven, Conn.: Yale University Press, 1967), pp. 273–75, Ricardo Quintana, *Oliver Goldsmith: A Georgian Study* (New York: Macmillan, 1967), pp. 110–13; and Hopkins, *True Genius*, pp. 209–16. An attempt to reconcile the novel's satiric and Sentimental aspects is undertaken by George E. Haggerty, "Satire and Sentiment in *The Vicar of Wakefield*," *The Eighteenth Century* 32(1) (1991), pp. 25–38.

4. Jaarsma, in "Satiric Intent," does in fact deal with certain secular issues in *The Vicar*, as does Hopkins in "Social Stratification and the Obsequious Curve: Goldsmith and Rowlandson," *Studies in the Eighteenth Century* III (Toronto: University of Toronto Press, 1976), pp. 55–71, and in "Matrimony in *The Vicar of Wakefield* and the Marriage Act of 1753," *Studies in Philology* 74(3) (July 1977), pp. 322–39.

5. Daniel Defoe, *Robinson Crusoe* (Oxford: Basil Blackwell, 1927), p. 3

6. Peter Earle, *The Making of the English Middle Class: Business, Society and Family Life in London, 1660–1730* (Berkeley: University of California Press, 1989), p. 10.

7. Paul Langford, *A Polite and Commercial People: England 1727–1783* (Oxford: Clarendon Press, 1989), p. 68.

8. Donald Davie, "Notes on Goldsmith's Politics" in Swarbrick, *Art of Oliver Goldsmith*, pp. 79–89. See also John Bender, "Prison Reform and the Sentence of Narration in *The Vicar of Wakefield*," in *The New Eighteenth Century: Theory, Politics, English Literature*, ed. Felicity Nussbaum and Laura Brown (New York: Methuen, 1987), p. 173.

9. Earle, *Making of the English Middle Class*, pp. 336, 334.

10. All citations of Goldsmith other than *The Vicar of Wakefield* refer to *The Collected Works of Oliver Goldsmith*, ed. Arthur Friedman (Oxford: Clarendon Press, 1966).

11. Paul Langford, *Public Life and the Propertied Englishman 1689–1798* (Oxford: Clarendon Press, 1991), p. 502.

12. All references to *The Vicar of Wakefield* are from the Penguin Edition, ed. Stephen Coote (Harmondsworth, UK: Penguin, 1982). Parenthetical references in text are to page numbers in this edition.

13. Jaarsma, "Satiric Intent," p. 337

14. Thomas R. Preston, "The Uses of Adversity: Worldly Detachment and Heavenly Treasure in *The Vicar of Wakefield*," *Studies in Philology* 81(2) (Spring 1984), p. 237.

15. See Langford, *Public Life*, p. 502.

16. Goldsmith's fellow novelist John Potter, author of *The Curate of Coventry, A Tale*, 1771, opines that people of rank, "being independent of the lesser cares of life, from their situation, seldom pay a proper regard to their moral duties, which are the very cement and bond of society." Such bashing of the upper classes, says Langford, "appealed equally to writers who exploited the cult of feeling and bourgeois honesty." See Langford, *Public Life*, p. 540.

17. Peter Earle, *The World of Defoe* (New York: Atheneum, 1977), p. 193. See also Maximillian E. Novak, *Economics and the Fiction of Daniel Defoe* (Berkeley: University of California Press, 1962), pp. 136–38.

18. The phrase is Raymond Hilliard's from "The Redemption of Fatherhood in The Vicar of Wakefield," *SEL* 23(3) (Summer 1983), p. 473.

19. Hopkins, *True Genius*, pp. 186–91, provides a catalogue of the Vicar's yearnings for upward mobility.

20. Adelstein, "Duality," p. 318.

21. For a discussion of Primrose's failings as a paterfamilias, see Hilliard, "Redemption," pp. 465–72.

22. As Earle makes clear, this view is quite similar to Defoe's (Earle, *World of Defoe*, p. 162).

23. Langford, *Public Life*, p. 506.

24. Battestin, *Providence of Wit*, pp. 193–214.

25. John A. Dussinger, in *The Discourse of Mind in Eighteenth-Century Fiction* (The Hague: Mouton, 1974), pp. 162–63, also draws attention to the bourgeois character of this lyric and the implications of Olivia's rendition of it.

26. For an intriguing discussion of Goldsmith's possible authorship of a didactic children's book, see Neil McKendrick, John Brewer, and J. H. Plumb, *The Birth of a Consumer Society: The Commercialization of Eighteenth-Century England* (Bloomington: Indiana University Press, 1982), pp. 300–303.

27. Hopkins, "Obsequious Curve," p. 69; Dussinger, *Discourse of Mind*, p. 171.

28. See Nancy Armstrong, *Desire and Domestic Fiction: A Political History of the Novel* (New York: Oxford University Press, 1987), pp. 108–34, for an explication of the contest between Richardson's Pamela and Mr. B as a struggle between bourgeois and aristocratic conceptions of gender, marriage, and the household establishment. Also see Hopkins, "Matrimony," p. 338.

29. Quintana, *Oliver Goldsmith*, p. 113.

30. Adelstein, "Duality," p. 318.

31. Hopkins, *True Genius*, p. 208. In a puzzling turn, Hopkins writes that the novel's "exaggeration of *structure* [italics mine] particularly toward the conclusion, represents Dr. Primrose's being carried away by his own story: he uses all of the stock *situations* [italics mine] normally used in sentimental romance and stage comedy." Unless he would have us believe that Goldsmith means for us to perceive the Vicar as *lying* about the *events* of the tale's climax—never a real possibility—

I can't understand what he is claiming here. Hopkins is generally much more persuasive when dealing with the first half of the novel than with the second.

32. *Encyclopedia Britannica*, 11th ed., p. 216.

33. Maurice Z. Shroder, "The Novel as Genre," in *The Theory of the Novel*, ed. Phillip Stevick (New York: Free Press, 1967), pp. 22, 24.

34. Jaarsma, "Satiric Intent," p. 339.

35. Some critics think this story is also a parody of Sentimental novels—see Hopkins, *True Genius*, pp. 97–98.

36. Quintana, *Oliver Goldsmith*, p. 106.

37. Mikhail Bakhtin, *The Dialogic Imagination*, ed. Michael Holquist, trans. Caryl Emerson and Michael Holquist (Austin: University of Texas Press, 1988), p. 397.

38. Langford, *A Polite and Commercial People*, p. 464.

39. Battestin, *Providence of Wit*, p. 199.

Chapter 3. *The Anti-Romantic Polemics of* Mansfield Park

1. D. A. Miller, *Narrative and Its Discontents: Problems of Closure in the Traditional Novel* (Princeton, N.J.: Princeton University Press, 1981), pp. xiv, 3.

2. Ibid., p. 54.

3. Marilyn Butler finds a similar conflict between anti-Jacobin ideas and novelistic form in *Jane Austen and the War of Ideas* (Oxford: Clarendon Press, 1975), pp. 247–49. She concludes that Fanny's failure as a character "lies in the incongruity of the old absolutes to the novel, a form which historically is individualistic and morally subversive." She goes on to say that "the failure lies not so much in the ideas [themselves], as in the attempt to use the inward life of a heroine as a vehicle for them."

4. Butler, *Jane Austen*, asserts (p. 242) that "Fanny's story undoubtedly takes on colouring of a special kind from the period in which it was written. There can be no doubt that many of the central themes of the book have been modified by the spirit of Evangelicalism." It is of course possible that such an influence could have increased Austen's dissatisfaction with Gothic and Byronic tests, but the whole argument for her evangelical semiconversion seems to rest upon meager evidence.

5. Tony Tanner, *Jane Austen* (Cambridge, Mass.: Harvard University Press, 1986), p. 143.

6. Attempts to paint Jane Austen as a more or less thorough Romantic include a special edition of *The Wordsworth Circle* 7(4) (Autumn 1976); Susan Morgan, *In the Meantime: Character and Perception in Jane Austen's Fiction* (Chicago: University of Chicago Press, 1980); and Nina Auerbach, both in "Jane Austen and Romantic Imprisonment," in *Jane Austen in a Social Context*, ed. David Monaghan (Totowa, N.J.: Barnes & Noble, 1981), pp. 9–27, and in "Jane Austen's Dangerous Charisma: Feeling as One Ought about Fanny Price," *Women and Literature* 3 (1988), pp. 208–23. In the latter, Auerbach cites Fanny's tendency to be a killjoy and then goes so far as to assert that "this elevation of one's private bad feelings into a power alternate to social life associates Fanny not merely with early Romantic outcasts, but with such dashingly misanthropic hero-villains as Byron's Childe Harold, Mary Shelley's Frankenstein, and Maturin's Melmoth" (p. 210).

7. Frank W. Bradbrook, *Jane Austen and Her Predecessors* (Cambridge: Cambridge University Press, 1967), pp. 78, 107–8; Stuart M. Tave, "Jane Austen and

One of Her Contemporaries," in *Jane Austen: Bicentenary Essays*, ed. John Halperin (Cambridge: Cambridge University Press, 1975), pp. 61–74. See also Jay Clayton, *Romantic Vision and the Novel* (Cambridge: Cambridge University Press, 1987), p. 61.

8. All references to *Mansfield Park* refer to the Penguin edition (Harmondsworth, UK: 1985). Parenthetical references in text are to page numbers in this edition, except as noted.

9. George Levine, *The Realistic Imagination: English Fiction from* Frankenstein *to* Lady Chatterley (Chicago: University of Chicago Press, 1981), pp. 6, 17, 35.

10. Fanny is also allowed to quote from Scott at Southerton's chapel, but then Scott is no Romantic. His narratives, no matter their violent subject matter or exotic historical setting, are at all points interfused by a calm, thoroughly Augustan intelligence. It is little wonder that the two authors admired each other.

11. "Lyrical Ballads," Preface of 1800.

12. Robert Kiely, *The Romantic Novel in England* (Cambridge, Mass.: Harvard University Press, 1972), p. 22.

13. Levine, *The Realistic Imagination*, p. 35.

14. John Ruskin, "Of Queens' Gardens," in *Works*, The Illustrated Cabinet Edition, vol. 26 (Boston: Dana Estes & Company), p. 93.

15. Joseph Conrad, *Heart of Darkness* (Harmondsworth, UK: Penguin, 1983), pp. 113–14.

16. These useful terms were first suggested to me by Anthony Winner.

17. These elaborations on the meaning of "mediated" and "absolute" are largely, though not wholly, taken from the terminology of Joseph Wiesenfarth, who, in his *Gothic Manners and the Classic English Novel* (Madison: University of Wisconsin Press, 1988), pp. 11–15, proposes a set of distinctions by which the concerns of what he terms "the new Gothic novel" can be differentiated from those of the "novel of manners." I employ some of his categories fully realizing that I am lifting them out of context, for while it is true that Wiesenfarth sees Austen as perhaps the quintessential novelist of manners, he uses the term "*new* Gothic" to refer to a set of novels published after—sometimes well after—*Mansfield Park* and different in many important ways from their Radcliffian precursors. Nevertheless, I feel justified in adopting his terms (again, with appropriate adjustments) for two reasons. First of all, I am certain that most readers will see enough of what Wiesenfarth considers to be "new Gothic" concerns in the "old Gothic" of Radcliffe, Lewis, etc., to absolve me of the charge of complete anachronism. Second, what he labels as the stuff of the "new Gothic" is uncannily descriptive of what is contained in *Childe Harold's Pilgrimage* and *The Giaour*.

18. *The Giaour* appeared in June 1813. Austen was working on revisions of *Mansfield Park* up until December of that year. See John Halperin, *The Life of Jane Austen* (Baltimore: Johns Hopkins University Press, 1984), pp. 231, 233–34.

19. An anonymous review of the volume containing *Northanger Abbey* and *Persuasion* in *Scots Magazine . . .*, vol. 81, pt. 1 (May 1818), pp. 453–55. Reprinted in B. C. Southam, ed., *Jane Austen: The Critical Heritage* (London: Routledge and Kegan Paul, 1968), pp. 266–68.

20. All citations from *Northanger Abbey* and *Persuasion* refer to the Penguin editions (Harmondsworth, UK: Penguin, 1985).

21. Jane Austen, *Minor Works*, ed. R. W. Chapman (Oxford: Oxford University Press, 1954), p. 403–4.

22. Richard Simpson, unsigned review of "Memoir of Jane Austen," *North British Review* 52 (1870), pp. 129–52; reprinted in *Critical Heritage*, p. 244.

23. Tanner, *Jane Austen*, p. 163.

24. Auerbach, "Romantic Imprisonment," pp. 13–14, 16.

25. Mikhail Bakhtin, *Problems of Dostoevsky's Poetics*, ed. and trans. Caryl Emerson (Minneapolis: University of Minnesota Press, 1984), pp. 193, 197.

26. Bakhtin, *Problems*, p. 195.

27. Ibid., p. 195.

28. Auerbach, "Romantic Imprisonment," pp. 21–22.

29. The phrase is employed, in the midst of a broadly similar argument concerning *Northanger Abbey*, by Claudia L. Johnson, *Jane Austen: Women, Politics, and the Novel* (Chicago: University of Chicago Press, 1988), p. 47. Also see Levine, *The Realistic Imagination*, p. 64.

30. James Thompson, *Between Self and World: The Novels of Jane Austen* (University Park: Pennsylvania State University Press, 1988), p. 33.

31. Butler, *Jane Austen*, p. 244.

32. Bakhtin, *Problems*, p. 196.

33. Tanner, *Jane Austen*, p. 18.

34. Bakhtin, *Problems*, p. 195.

35. The frequent use of such words is noted by Avrom Fleishman, *A Reading of* Mansfield Park (Minneapolis: University of Minnesota Press, 1967), pp. 51–52.

36. Michiel Heyns, "Shock and Horror: The Moral Vocabulary of *Mansfield Park*," *English Studies in Africa: A Journal of the Humanities* 29(1), pp. 13–16. A rather intricate defense of Fanny, and to some extent of the novel as a whole, is mounted by Roger Gard, *Jane Austen's Novels: The Art of Clarity* (New Haven, Conn.: Yale University Press, 1992), pp. 121–44.

37. Lionel Trilling, *The Opposing Self* (New York: Viking Press, 1955), p. 208.

38. Tanner, *Jane Austen*, p. 143.

39. Heyns, "Shock and Horror," p. 16.

40. Janet Burroway, "The Irony of the Insufferable Prig: *Mansfield Park*," *Critical Quarterly* 9(2) (Summer 1967), p. 130.

41. Levine, *The Realistic Imagination*, pp. 19, 36.

42. Burroway, "Irony," p. 130, and Butler, *Jane Austen*, pp. 237–38.

43. Sydney McMillen Conger, "Reading 'Lovers' Vows': Jane Austen's Reflections on English Sense and German Sensibility," *Studies in Philology* 85(1) (Winter 1988), p. 113, and Burroway, "Irony," pp. 135–38.

44. Leroy W. Smith, "Mansfield Park: The Revolt of the 'Feminine' Woman," *Social Context*, pp. 154–57.

45. Trilling, *Opposing Self*, pp. 212–13. Levine, *The Realistic Imagination*, p. 75, calls Fanny "a sentimental heroine, a Pamela without Pamela's energy."

46. David Lodge, *Language of Fiction: Essays in Criticism and Verbal Analysis of the English Novel* (New York: Columbia University Press, 1966), p. 97.

47. Butler, *Jane Austen*, p. 247.

48. Clayton, *Romantic Vision*, p. 63.

49. Tony Tanner, *Adultery and the Novel: Contract and Transgression* (Baltimore: Johns Hopkins University Press, 1979), p. 105.

50. Fleischman, *Reading*, p. 64, and Auerbach, "Dangerous Charisma," p. 210.

51. Trilling, *Opposing Self*, p. 227.

52. It seems to me that Bakhtin's notion of dialogic engagement can refine the

assertions of Tanner (*Jane Austen*, p. 39) and other critics that the enemies of Austen's ideology all come from within that same ideology, for according to Bakhtin, *Mansfield Park* both pursues and eschews genuine dialogue with an "alien" discourse.

53. Mikhail Bakhtin, *The Dialogic Imagination*, ed. Michael Holquist, trans. Caryl Emerson and Michael Holquist (Austin: University of Texas Press, 1988), p. 400.

54. Bakhtin, *Problems*, p. 64

55. 5 March 1814, quoted in Halperin, *Life of Jane Austen*, p. 252.

Chapter 4. Bildungsromans That Aren't

1. John Ruskin, "Of Queens' Gardens," in *Works*, The Illustrated Cabinet Edition, vol. 26 (Boston: Dana Estes & Company), p. 87.

2. Ibid.

3. Ibid., p. 122.

4. All citations from *Agnes Grey* refer to the Oxford Edition (Oxford: Clarendon Press, 1988). Parenthetical references in text are to page numbers in this edition.

5. M. M. Bakhtin, *The Dialogic Imagination*, ed. Michael Holquist, trans. Caryl Emerson and Michael Holquist (Austin: University of Texas Press, 1981), p. 106.

6. Gary Saul Morson and Caryl Emerson, *Mikhail Bakhtin: Creation of a Prosaics* (Stanford, Calif.: Stanford University Press, 1990), pp. 380–81.

7. Ibid., p. 382.

8. Bakhtin, *Dialogic Imagination*, p. 392–93.

9. Maurice Z. Shroder, "The Novel as a Genre" in *The Theory of the Novel*, ed. Phillip Stevick (New York: Free Press, 1967), p. 16.

10. Bakhtin, *Dialogic Imagination*, p. 392.

11. P. J. M. Scott, *Anne Brontë: A New Critical Assessment* (Totowa, N.J.: Barnes & Noble, 1983), pp. 26–27.

12. Tom Winnifrith, *The Brontës* (New York: Macmillan, 1977), pp. 69–70.

13. Scott, *Anne Brontë*, pp. 20–22.

14. W. A. Craik, *The Brontë Novels* (London: Methuen & Co., 1968), p. 211.

15. Winnifrith, *The Brontës*, p. 70.

16. M. M. Bakhtin, *Speech Genres and Other Late Essays*, ed. Caryl Emerson and Michael Holquist, trans. Vern W. McGee (Austin: University of Texas Press, 1986), p. 21.

17. Terry Eagleton, *Myths of Power: A Marxist Study of the Brontës* (London: Macmillan, 1975), p. 128.

18. Ibid.

19. Phillip Collins, *Dickens and Education* (London: Macmillan & Co., 1963), pp. 184–85.

20. Angus Wilson, "Introduction" to the Penguin Edition (Harmondsworth, UK: Penguin, 1985), p. 26.

21. Steven Marcus, *Dickens: From Pickwick to Dombey* (New York: Basic Books, 1965), p. 80.

22. Grahame Smith, *Dickens, Money, and Society* (Berkeley: University of California Press, 1968), pp. 33, 13.

23. Ibid., p. 13.

24. All references to *Oliver Twist* are from the Penguin edition (Harmondsworth, UK: Penguin, 1985). Parenthetical references in the text are to page numbers in this edition.

25. Barry Westburg, *The Confessional Fictions of Charles Dickens* (De Kalb: Northern Illinois University Press, 1977), p. 6.

26. Torsten Pattersson also nominates Dickens as a naturalist, though for different reasons, in "Enough to Have Bodies? Two Incongruities in *Oliver Twist*," *Orbis Litterarum* 45 (1990), pp. 341–50.

27. Westburg, *Confessional Fictions*, p. 13.

28. W. J. Harvey, *Character and the Novel* (Ithaca, N.Y.: Cornell University Press, 1965), pp. 134, 137.

29. Benjamin Disraeli, *Coningsby* (Oxford: Oxford University Press, 1982), p. 148.

30. William T. Lankford, "'The Parish Boy's Progress,': The Evolving Form of *Oliver Twist*," *PMLA* 93(1) (January 1978), pp. 20–21.

31. Westburg, *Confessional Fictions*, p. 1.

32. See Janet L. Larson, *Dickens and the Broken Scripture* (Athens: University of Georgia Press, 1985), p. 71.

33. Morson and Emerson, *Mikhail Bakhtin*, p. 202.

34. Charles Dickens, *David Copperfield* (Harmondsworth, UK: Penguin, 1983), p. 208.

35. For a longer discussion of the biographical aspects of *Oliver Twist*, see Morris Golden, "Dickens, Oliver, and Boz," *Dickens Quarterly* 4(2) (June 1987), pp. 65–77.

36. John Carey, *Here Comes Dickens: The Imagination of a Novelist* (New York: Schocken Books, 1974), p. 149.

37. For a Bakhtinian account of the blacking warehouse's effects on Dickens's fiction, see Stanley Tick, "Dickens, Dickens, Micawber . . . and Bakhtin," *Victorian Newsletter* 70 (Spring 1991), pp. 34–37.

38. For another discussion of Wordsworth and *Oliver Twist*, see Rosemarie Bodenheimer, *The Politics of Story in Victorian Social Fiction* (Ithaca, N.Y.: Cornell University Press, 1988), pp. 119–30.

39. This is pointed out by Larson, *Broken Scripture*, p. 54. Also see David Grylls, *Guardians and Angels: Parents and Children in Nineteenth-Century Literature* (London: Faber & Faber, 1978), pp. 140–42.

40. J. Hillis Miller, *Charles Dickens: The World of His Novels* (Bloomington: Indiana University Press, 1969), pp. 78, 81.

41. Harvey, *Character*, p. 137.

42. See, for instance, Wilson, "Introduction," pp. 25–26; Humphry House, "Introduction," *Oliver Twist* (Oxford: Oxford University Press, 1985), pp. v–vi; and Joseph Sawiki, "Oliver (Un)Twisted: Narrative Strategies in *Oliver Twist*," *Victorian Newsletter* 73 (Spring 1988), p. 27.

43. Westburg, *Confessional Fictions*, pp. 7–8.

44. Lawrence Frank, *Charles Dickens and the Romantic Self* (Lincoln: University of Nebraska Press, 1984), pp. 22, 28.

45. H. M. Daleski, *Dickens and the Art of Analogy* (London: Faber & Faber, 1970), p. 60.

Chapter 5. Foucault, Neo-Marxism, and the Cultural Conversation

1. Gerald Graff notes the connection between "the later Foucault," new historicism, and a criticism of political despair in "Co-optation," *The New Historicism*, ed. H. Aram Veeser (New York & London: Routledge, 1989), pp. 168–81.

2. See Terry Eagleton, "Wittgenstein's Friends," in *Against the Grain: Essays, 1975–1985* (London and New York: Verso, 1986), p. 116.

3. Michel Foucault, *Power/Knowledge: Selected Interviews and Other Writings, 1972–1977*, ed. Colin Gordon (New York: Pantheon, 1980), p. 98.

4. Frank Lentricchia, *Ariel and the Police: Michel Foucault, William James, Wallace Stevens* (Madison: University of Wisconsin Press, 1988), pp. 68, 69.

5. Michel Foucault, *Discipline and Punish: The Birth of the Prison*, trans. Alan Sheridan (New York: Random House, 1979), p. 26.

6. Hubert L. Dreyfus and Paul Rabinow, *Michel Foucault: Beyond Structuralism and Hermeneutics*, 2d ed. (Chicago: University of Chicago Press, 1983), p. 147.

7. As Edward Said has commented, Foucault "by his analysis of power [revealed] its injustice and cruelty, but by his theorization . . . let it go on more or less unchecked." "Foucault and the Imagination of Power" in *Foucault: A Critical Reader*, ed. David Couzens Hoy (Oxford: Basil Blackwell, 1986), p. 152.

8. Gary Saul Morson and Caryl Emerson, *Mikhail Bakhtin: Creation of a Prosaics* (Stanford, Calif.: Stanford University Press, 1990), p. 28.

9. Mikhail Bakhtin, *The Dialogical Imagination*, ed. Michael Holquist, trans. Caryl Emerson and Michael Holquist (Austin: University of Texas Press, 1981), pp. 262–63.

10. Foucault, *Power/Knowledge*, p. 188.

11. Ibid., p. 141–42.

12. A typical formulation appears in Foucault, *Power/Knowledge*, pp. 162–64, where he asserts that "resistances to the Panopticon will have to be analyzed in tactical and strategic terms, positing that each offensive from the one side serves as leverage for a counter-offensive from the other."

13. Personal communication from Foucault, quoted in Dreyfus and Rabinow, *Michel Foucault*, p. 187.

14. Alan Sheridan, *Michel Foucault: The Will to Truth* (New York and London: Tavistock, 1980), pp. 185.

15. Stephen Greenblatt, *Renaissance Self-Fashioning: From More to Shakespeare* (Chicago: University of Chicago Press, 1980), p. 209. To be fair, some of Greenblatt's recent studies seem to paint a more balanced picture of the possibilities for both cooptation and subversion within literary texts.

16. Mark Seltzer, *Henry James and the Art of Power* (Ithaca, N.Y.: Cornell University Press, 1984), p. 18.

17. D. A. Miller, *The Novel and the Police* (Berkeley: University of California Press, 1988), p. x.

18. Peggy Knapp, *Chaucer and the Social Contest* (New York and London: Routledge, 1990), p. 3.

19. Foucault, *Power/Knowledge*, p. 82.

20. Knapp, *Chaucer*, pp. 4–5.

21. Bakhtin, *Dialogic*, pp. 293–94.

22. Paul Smith, *Discerning the Subject* (Minneapolis: University of Minnesota Press, 1988), p. 6.

23. Bakhtin, *Dialogic*, p. 345.

24. See ibid., pp. 344–47.

25. Ibid., pp. 346, 348.

26. Ibid., p. 345.

27. Smith, *Discerning the Subject*, p. 158.

28. See Louis Althusser, "Ideology and Ideological State Apparatuses," in *"Lenin and Philosophy" and Other Essays* (London: NLB, 1971).

29. Susan Stewart, "Shouts on the Street: Bakhtin's Anti-Linguistics," in *Bakhtin: Essays and Dialogues on His Work*, ed. Gary Saul Morson (Chicago: University of Chicago Press, 1986), p. 52.

30. V. N. Voloshinov, *Marxism and the Philosophy of Language*, trans. Ladislav Matejka and I. R. Titunik (New York and London: Seminar Press, 1973), p. 38.

31. Morson and Emerson, *Mikhail Bakhtin*, p. 218.

32. For a full discussion, see Caryl Emerson, "The Outer World and Inner Speech: Bakhtin, Vygotsky, and the Internalization of Language," in *Bakhtin: Essays and Dialogues on His Work*, ed. Gary Saul Morson (Chicago: University of Chicago Press, 1986), pp. 21–40.

33. Morson and Emerson, *Mikhail Bakhtin*, pp. 200–203.

34. Voloshinov, *Marxism*, pp. 85–86.

35. Ibid., p. 34.

36. Foucault, *Power/Knowledge*, p. 188.

37. Mikhail Bakhtin, *Problems of Dostoevsky's Poetics*, ed. and trans. Caryl Emerson (Minneapolis: University of Minnesota Press, 1984), p. 59.

38. Raymond Williams, *Marxism and Literature* (Oxford: Oxford University Press, 1977), p. 110.

39. Ibid., p. 114.

40. The terms are Raymond Williams's. See *Marxism and Literature*, pp. 121–27.

41. Terry Eagleton, *Criticism and Ideology: A Study in Marxist Literary Theory* (Thetford, UK: Verso, 1978), p. 101.

42. Tony Bennett, *Formalism and Marxism* (London and New York: Methuen, 1979), p. 109. In fairness to Eagleton, his subsequent writings seem to offer a way around this objection, for he states in *Literary Theory: An Introduction* (Minneapolis: University of Minnesota Press, 1983), pp. 10–16, that "literature, in the sense of a set of works of assured and unalterable value, distinguished by certain shared inherent properties, does not exist" but is rather "a *construct*, fashioned by particular people for particular reasons at a certain time." Thus, when he goes on to say that the "value judgements [by which literature is constituted] have a close relation to social ideologies," I think we may take him to mean that decisions about what a given culture defines as literature *tend to be* saturated with political implications and that therefore works denominated as literary can *often* be examined in a manner potentially revelatory of their culture's ideological assumptions. I don't think he means to contend that literary texts are always and everywhere supremely privileged windows into the workings of hegemony or that other, nonliterary texts would be chronically incapable of exposing such social processes to better effect.

43. Bakhtin, *Dialogic*, pp. 296–97.

44. Ibid., p. 7.

45. Ibid., p. 11.

46. Nancy Glazener, "Dialogic Subversion: Bakhtin, the Novel and Gertrude Stein," in *Bakhtin and Cultural Theory*, ed. Ken Hirschkop and David Shepherd (Manchester and New York: Manchester University Press, 1989), p. 109.

47. Bakhtin, *Dialogic*, pp. 325–26.

48. Ibid., p. 333.

49. See Morson and Emerson, *Mikhail Bakhtin*, p. 310.

50. Bakhtin, *Dialogic*, pp. 369–69.

51. Foucault, *Power/Knowledge*, p. 131.

52. Bakhtin, *Dialogic*, p. 333.

53. Ann Jefferson, "Realism Reconsidered: Bakhtin's Dialogism and the 'Will to Reference,'" *Australian Journal of French Studies* 23(3) (May–August 1986), p. 177. Also, David Carroll, "The Alterity of Discourse: Form, History, and the Question of the Political in M. M. Bakhtin," *Diacritics* 13(2) (Summer 1983), p. 77.

54. Bakhtin, *Problems*, p. 68.

55. Graham Pechey, "On the Borders of Bakhtin: Dialogisation, Decolonisation," in *Bakhtin and Cultural Theory*, ed. Ken Hirschkop and David Shepherd (Manchester and New York: Manchester University Press, 1989), p. 66.

56. Bakhtin, *Problems*, p. 69.

57. See Wayne Booth's "Introduction" to Bakhtin, *Problems of Dostoevsky's Poetics*, pp. xiii–xxvii.

58. Morson and Emerson, *Mikhail Bakhtin*, p. 132.

59. Richard Rorty, *Contingency, Irony, and Solidarity* (Cambridge: Cambridge University Press, 1989), pp. 39–40.

60. Ken Hirschkop, "Introduction: Bakhtin and Cultural Theory," in *Bakhtin and Cultural Theory*, ed. Ken Hirschkop and David Shepherd (Manchester and New York: Manchester University Press, 1989), p. 18.

61. Rorty, *Contingency*, p. 94.

62. Rorty too credits some novelists who predate Proust. See, for instance, *Contingency*, p. 141.

63. Bakhtin, *Dialogic*, p. 331.

Chapter 6. Interminable Conversations

1. Raymond Williams, *Culture and Society: 1780–1950* (New York: Columbia University Press, 1983), pp. 87, 91.

2. Enid L. Duthie, *The Themes of Elizabeth Gaskell* (Totowa, N.J.: Rowman & Littlefield, 1980), p. 84.

3. Williams, *Culture and Society*, pp. 91–92.

4. *The Letters of Mrs. Gaskell*, ed. J. A. V. Chapple and Arthur Pollard (Cambridge, Mass.: Harvard University Press, 1967), Letter 72a, p. 119.

5. Deirdre David, *Fictions of Resolution in Three Victorian Novels* (New York: Columbia University Press, 1981), p. 4.

6. All citations of *Mary Barton* refer to the Penguin edition, ed. Stephen Gill (Harmondsworth, UK: Penguin, 1979). Parenthetical references in text are to page numbers in this edition.

7. Patsy Stoneman has suggested that Gaskell, in trying to debunk specifically male attitudes toward power, portrays the millowners of *Mary Barton* as refusing dialogue with the workers "because to engage in speech with them would be to accept them as 'adults' and thus legitimate their access to the dominant 'language' of vengeance" (*Elizabeth Gaskell* [Bloomington: Indiana University Press, 1987], p. 75). It would be more accurate, I think, to propose that, as far as Gaskell is concerned, dialogue and violence are mutually exclusive, each being the product and producer of the other's suppression, and that the risk of alienating (and arm-

ing) Caliban arises from the maintenance of a stony silence rather than from the sharing of a supposedly murderous linguistic gnosis.

8. Marjorie Stone, in "Bakhtinian Polyphony in *Mary Barton:* Class, Gender, and the Textual Voice," *Dickens Studies Annual* 20 (1991), pp. 175–200, convincingly argues that Gaskell's earlier novel both depicts a good deal of diversity among the varying vocabularies of the working class and dialogizes gender-based languages to a significant extent.

9. Mikhail Bakhtin, *Problems of Dostoevsky's Poetics,* ed. and trans. Caryl Emerson (Minneapolis: University of Minnesota Press, 1984), p. 166.

10. Igor Webb, *From Custom to Capital: The English Novel and the Industrial Revolution* (Ithaca, N.Y.: Cornell University Press, 1981), p. 196.

11. Bakhtin, *Problems,* p. 64.

12. William Wordsworth, "Prospectus" to *The Recluse,* ll. 50–51, 55, 59.

13. See especially Stoneman, *Elizabeth Gaskell,* and Catherine Gallagher, *The Industrial Reformation of English Fiction 1832–1867* (Chicago: University of Chicago Press, 1985).

14. Bakhtin himself is sometimes taken to task for resting satisfied with a form of political resistance that manifests itself only "inside" literary texts. See, for instance, Michael Gardiner, *The Dialogics of Critique: M. M. Bakhtin and the Theory of Ideology* (New York: Routledge, 1992), pp. 176, 186–87.

15. Stephen Gill, "Introduction" to the Penguin edition of *Mary Barton,* pp. 24–25. Likewise John Lucas, *The Literature of Change: Studies in the Nineteenth-Century Provincial Novel* (New York: Harper & Row, 1977), p. 45: "Death, exploitation, misery, suffering, injustice, and the sheer detail with which the novel abounds: these go clean counter to her recommendations. . . . For what she recommends cannot cope with the state of affairs that *Mary Barton* reveals."

16. *Letters,* No. 72, p. 116.

17. W. A. Craik, *Elizabeth Gaskell and the English Provincial Novel* (London: Methuen, 1975), p. 97.

18. All citations to *North and South* refer to the Oxford edition, ed. Angus Easson (Oxford: Oxford University Press, 1973). Parenthetical references in the text are to page numbers in this edition.

19. Carol Landsbury, *Elizabeth Gaskell: The Novel of Social Crisis* (New York: Harper & Row, 1975), pp. 108–9.

20. Gary Saul Morson and Caryl Emerson, *Mikhail Bakhtin: Creation of a Prosaics* (Stanford, Calif.: Stanford University Press, 1990), p. 126.

21. Gallagher, *Industrial Reformation,* pp. 170–71.

22. Rosemarie Bodenheimer, "*North and South*: A Permanent State of Change," *Nineteenth-Century Fiction* 34(3) (December 1979), p. 287.

23. Bakhtin, *Problems,* pp. 6–7.

24. John Lucas, "Mrs. Gaskell and Brotherhood," in *Tradition and Tolerance in Nineteenth-Century Fiction,* ed. David Howard, John Lucas, and John Goode (London: Routledge & Kegan Paul, 1966), p. 147.

25. For another discussion of the mutual incomprehensibility of the social languages in *North and South,* see Hilary M. Schor, *Scheherezade in the Marketplace: Elizabeth Gaskell and the Victorian Novel* (New York: Oxford University Press, 1992), pp. 124–36.

26. Bodenheimer, "Permanent Change," p. 291.

27. Stoneman, *Elizabeth Gaskell,* p. 134.

28. Landsbury, *Social Crisis*, pp. 108–9.

29. Bodenheimer, "Permanent Change," p. 301.

30. Fredric Jameson, *The Political Unconscious: Narrative as a Socially Symbolic Act* (Ithaca, N.Y.: Cornell University Press, 1981), pp. 287–91.

31. Morson and Emerson, *Mikhail Bakhtin*, p. 397.

32. Lucas, "Mrs. Gaskell and Brotherhood," p. 201.

Chapter 7. Individual versus Collectivity

1. See Ian Watt, *The Rise of the Novel: Studies in Defoe, Richardson, and Fielding* (Berkeley: University of California Press, 1957); and J. W. Harvey, *Character and the Novel* (Ithaca, N.Y.: Cornell University Press, 1965).

2. Mikhail Bakhtin, *The Dialogic Imagination*, ed. Michael Holquist, trans. Caryl Emerson and Michael Holquist (Austin: University of Texas Press, 1981), p. 350–51.

3. George Woodcock, "Introduction," *A Tale of Two Cities* (New York: Penguin, 1970). All subsequent citations from the novel refer to this edition.

4. See J. M. Rignall, "Dickens and the Catastrophic Continuum of History in *A Tale of Two Cities*," *NLH* 51(3) (Fall 1984); and Jack Lindsay, "A Tale of Two Cities," in *Twentieth-Century Interpretations of "A Tale of Two Cities*,*"* ed. Charles E. Beckwith (Englewood Cliffs, N.J.: Prentice-Hall, 1972).

5. See Catherine Gallagher, "The Duplicity of Doubling in *A Tale of Two Cities*," *Dickens Studies Annual* 12 (1983), pp. 125–45.

6. Bakhtin, *Dialogic Imagination*, pp. 365–66.

7. Franklin Court, in "Boots, Barbarism, and the New Order in Dickens' *A Tale of Two Cities*," *Victorians' Institute Journal* 9, p. 34, points out that "by employing this particular stylistic device, Dickens can more convincingly present thousands of people—either the mob or the aristocracy—as a single power. The footsteps raging in Saint Antoine and echoing simultaneously in London can be viewed, therefore, as one gigantic, inanimate foot of a body that, in this instance, is the revolutionary mob."

8. Richard Dunn, "A Tale for Two Dramatists," *Dickens Studies Annual*, 12 (1983), p. 121; and Michael Timko, "Splendid Impressions and Picturesque Means: Dickens, Carlyle, and the French Revolution," pp. 186–87.

9. Gallagher, "Duplicity," pp. 140–41.

10. Sylvère Monod, "Dickens' Attitudes in *A Tale of Two Cities*," *Nineteenth-Century Fiction* 24(4) (March 1970), p. 497.

11. Rignall, "Catastrophic Continuum," p. 577.

12. Gallagher, "Duplicity," pp. 133–34.

13. Albert Hutter, "Nation and Generation in *A Tale of Two Cities*," *PMLA* 93(3) (May 1978), p. 453.

14. Rignall, "Catastrophic Continuum," p. 583.

15. Ibid.

16. Chris R. Vanden Bossche, "Prophetic Closure and Disclosing Narrative: *The French Revolution* and *A Tale of Two Cities*," *Dickens Studies Annual* 12 (1983), p. 211.

17. George Levine, *Darwin and the Novelists: Patterns of Science in Victorian Fiction* (Cambridge, Mass.: Harvard University Press, 1988), p. 166.

18. Charles Dickens, *Little Dorrit* (New York: Penguin, 1978).

Conclusion

1. Michael Holquist, for instance, seems much less interested in carnival than in dialogism, as is evidenced by the title and contents of his interesting study, *Dialogism: Bakhtin and His World* (New York: Routledge, 1990).

2. See Michael Gardiner, *The Dialogics of Critique: M. M. Bakhtin and the Theory of Ideology* (New York: Routledge, 1992). As will become clear, I am in broad agreement with what Gardiner has to say about dialogism and part company with him only on the question of carnival's political import. To be fair, Gardiner himself is not without his doubts about the historicity and subversive potential of the carnivalesque.

3. Gary Saul Morson and Caryl Emerson, *Mikhail Bakhtin: Creation of a Prosaics* (Stanford, Calif.: Stanford University Press, 1990), p. 67.

4. Lennard J. Davis, "The Monologic Imagination: M. M. Bakhtin and the Nature of Assertion," *Studies in the Literary Imagination* 23(1) (Spring 1990), p. 39.

5. M. M. Bakhtin, *Rabelais and His World*, trans. Helene Iswolsky (Bloomington: Indiana University Press, 1984), pp. 33–34.

6. Ibid., p. 18.

7. Robert Young, "Back to Bakhtin," *Cultural Critique* 2 (1985–86), p. 84.

8. Simon Dentith, "Dickens and Popular Laughter" (Paper delivered at the Sixth International Bakhtin Conference in Cocoyoc, Mexico, July 1993), abstract.

9. Davis, "Monologic," p. 40.

10. Bakhtin, *Rabelais*, p. 75.

11. Terry Eagleton, "Wittgenstein's Friends," in *Against the Grain: Essays 1975–1985* (London: Verso, 1986), p. 129.

12. M. M. Bakhtin, *Speech Genres and Other Late Essays*, ed. Caryl Emerson and Michael Holquist, trans. Vern W. McGee (Austin: University of Texas Press, 1986), p. 138.

13. Ibid., p. 149.

14. John Brenkman, "Multiculturalism and Criticism," in *English Inside and Out: The Places of Literary Criticism*, ed. Susan Gubar and Jonathan Kamholtz (New York: Routledge, 1993), p. 99.

15. Gardiner, *Dialogics of Critique*, p. 166.

16. Bakhtin, *Speech Genres*, p. 139.

17. Gardiner, *Dialogics of Critique*, p. 75. Gardiner is paraphrasing Allon White in "The Struggle over Bakhtin: Fraternal Reply to Robert Young," *Cultural Critique* 8, pp. 217–41.

18. Ibid., p. 176.

19. Young, "Back to Bakhtin," p. 85.

20. Robert Stam, *Subversive Pleasures: Bakhtin, Cultural Criticism, and Film* (Baltimore: Johns Hopkins University Press, 1989), p. 16.

21. Michael Holquist, "Introduction: The Architectonics of Answerability," in M. M. Bakhtin, *Art and Answerability: Early Philosophical Essays*, ed. Michael Holquist and Vadim Liapunov, trans. Vadim Liapunov and Kenneth Bronstrom (Austin: University of Texas Press, 1990), p. xlii.

22. See, for instance, Patricia Yaeger, *Honey-Mad Women: Emancipatory Strategies in Women's Writing* (New York: Columbia University Press, 1988), and *Feminism, Bakhtin, and the Dialogic*, ed. Dale M. Bauer and S. Jaret McKinstry (Albany: State University of New York Press, 1991).

23. Young, "Back to Bakhtin," p. 84.

24. Davis, "Monologic," p. 40.

25. Gardiner, *Dialogics of Critique*, p. 187.

26. Young, "Back to Bakhtin," p. 86.

27. David K. Danow, *The Thought of Mikhail Bakhtin: From Word to Culture* (New York: St Martin's Press, 1991), p. 114.

28. M. M. Bakhtin, *The Dialogic Imagination: Four Essays by M. M. Bakhtin*, ed. Michael Holquist, trans. Caryl Emerson and Michael Holquist (Austin: University of Texas Press, 1981), p. 28.

29. P. N. Medvedev, *The Formal Method in Literary Scholarship*, trans. Albert J. Wehrle (Cambridge, Mass.: Harvard University Press, 1985), p. 131.

30. Stam, *Subversive Pleasures*, p. 222.

31. Gary Saul Morson, "Bakhtin and the Present Moment," *American Scholar*, 60(2) (Spring 1991), p. 208.

32. George Eliot, *Adam Bede*, ed. Stephen Gill (Harmondsworth, UK: Penguin, 1982), p. 222.

33. Stam, *Subversive Pleasures*, p. 21.

34. Gardiner, *Dialogics of Critique*, p. 90.

35. Ibid., p. 3.

36. Patricia S. Yaeger, " 'Because a Fire Was in My Head": Eudora Welty and the Dialogic Imagination,' " in *Welty: A Life in Literature*, ed. Albert J. Devlin (Jackson: University Press of Mississippi, 1987), p. 145.

37. Peter Hitchcock, "Radical Writing" in *Feminism, Bakhtin, and the Dialogic*, ed. Dale M. Bauer and S. Jaret McKinstry (Albany: State University of New York Press, 1991), p. 115.

38. See Julia Kristeva, "The Ruin of a Poetics" in *Russian Formalism: A Collection of Articles and Texts in Translation* (Harper & Row, 1973), pp. 102–19; and Eagleton, "Wittgenstein's Friends," p. 116.

Index

*

UNIVERSITY PRESS OF NEW ENGLAND publishes books under its own imprint and is the publisher for Brandeis University Press, Brown University Press, Dartmouth College, Middlebury College Press, University of New Hampshire, University of Rhode Island, Tufts University, University of Vermont, Wesleyan University Press, and Salzburg Seminar.

LIBRARY OF CONGRESS CATALOGING-IN-PUBLICATION DATA

Baldridge, Cates.

The dialogics of dissent in the English novel / Cates Baldridge.

p.   cm.

Includes bibliographical references and index.

ISBN 0–87451–666–8 (cl)

1. English fiction—History and criticism.   2. Politics and literature—Great Britain—History.   3. Literature and society—Great Britain—History.   4. Social problems in literature. 5. Dissenters in literature.   I. Title.

PR830.P6B35   1994

823.009'358—dc20   93–41021

∞